# THE CHALLENGE OF EXISTENTIAL SOCIAL WORK PRACTICE

# THE CHALLENGE OF EXISTENTIAL SOCIAL WORK PRACTICE

MARK GRIFFITHS

First published 2017 by
PALGRAVE

Palgrave in the UK is an imprint of Macmillan Publishers Limited, registered in England, company number 785998, of 4 Crinan Street, London, N1 9XW.

Palgrave® and Macmillan® are registered trademarks in the United States, the United Kingdom, Europe and other countries.

ISBN 978–1–137–52829–2 paperback

This book is printed on paper suitable for recycling and made from fully managed and sustained forest sources. Logging, pulping and manufacturing processes are expected to conform to the environmental regulations of the country of origin.

A catalogue record for this book is available from the British Library.

A catalog record for this book is available from the Library of Congress.

# CONTENTS

# LISTS OF TABLES AND BOXES

## Tables

## Case Examples

# Reflective Exercises

# ACKNOWLEDGEMENTS

I would like to thank my primary supervisor, Professor Bob Pease, and associate supervisor, Dr Mathew Sharpe, for their encouragement, support and criticism in the supervision of my PhD on existential social work practice. I would also like to thank all the social workers who participated in the existential social work focus groups facilitated through the Australian Association of Social Workers, particularly Peter Greasley, private practitioner Pamela Trotman, and existential psychotherapist and social worker Rowena Bianchino. I would like to thank Professor Catherine Bennett, head of the School of Health and Social Development at Deakin University, for her encouragement and support, and the University of Tasmania and the School of Social Sciences for their assistance. I want to acknowledge the profound contribution made by previous social work writers on applying existential thought to social work practice. I would also like to acknowledge the influence of author Robert Sutton, and his work *Human Existence and Theodicy*, which I found quite an inspiration as I explored the intellectual maze that is existential thought. This publication was supported by an Australian Government Research Training Scholarship.

Finally, this book is dedicated to all the social workers in our direct practice human services across the globe, working to deliver a range of forms of assistance to overwhelming numbers of clients. I hope this book provides you with the inspiration to continue this vital human service with joy and with the certain knowledge that your efforts to implement the existential social work ideas in this work will make a real difference.

# 1

# BEING-IN-THE-SOCIAL WORK-WORLD

What does it mean to be a social worker today, working in a social work world? The lived experience of social work practice is the starting point for existential social work. In existential thought, our consciousness is not separate from our world but exists within the worlds we inhabit. By the time of starting their first job, the social work graduate is immersed in the daily challenge of delivering social work services. Social work theory that pays little attention to the lived experience of direct service work can appear remote and irrelevant. After all their essays have been written and marked, the tendency is for graduates to leave social work theory behind and to focus on the functional aspects of the job. The pressure of frontline social work services and the high levels of accountability expected in this new risk-averse work environment can encourage a complete disjunction from the reflective emphasis of academic training. The heavy administrative requirements of most direct service social work jobs can consume huge amounts of work time. Suddenly, the job can feel quite onerous and bureaucratic, miles from the expectations of student days.

The first conceptions of social work were created from the lived experience of the first caseworkers. They created the social work world that we inhabit, whether, as a social worker, you are working with many colleagues in a public hospital, as the only social worker in an isolated rural community, or in an emergent field such as an internet-based service. Other social work texts focus on the context of practice or on the politics of social services; these texts assume that the bigger picture is shaping social work at the coalface. Social work is indeed being shaped by larger external forces, like information technology, managerialism, disruption, increased accountability, and risk management. An appreciation of how these forces affect direct service is required. However, focusing exclusively on these forces leaves social work students confused and perplexed about the value of direct service.

The existential approach takes seriously the lived experience of social worker and client. How can we make this experience more valuable and enjoyable? Isn't the reason social workers come into this work to help other people? Direct service workers (which includes most early-career social workers) seek to change the world, client by client. Levinas, an existential philosopher, argues that our first lived experience of the world is one of dwelling in enjoyment – think of a newborn baby and her mother; dwelling in social work means finding a way to really enjoy your practice.

## Being-in-a-social work-world

The phrase 'being-in-a-social work-world' contains an existential concept: that our existence is essentially immersed in the world in which we work and live. Taking this view, there is no subject–object divide. As a social worker, you operate in a 'social work world' that has particular and established ways of sharing activities, having discussions, and doing things. The more comfortable and familiar you become with this world, and the more time you allow yourself to appreciate and understand it, the more you will feel as though you can dwell in it. You have to work hard in this arena, and must be able to perform to its requirements, because there is always a human need to meet. The practical, 'how to do it' part of social work is important to grasp, but you also need to recognize that there will always be more to learn. More possibilities will become apparent for you as you begin to shape this world. An important part of this social work world is the meanings that are created to make sense of it. For example, in my current work with men in family violence, we invite men to become 'card carrying adults', accepting their responsibilities as fathers, as partners, and in other roles.

Being-in-a-social work-world means being in a place where there are pre-existing agencies, where services are delivered, and where there are programs in which standards, guidelines, policies, and operational procedures are followed. It means there is a 'way we do business around here'. How do you make sense of a world in which some clients don't fit the parameters of the program? Everything appears to be immediately at hand in the sense that we begin within an existing service system, and there is a tendency to think that our job is simply to adjust to the 'way business is done around here'.

As Neil Thompson, a prominent existential social work author, has pointed out, often the new graduate is discouraged from asking questions and from developing a deeper knowledge base; they are urged instead 'to get on with the job' (Thompson, 2010, p. 11). As professional social workers we have to make sense of this world for ourselves, which usually involves a deep engagement with the world of meaning that already exists in the given workplace. Imagine an agency in which every social worker could choose for themselves how and in what format to record their case notes. Chaos would ensue. So we 'learn the ropes'. We fit in, without really understanding why things have been shaped in the way they are. At the same time, and often in small ways, we start to shape our world a little, to gain a deeper understanding of practice, and we begin to ask questions about why things are done this way or that. We might observe a practitioner suggest some changes that are accepted by management. Suddenly, a new practice has evolved.

But what does it mean to dwell in social work, to enjoy it like a baby enjoys their bath? It means you feel that 'this is exactly where I should be, right here, doing this job, at this time, in my career'. This is what is meant by 'being-in-a-social work-world'. It means finding a way to be thoroughly nurtured and supported by the work and by the camaraderie of the team, so that the practical doing of the job comes from a place of nurture and giving rather than obligation and duty. It provides opportunities (and encourages you) to question practices and to suggest new ways of doing things. Of course, there can be valid reasons why some new ideas for improving service should themselves be questioned and rejected. Further learning takes place when explanations are provided that help us to understand the limitations of our suggestions.

It is impossible to imagine social work separate from the world in which it exists. As Bertha Reynolds, one of the founding social workers, wrote more than sixty years ago:

It is not possible to do good social work without equipment. Buildings are necessary in order to meet people, facilities for administration ... or whatever the program of the agency demands. In addition an agency works through community contacts, influential people and other social institutions. A new agency has to gather these facilities and win the respect and confidence of its community. (Reynolds, 1951, pp. 2–3)

A social work agency is a living world, and 'being thrown' into this world thrusts us into a given social work world. Our facticity or the given facts of our human existence, which limit our existence, include the many givens in our lives, such as our gender, race, age, family, culture, and even chance historical events, such as where we did our first social work placements. The first clients you work with and the challenges that work presents are experiences into which you are, in a sense, 'thrown', and this is just part of the 'facticity of the world'. The way you respond to these experiences presents you with some choice in the experience of being thrown in (Van Deurzen and Kenward, 2005). The idea of being thrown is reminiscent of this famous gendered quote from Karl Marx:

> Men make their own history, but they do not make it just as they please; they do not make it under circumstances chosen by themselves, but under circumstances directly encountered, given and transmitted from the past. The tradition of all the dead generations weighs like a nightmare on the brain of the living. (1852, p. 1)

An existential version of a similar thought describes history as being 'the risk of the possible and the pinch of the real' (Flynn, 1997, p. 11).

We are historical beings, and as social workers we live within a definite period of social work's history, a period in which there are possibilities and limitations. Jessie Taft, one of the founders of an early existential approach to social work practice, wrote: 'To talk about the spirit of social work is to assume an appreciation of its past as well as a vision of its future, for we want no visions which have not grown out of experience' (Taft, 1928, p. 103).

Some traditions that older generations of social workers pass on to us can be very valuable tools, practice wisdoms and theoretical understandings that we ought to cherish and maintain. Not everything that is passed on is a nightmare on the brain of the living. In the first practice vignette below, the challenge of learning the ropes and applying your social work knowledge and skills is framed as the process of gaining some street-level credibility. This framing is derived from a study by Michael Lipsky (2010), titled *Street Level Bureaucracy*, in which Lipsky argues that social workers and other direct human services workers use their discretion when applying rules and regulations during coalface interactions. This finding has been confirmed in subsequent studies, and it suggests, paradoxically, that direct service workers do in fact have some discretion in the way they interpret procedures and implement policy. Is this, perhaps, where social work theory can shape practice by helping new practitioners know what is really important in client encounters and how to respond?

---

Reflective Exercise 1.1: Learning the ropes in social work

In your first social work job or placement the task is mastering 'the way we do business around here'. Can you do the job as it is now? Demonstrate this capacity before offering any opinions about ways to improve service delivery. Can you think of some smart ways to gain 'street-level credibility' within your job or placement?

---

Jessie Taft considered there to be 'growing points' in the history of social work just as there are in individual social workers' histories (Taft, 1928, p. 103). These are the turning points at which a dramatic change takes place in practice. This change may affect a small aspect of practice, but it is this aspect that is the 'most alive', to use her term. Taft describes her own development, in which she felt guilt and obligation in working with poor families. Alms-giving hid a motivation of personal salvation. The unworthiness of 'doing good' as a motivation in social work drove theorists to search for 'scientific' approaches to addressing human need. Social work clients became participants in objective studies called 'assessments'. But beyond this objectivity, some clients have a way of calling attention to their *subjective* reality: they bring their own perspective to their social worker.

In 1928, social work theorists were beginning to discover psychology and the ways in which our hidden inner world shapes our behaviour. Was the social worker really capable of focusing on the other person if they were striving to be a purely objective observer, rather than also being aware of that person's subjective inner state and their own inner state? If I am frightened about my own performance as a social worker, how does that play out in a client interview? If I am unaware of my own emotional turmoil and pain, how might it affect my capacity to hear the client's? Taft (1928) responds that the increasingly important point in social work was an awareness that the social worker participated in the situation, and that facing the responsibility of helping someone involved taking responsibility for oneself as a professional helper. Taft went on to develop the first existential social work approach, called the Functional School, which I will discuss further in the second chapter of this book. She sought out this kind of professional emotional help for herself from Otto Rank, one of the first psycho-analysts, who became a mentor to her and to the Functional social work school.

Towards the end of this chapter, I argue for a preliminary definition of existential social work practice. The term 'existential social work' refers to a broader range of theories and approaches than does 'existentialist social work', which tends to be identified exclusively with existentialism, a twentieth-century philosophical movement in which Sartre and de Beauvoir were prominent figures. In this work I have incorporated insights about social work from other sources including Camus, Levinas, Marcel, Stein, and Heidegger, as well as Sartre. Existential social work aims to focus on the real, lived experience of doing social work rather than on theoretical or abstract ideas about social work that are separated from practice. As other philosophical social work texts have noted, some social workers can find philosophy a bit tiresome and can see it as irrelevant. This view probably reflects their anxiety and sense of urgency at getting on with the practical tasks of the job. However, because of the inherent philosophical dilemmas involved in intervening in other people's lives, social work is a form of 'doing philosophy' (Ragg, 1980, p. 231). As Ragg has stated, social work is 'working with real life problems rather than with the philosophical problems, that philosophers study' (p. 232).

Philosophy in social work is more like a genuine conversation involving the experience of understanding, a conversation in which meaning emerges in a dialectic beyond the intention of the participants. As Gadamar (1989) describes it:

> To reach an understanding in a dialogue is not merely a matter of putting oneself forward and successfully asserting one's point of view, but being transformed into a communion in which we do not remain what we are. (p. 387)

As part of 'being-in-the-social work-world', the social worker must be open to the client world, the agency world, and the world of other workers and agencies to enable this genuine dialogue and creative fusion to occur.

Social work philosophy is lagging behind the technical and methodical advances of the profession (Reamer, 1993), although recent publications have aimed to address this issue (Grimwood, 2016). A common analytical approach examines the political context of social work practice, including political and moral philosophy. Priority is given in this approach to issues external to social work practice but that impinge upon it. It moves from abstract philosophical issues to their concrete implications for social work practice. While this approach is reasonable, I wish to explore the topic of philosophy in social work from the opposite direction, from the lived experience of social work itself, using existential philosophy to explore whether this experience can be useful in understanding social work practice. I am suggesting, by taking this approach, that the techniques of social work (i.e. its methods, like casework, group work, social action, etc.) is not the essence of social work. However, the techniques of social work do reveal something about its essence, and they hide the work's other aspects. The techniques or methods used in social work are changing and will continue to change, but is there something about social work that is deeper than its methods?

I am not suggesting that social work is a phenomenon that has a unique identity or essence, outside of historical time. Richard Turner (1973), a South African existential philosopher who studied with Sartre and was murdered during the apartheid era, states that to understand dialectically means to 'unravel the ways in which [things are] related to other things. We have to treat [them] as [...] interdependent part[s] of a totality, rather than a self-sufficient identity' (p. 31).

In addition to understanding social work dialectically, as a living profession that projects future change by negating present givens, we also need to appreciate its capacity to reach beyond itself and thus to surpass itself.

## Social casework emerges

In taking this existential approach, I am following in the footsteps of Mary Richmond, the first theoretician of the social casework method. In her second book, *What is Social Casework?*, Richmond (1922) argues that 'there was social casework long before social workers began' (p. 5), and she proceeds to offer the first definition of social casework, based on a number of cases. Starting in this way, Richmond returns to first principles and asks '*what* social casework is and *why*' (p. 26). Richmond gave the first two chapters of this book the same title, 'Social Case Work in Being', and chose example cases from a range of fields, including social casework conducted by social workers, and by other professionals, such as teachers and nurses. Many of the first social workers were, in fact, people of other professions, and in their practice they set aside their prior skillsets to create the field of social casework (Lubove, 1965).

Richmond had already (in 1917) published *Social Diagnosis*, which borrowed the medical diagnostic model and applied it to social investigation, to be conducted by a social worker. In her second publication, she expands upon her thorough analysis of the social evidence to conclude that social casework should aim for the 'development of personality' because 'personality is a far more inclusive term' (Richmond, 1922, p. 90). She lists social and other environmental factors likely to shape personality, including communities and institutions, noting no conflict between the ideas of relatedness (her term for what we might today call the 'relational supports' of the client) and individual differences. Richmond had a theory of the wider self that incorporated all of a person's social relationships (Lubove, 1965).

While the terminology is somewhat outdated, what is important here is that when professional social work emerged for the first time, as social casework, it was thought through by one of its founders from first principles, using existential language. The definitions created to describe social casework were based on the lived experiences of social workers, and others, doing social casework. Finally, the definition of social casework, as derived from Richmond's case examples, shows a primordial form of existential social work practice in its emphasis on creative engagement and involvement with the client in their social situation and in its vital highlighting of client participation and of the need for recognition of difference (or differential approaches), because no two clients' circumstances are ever the same.

This brief exploration of the first emergence of social work as a profession gives us hints about its present shape. The existential view is that we live in historical temporality, involving past, present, and future. According to Heidegger, 'our past is not something that follows along after us, but goes ahead of us' (Heidegger, 1962, p. 41). What he means by this is that the present includes aspects of our past, and of our future, which we plan in the present, and which can also take account of our past (if this future is to be informed by it). We need to 'discover this (social work) tradition, preserve it and study it explicitly' (p. 41).

# What does the term 'social work' mean?

The meaning of 'social' has been a central issue for the profession. Many of the profession's internal conflicts reflect different perspectives on the meaning of this word. A core curriculum subject in most social work courses, which attempts to bridge the gap between basic disciplines and social work practice, is often called 'human behaviour and the social environment' (Bisno and Cox, 1997, p. 5). It attempts to create the social in social work as professional knowledge but often ends up being described as a 'multidisciplinary potpourri' (p. 5). The 'work' in social work refers to the action taken, but also distinguishes it from the word 'professional'. Something of the humble origins of social work is preserved in the name of the profession itself. A certain lack of status is implicit in the name and has been a constant concern since the field's inception. There is a dialectical contradiction or tension inherent in social work. It receives its mandate from a society that it must also occasionally oppose in some way in order to advocate for the weakest and most marginalized within that same society. An inauthentic anxiety about the status of social work can also be observed in the search for status, in which emphasis is placed on function over cause and technique over goals and on the embrace of dominant ideologies (Bisno, 1956). The tendency today is to ignore the humble beginnings of the profession and its 'worker' status.

# Social work in the technological age

What does it mean to 'be a social worker' in the twenty-first century? Social workers typically risk-manage cases in narrowly defined and highly prescribed sub-areas of a more narrowly defined practice setting, such as child protection. This specialization of social work continues in our technologically advanced era. A descriptive 'average, everyday' account of what social workers do in a range of fields of practice is what generally passes for an account of social work as a profession. One description analyses social work as containing five essential elements: purpose, values, sanction, knowledge, and skills (Williams and Joyner, 2008). The social worker uses knowledge, values, and skills with the sanction of society for the purpose of promoting positive change or of preventing further harm. But is social work more than what we do? What is the essence of social work? When social work is stripped of its usual defining qualities, such as where you practice it, who you see, what program you operate in, and what your role is, how would you describe what it is you do as a social worker?

---

Reflective Exercise 1.2: Your essence

Does social work have an essence or core independent of place, time, function, and method? What is your essence (stripped of your job, student status, family, relationships, where you live, what you do for fun, etc.)?

---

It is actually quite difficult to answer these questions. One thing you can say with certainty is that you exist. Social work exists, too. One day it might not exist, but we know for sure that we ourselves will not exist. Here I am asking an ontological question about social work itself. What does it mean to be a social worker now? The important thing is that social work exists in the world. Some existentialists argue that our existence precedes our essence. In this view, the existence of social work is more important than any effort to describe or prescribe its essence as a stable entity. Social workers are shaping social work today and its future tomorrow. We are shaped by our past and by many forces outside our control, such as economic, political, and technological changes. This means, paradoxically, that it would be impossible to construct social work anew as it exists today. The field's history, traditions, and proven track record in certain fields and lack of success in others will also have a significant bearing on where it thrives and disappears. Outside forces, such as social changes, technological developments, social reforms, and environmental change, will also shape the future of social work.

But is there something unique about social work that separates it from other helping professions like youth work, medicine, law, and nursing? Does it matter? This is a question that has occupied the thinking of social workers, and they have come up with some answers. Neil Thompson thinks social work can be best described as a 'contested entity', but this conceptualization of social work as an entity takes us away from the being of social work. His description of social work as 'doing society's dirty work' resonates with the difficult problems social workers have to deal with (Thompson, 2009, p. 6).

All theoretical perspectives on social work start with certain assumptions, which then shape their account of what social work is. A 'maintenance' view expresses acceptance of the political status quo and argues that social workers expressing political views falls outside the proper social work agenda. In this view, we are the 'maintenance mechanics oiling the interpersonal wheels of the community' (Davies, 1985, p. 28). This potentially pejorative view of social work implies that the work, which merely keeps people surviving, coping in their world, is inferior to social work that is aimed at social change. Even worse, social work has been considered a form of social control: by helping people cope in the existing system it reinforces the inequality and oppression inherent in that system.

The existential view recognizes these aspects of social maintenance and social change in social work. Much of social work helps maintain systems, people, and programs. It is simply hidden from view, yet it is vital to good practice and to helping people cope day to day. Similarly, social work maintains lives by doing lots of routine things like keeping good records, running planning meetings, ensuring ongoing service delivery, and helping people connect to appropriate services. Helping people home from hospital with proper supports frees up hospital beds for other patients and saves resources. Should social workers be concerned about saving public money and avoiding waste (such as by helping to avoid missed appointments and managing waiting lists), non-compliance, and non-attendance in a finite world with infinite potential needs? What remains hidden from view is what we have chosen to place in the background. When routine tasks are not done, they suddenly become visible. An existential social work approach embraces the depth of everyday practice and celebrates its value in keeping things in good order, in servicing clients, and in noticing the small things that ensure good services, while also questioning whether our routines and maintenance tasks of helping people cope with life can be done more effectively.

---

Reflective Exercise 1.3: Social work as social maintenance

Do you think social workers have a responsibility to minimize program wastage, such as professional time-wasting? Or is this just the responsibility of outside auditors, line managers, or researchers?

Why are good, orderly processes important in social work?

Malcolm Payne, in *Modern Social Work Theory* (2005), argues for a moderate 'social constructionist' view of social work, which he says involves three competing discourses within the profession. These competing discourses are the therapeutic or clinical practice view, the individual reformist social order view (which includes the maintenance perspective above), and the transformational or critical view, concerned with challenging oppression and inequality in society. Payne maintains that we construct our practice from within these competing and, in some ways, overlapping views. While there is much to like about Payne's constructionist perspective on social work, I am concerned that it lacks grounding or substance in its description of social work in terms of competing discourses. Certain discourses also seem to be overlooked in the process, such as the ecological and the spiritual, although there is a developing literature on green social work and on spiritually sensitive practice. The word 'discourse' implies language, and the question arises whether there is something in this relational sphere that grounds these different views of social work.

Is there some settled configuration of social work that can provide grounds upon which the world of social work can grow and flourish amongst competing discourses? Mary Richmond excluded from her description and definition of social casework what she considered to be inferior practice. She focused on long-term, intensive social casework of two to six years' duration, something that is strikingly rare today. She eliminated work done by inexperienced practitioners, work conducted in secondary settings, or what she described as work that was subsidiary to the dominant professional intervention, such as that conducted alongside a medical practitioner. Richmond (1922) considered restricted social work to be that which was limited by rules or prescribed ways of proceeding, as well as any practice that 'crippled professional discovery and development' (pp. 87–89). Most social work practice today would be excluded from her study. Richmond was trying to create the best conditions possible to allow this new social casework practice to emerge, or 'show up', in all its glory. Richmond's was an age of objectivity, and social work emerged as a product of modernity. Clients would be objectively studied and the social facts obtained. We are emerging from that age into a technological age in which service industries are being shaped by rapidly evolving technology that denies limitations to service and provides maximum choice while eliminating, as far as possible, identity, locality, and non-technological perspectives. What matters in this new age is efficiency and 'getting things right'. There appears to be no essence, spirit, or soul that has to be respected. The goal for humans is adaptation to technological requirements. Heidegger described the essence of modern technology as turning everything in the world into 'standing reserve'. He meant that modern technology orders, extracts, regulates, secures, or places on call all resources, including human resources, and makes them available for human use on an as-needed basis (Heidegger, 1977). This description of technology suggests that we may end up in some twenty-four-hour service delivery system. We can already see the beginnings of this in the way that new information technology quickly reshapes social work practice, and not always for the better (Parton, 2006).

One of the first challenges of the social worker in this new age is to be able to do the job required in the appropriate manner, using all the technology required. Social workers are employed by organizations that expect them to be able to handle all these requirements. There is a much higher level of prescription in how things are done and in what the reporting requirements are. The mood tends to be one of ambivalence towards the technological world: on the one hand, it offers immense potential for improved service delivery, but on the other, it can stultify and deaden practice through loss of connection and identity and through chronic over-prescription of practice. When child protection workers were asked about the most frustrating part of their work, human resources staff expected them to talk about difficult clients. They were surprised to find that it was their paperwork and computer systems that caused them the most frustration, often consuming between 80% and 90% of their work time (Griffin, 2011).

An example of this kind of technological impediment is where a comput-erized case management system prescribes the case assessment process, regulatory processes, and administrative tasks, consuming huge amounts of time; lengthy court appearances then absorb much of the time that remains. Social workers report squeezing client contact time, including home visits, phone contact and interviews, into the remaining 10–20% of their shifts, quite the reverse of their pre-employment expectations. Many of the human services and health information systems remain cumbersome and uncoordi-nated, resulting in excessive screen-based work time (Department of Human Services, 2011). The work of Eileen Munro in the Munro review of Child Pro-tection in the United Kingdom represents an attempt to remove the bureau-cracy imposed on child protection workers over the last thirty years and to encourage more professional decision making to be based on direct engage-ment with clients by child protection workers (Munro, 2010; Parton, 2012).

# Existential social work in the technological age

One of the challenges for existential social work today is to provide meaning, purpose, and spirit to social work in this modern, technological era. How do we bring about the full potential of social work practice in such an era? I would suggest that, in this new age, the existential view provides one way to ground social work that allows the essence of social work to manifest itself. This would not be a nostalgic return to some golden age of social work, but a position that says 'social work matters and I want it to thrive in this new technological era. I expect to live my social work in the conditions that exist in this world now.' This means being receptive to the relational world, where hidden opportunities abound. It also means establishing a personal relationship to social work's history and recognizing that all those established practices, like casework, group work, critical social work practice, community action, and social policy analysis, are great technical innovations that fought for their opportunity to be recognized as legitimate tools and methods. Ask yourself this: How do these tools and methods relate to my purpose in social work today? One way of answering this question is to create a network of social work writers and mentors that can inspire your development as a social worker.

---

Reflective Exercise 1.4: Developing your network of social work inspirations

Can you identify a social work writer who really inspires you?

Do you know any social workers who inspire you?

Write down your thoughts on how you can connect with social work's rich history.

For example, my reading of *Rebellious Spirit* (2005), by professor of social work Janice Andrews-Schenk on Gisela Konopka, provided real inspiration in my social work career because it showed how much Konopka was able to contribute to social work and social group work despite her character flaws and feelings of personal inadequacy. Konopka worked hard at what she was good at and had a very good personal support network on which she relied.

---

I want to suggest a way forward that will help to ground social work in its existential essence. How do we do this? One way is look at things the way the creators of social work saw them. Put yourself in their shoes. See their efforts as various existential projects – which they were – as steps into unknown territory. Remember that all our projects in life always have unforeseen (and unintended) consequences. We cannot interpret solely on the basis of intended results. Heuristic interpretation requires that we look at the whole in its parts and the parts in their whole. An existential dialectical approach to understanding things requires us to ask three questions:

1   What are we studying? (The answer should be a good description of what we are interested in, namely a period of social work. This is called the phenomenological description stage.)

2   How and when did it appear or show up? (This is the analytic regressive stage, looking at the internal and external elements that shaped the emergence of the phenomenon.)

3   Why is it significant for us today and into the future? (This is the progressive synthesis stage, which involves the application of the being-in-the-world concept in that you are part of the story you are investigating.) (Farrar, 1994).

---

Reflective Exercise 1.5: Your favourite social worker

Choose a historical social worker and use the progressive regressive method above to investigate

● What they were setting out to do,

● What their circumstances were (their social work world and constraints),

● How their initiative went as a project (successes, failures, any unintended or unforeseen consequences), and

● Why it is important to you, today, and into your social work future.

One of the features of social work that remains essential is that the social worker has very little external equipment with which to work. The social worker's 'implements' are their person: their personality, intelligence, skills, temperament, demeanour, care and concern for the client, and other qualities that are intrinsic to the worker. Social work can be viewed as a practical 'performance', involving such activities as casework, meetings, phone calls, report writing, and many other activities. The problems social workers face can often be challenging, involving deeply entrenched, chronic, or 'wicked' problems (Australian Public Service Commission, 2007). This level of complexity often leads to a response that tries to simplify the solutions. So typically you have a pragmatic response, a no-nonsense approach that emphasizes practical solutions. Others can adopt an ideological mindset in which an explicit framework is used to perceive all issues, resulting in standard solutions being prescribed.

## Is there an authentic social work?

Are some approaches to social work more authentic than others? Is it possible to say that some forms of practice in social work are inauthentic? Contrary to popular belief, we learn to be authentic by being inauthentic. What does this mean? We learn by watching how 'they' do things. We follow others who are more experienced, but gradually we are able to shape our own practice, in small ways at first, and over time, hopefully, we become accomplished at some things, or even an expert. This was how I learned basic counselling skills in social work. For example: How do I show empathy for a client? Or, at an even more basic level: How do I ask open-ended questions that might encourage a client to explore their issues? Awkwardly at first, we learn the 'right' phrases, like 'I'm hearing you say ... and I guess that makes you feel...'. These forms of words can sound inauthentic to the social worker and to the client. The challenge for the social worker is in reframing these standard phrases to make them fresh and meaningful on each occasion, to each client.

Just like a musician imitating their favourite inspiration, we learn gradually, by rote and through practice, and by applying practice to theory we become more accomplished and more of 'us' begins to appear in the dialogue. We sound more real, even if the words have not changed that much. Things are less awkward. They are more inspired and impromptu at times, and when we make mistakes, we accept that we are human and that these learning moments allow clients to sense our genuineness and humility. Social work is more than a technical exercise, but the analogy above does suggest that authenticity in social work demands an artistic commitment to the practice. An artist, according to Otto Rank, faces their neurosis and creates something from it by bringing something new into the world (Kramer, 1996, pp. 189–200; Stein, 2010, pp. 116–131). We are all artists, says existential philosopher and theologian Paul Tillich, when we find the courage to face our anxieties and press ahead, despite finality, lack of meaning, and a sense of inadequacy, to try to create meaning from life and accept our limitations and those of others (Tillich, 1974, pp. 48–49).

As social workers, we are thrown into new challenges at every stage of our careers. Your career will commence somewhere, probably in direct service work; then you may get a promotion to a supervisory position after you have demonstrated some capacity in this area. You may do some research or policy development work, run a new pilot program, or move into agency management. Eventually your social work career will end. There is also a sense in which you commence each challenge unprepared or not fully prepared. This is the meaning of being 'thrown'. There will always be anxiety and guilt in your career until it ends. This guilt comes from the very nature of our thrown-ness and our almost total dependency on others. The existential view suggests that the way forward is to simply accept that some level of anxiety and guilt is part of acting in the world.

---

Reflective Exercise 1.6: Becoming a more authentic social worker using your unique qualities

What have been some of your *lived experiences* to date?

Just *describe them* – don't evaluate anything about them. This is called phenomenology – the description of lived experience.

In what way was it a privileged or oppressed existence, or did it contain elements of both?

What makes you unique, one of a kind, never to be repeated, different?

Do you have any gifts (these are things people notice about you or that you know you do rather well or find really easy to do but that others struggle with)?

Equally, do you have any problems, issues, burdens that you are struggling with? Many social workers have turned their own problems into a direction in their career path. Here the idea of the 'wounded healer' is used to describe a person who helps others overcome problems that he or she has dealt with, such as a former addict being a wounded healer in addiction recovery work.

What really attracted you to social work? What hooked you in?

# The end of your social work career

One day your social work career will be complete. Imagine that day now. Ask yourself this question: Will you have lived the social work career that only you could have lived? To existentialists, the death of something is an opportunity. It is a non-relational event. In one sense, only you experience your career's end. How many people come to the end of their lives or careers thinking 'I have not really done the things I really wanted to do'? By thinking clearly about your eventual demise (as a social worker, now), you can create a wonderful opportunity to answer these questions.

Reflective Exercise 1.7: Imagining the end of your social work career

Imagine the end of your social work career now

Ask yourself these questions

- As I exist in historical time, what are my current strengths as a social worker and where could these be best demonstrated in this historical period?

- What do I need to do to become an expert in some social work practice that I am interested in?

- What makes me unique as a social worker? What is totally 'mine' that no one else can do or wants to do?

- Am I going to use these 'gifts' in this life, in this occupation, or am I going to let them stay packed away?

- How can I create opportunities with my gifts to bring something new to social work that has not existed before I came along?

- What social movements am I interested in? How can I combine with others to create a new social work 'world'?

Thinking and acting upon this reflective exercise will help you move towards a more authentic social work position, where you are shaping your career, as well as being shaped by events, opportunities, and coincidences.

Inauthenticity is our normal state. Heidegger describes it as 'they thinking' or 'average everydayness'. When busy, excited, or ready for enjoyment, or when we are just 'following orders', for example, we are falling into 'they' living. We are all capable of falling back into inauthentic activities, like what Heidegger calls idle talk. By contrast, when authentic we become fascinated by the world with which we are concerned. Heidegger describes authenticity as a form of anticipatory resoluteness. This resolute, authentic approach enables the social worker to inspire or facilitate the development of authenticity in others. Edith Stein (2007), in her critique of Heidegger's main work *Being and Time*, described authenticity as a fullness of being, the state of being so involved in the moment that a timeless element enters within our finite existence, bringing joy, happiness, and love (pp. 79–80).

It is important to note that Heidegger stopped using the word 'authenticity' in his later writings because he felt it had taken on too much of a connotation of self-assertion. In using the word here, I am taking account of his criticism of existentialism's adoption of his work in this area. Heidegger had in mind a more receptive notion of authenticity, something more like feeling comfortable in your own skin and with your world. But the concept of authenticity and inauthenticity is central to his philosophy. In *Building, Dwelling, Thinking*, Heidegger (1971) discusses what it means to dwell. He writes:

> The word for peace means free, preserved from harm and danger, safeguarded. To free means to spare. The sparing itself consists not only in the fact that we do not harm the one whom we spare. Real sparing is something positive and

takes place when we leave something beforehand in its own nature when we return it specifically to its being, when we 'free' it in the sense of the word into a preserve of peace. To dwell, to be set at peace, means to remain at peace within the free, the preserve, and the free space that safeguards each thing in its nature. The fundamental character of dwelling is this sparing and preserving. (p. 149)

I once stayed with an Aboriginal man on his own tribal land in the Northern Territory of Australia. He once pointed to the nearest mountain from his bush home, the place in which he dwelt, along with his son. A dingo lived on this mountain. A hawk was diving for meat that the man threw into the lagoon by the camp. The dingo was there but not seen. The mountain was the dingo's domain, where he dwelt.

This is an example of what I think Heidegger had in mind and what is meant by 'being-in-the-world'. We need to dwell in this world and create a peace by sparing or creating safe spaces for people (and animals) to grow and be their most authentic selves (with the knowledge that people will fall into inauthenticity and back again, too, just like us). Social work has a historical existential essence, and it needs space and preserving to enable further growth and development. Part of creating real justice and peace in our world is looking after the vulnerable and marginalized. This is the social work 'being of care and concern'. This is dwelling in social work.

Where does this concern for social justice come from? How does it relate to the being of social work? Is it related to social work virtue ethics? In existential social work, ethics is built into our being in the lived experience of our relational world. Ethics relates to the face of the other – and ourselves – that cries out for attention and care. Everyone you meet is always more than any theory can explain. This overflowing of the other that exceeds any description precedes and calls out to me, to take responsibility in not harming them and in making their life better. Being a social worker involves creating this fullness of being in other people's lives. In the next reflective exercise, I ask you to imagine yourself being visited by a social worker. Heather MacDonald (2011), a clinical psychologist, documented how responding to an unfortunate accident during a home visit provided her with an opportunity to be her authentic self and to draw out the same from an untrusting, fearful client.

---

Reflective Exercise 1.8: Imagine being visited by or visiting a
social worker

Imagine you are required to see a social worker.

As the client, what would it be important for you to say or to have be heard?

What would it mean to have a social worker be really present and available to you,
to hear your story?

An example: Heather MacDonald, a clinical psychologist, was visiting a 17-year-
old African American woman, Dedra, who was pregnant (with a male child) for an
assessment. MacDonald didn't realize that she had blood all over her face from a
minor cut on her hand, which she had wiped on her face by accident. She had cut
herself on some faulty equipment. This embarrassing event proved to be a breakthrough for the stilted communication that often occurred. As MacDonald (2011)
states in her article, our clients often endure our presence, which has not been
requested. MacDonald learned through this breakthrough that Dedra feared
bringing a male black child into an oppressive, racist society.

---

Amy Rossiter argues that 'at the heart of Levinas' ethics is the notion that
our representations of persons are always inadequate. Something always
overflows, escapes our knowledge, comprehension, conceptions' (Rossiter,
2011, p. 983). Rossiter argues that we do violence to the other person by
not acknowledging this reality and by framing their conversations within
our professional constructs. What happens is that we shut out the possibility
of really noticing the overflow. In the existential social work approach, we
acknowledge this infinite capacity within the finite human being, this
uniqueness of the moment of engagement with the person in front of you.

Social work is defined by our ethical obligations to the other in our lived
experiences with them. These ethical obligations are prior to our knowledge
of how to intervene and assist. They derive not from the virtues of social
work, but from the gravitas of the suffering of the other. It is precisely in the
particularity and personal subjectivity of the other that this infinite capacity
is found. It is infinite because it is unique, unsurpassable, and beyond history
in the sense that action is required if harm is to be addressed now and the
future changed. Levinas describes a person capable of recognizing this in

others as someone who 'lacks nothing, who possesses her being entirely, who is able to go beyond her plenitude and has the idea of the infinite' (Levinas, 1969, p. 103). This existence is found in the face of the other people that social work exists for. These suffering other people precede social work and seek its assistance with this unnecessary suffering. Social work takes its responsibility from the other persons it helps and builds its knowledge, skills, and methods on the basis of this ethical responsibility.

## Defining existential social work practice

Existential social work focuses on the lived relational existence of people, which is always more than any amount of thought can explain. It aims to support people to create their infinite potential in the concrete world. An existential approach aims to create safe and peaceful spaces for client and worker growth, to prevent further harm, and to enhance positive change processes. An existential approach creates this space, even in social control situations where statutory obligations are in force.

Being is difficult to describe, but perhaps this is where existential thought aims to create an experience of being fully alive, or of a more abundant life for ourselves and our clients. Social workers' and our clients' beings are threatened by external forces, such as technology, global warming, our own fallibility, frailty and death, the slow malaise of loss of purpose and meaning, and negative emotions, including rejection of self and others, and loss of destiny and identity.

Existential social work acknowledges the oppressive circumstances of clients' lives and how this shapes and determines their decision making and coping abilities. It aims to strengthen their abilities to grow, despite this oppression, and helps them take responsibility for shaping their own lives. To do this effectively requires the social worker to take responsibility, as a professional helper, for their own growth and development, and to live their life to the fullest extent (Taft, 1928). It requires that we work with others in social movements to challenge oppressive circumstances. Existential social work is not simply the application of existential therapy to social work practice, nor is it simply applying existential concepts to social work practice. Existential therapies and concepts are only part of the story of existential social work practice. Existential social work is an openness to the mystery of social work.

# Conclusion

In this chapter, I have argued that existential social work begins with the lived experience of social work practice. While there are many external forces shaping social work, an existential approach begins at the coalface of direct practice, where social work first emerged. Mary Richmond, the first theorist of social casework, used this approach to define what was unique about casework and then to create a new method.

I began by asking, 'what does it mean to be a social worker today, working in a social work world?' Using the French existential philosopher Levinas, I have described some of the features of the lived experience of social workers today and have suggested that we need to dwell within social work, enjoying both its maintenance and social change tasks and the challenges that it presents each step of the way. Social workers must combine theory from their academic training and their own reading with their practice experience to fully dwell within their field of service. The technological age in which we live can strip us of meaning and human connection through its dominant impact on service delivery and its striving for efficiency. The existential challenge to social work is for it to stand its ground in honouring the relational, the historical, uniqueness, and the presence of the other in the face of the client. No system can encompass the other. Their uniqueness overflows into infinity. This is the essence in existence of existential social work.

## KEY POINTS FROM CHAPTER 1

1  Social work was created from the lived experience of the first social caseworkers.
2  Existential language was used to define social casework from the beginnings.
3  The name 'social worker' helped us explore the humble historical essence of the profession.
4  Social work exists to serve and give voice to the vulnerable, marginalized, and oppressed.
5  An existential approach remains open to existence and refuses to define clients by any existing theory or approach.

# 2

## "IMMORTAL SOCIAL WORK": THE FIRST EXISTENTIAL SOCIAL WORK PRACTICE

The next two chapters cover the fragmented history of existential thought in social work. They are relevant today because they provide some insight into how social work can thrive in this technological age. Does working within the limits of our functional role as social workers actually give us and our clients more freedom to be creative? Every time a social worker sits with a client he or she gives testimony to the value of social casework, an individualized service that recognises the value of the professional relationship in helping a person talk through issues as a way of helping to solve them. The same applies to the participants or members of a group or community with whom a social worker is working. In these next two chapters, I want to pay homage to those existential social work writers who have come before me, for their help in shaping my views on this approach. In this chapter, I am exploring the first existential social work movement, which began with Jessie Taft and the Functional School of social work. In Chapter 3, I explore the contributions of Ruth Wilkes, Donald Krill, Neil Thompson, and Jim Lantz to existential social work practice.

As I explained in Chapter 1, social casework, as first defined by Mary Richmond (1922), was derived from the selective lived experiences of early caseworkers building upon a primordial form of existential social work – which she eventually defined as: 'those processes which develop personality through adjustments consciously effected, individual by individual between men [sic] and their social environment' (pp. 98–99).

Richmond's phrase is often portrayed as a social approach, in comparison to the psychological approaches that became dominant with the influence of psychoanalysis on social work. From the very beginning, social casework was focused on helping the individual person in a way that enhanced their innate potential, rather than leaving them more dependent on the helper. Good intentions were no longer enough. In defining the being of social casework, Richmond would have excluded most of the practices that make up social work today, and examined cases from her own practice and others' that were intensive and long term (from two to six years of professional work). Her description of social casework as the development of personality is thoroughly therapeutic in orientation, and this is not fully appreciated (Yelloly, 1980, p. 61). In part, this reflected social work's overriding and continuing search for status as a profession (Ehrenreich, 1985).

In Chapter 1, I mentioned that Otto Rank came into social work at the time of his growing alienation and eventual ostracism from the Freudian orthodoxy. Jessie Taft, the founder of the Functional School, was already an accomplished psychologist with a PhD, an author, and was two years Rank's senior, when she first heard his lecture on the 'Trauma of Birth' in 1924. Two years later, Taft entered therapy with Rank, mainly for professional development reasons. She became his friend, translator, and, finally, biographer.

Existential social work practice emerged in social work with the influence of Otto Rank on the development of the Functional School. Rank is described by another of his biographers, E. James Lieberman (1985), as an 'existential pathfinder and pioneer relationship therapist' (p. 38). Lieberman is referring to Rank's efforts to develop and improve psychoanalysis, based on Rank's own analytic experience. Rank had concerns about the limitations, errors, and inadequacies of Freud's thought up to the 1920s. When Rank was ostracized by the psychoanalytic movement, he developed his theory of Will Therapy. Will Therapy has an existential and relationship foundation and gives priority to what we make of our lives, against the things that determine the context in which our lives are lived. Much of Rank's writing is quite complex and psychoanalytically informed, but the existential elements are apparent in the central role of will and choice, including the positive view of resistance, the emphasis on the present and future over the past, the recognition of limitations in life, such as time, and, especially, in his unique view on creative work and the helping relationship.

Jessie Taft used the term 'the immortal social worker' to refer to the professional social work self. It sounds very grandiose. Taft is applying Rank's view that the artist is seeking immortality through his or her creative endeavours. While this may apply to famous artists, Taft is suggesting that social workers are seeking a kind of immortality through their influence on others when they apply their creative skills to the practice of social work. Helping others has its own rewards. Most social work is anything but immortal, but Rank had a very wide definition of creative endeavour, which included institutional creation, the creation of new programs, and creative work done in social work practice. Rank regarded the creative person or artist as someone trying in their work to immortalize their mortal life. Taft applied many of Rank's therapeutic ideas about creativity to social casework. I believe Taft aimed to focus on how this approach encourages the caseworker to bring their attention, focus, and imagination to the helping relationship. Rank uses the term 'difference' to refer to the unique qualities of the individual person and to his or her recognition of their own potential for growth, rather than necessarily forcing the individual to conform or adjust to some set societal standard. The latter aim was the focus of psychoanalytically informed social work practice and of the Mary Richmond social diagnostic approach. Rank states:

> Social Work has been forced to change from the 'inside' because it did not have the authority of science, nor the skill and power of the professions of law and medicine. The first step in training for social work is the acceptance of difference; the second, is the utilization of differentiation for growth and, the third, is to permit difference, i.e., to permit the other to grow. (cited in Taft, 1958, p. 231)

## Functional social work defined

In the Functional social work approach, the social worker needs to be capable of representing the purpose of the program or agency to the client and of working within the fullness and limitations of an agency's function. Paradoxically, Taft claims that this frees up the client and the worker to focus their efforts on creating solutions within this Functional arena. It is precisely the limitations of an agency's function that enable the imaginative potential of social work to be applied. Taft was very clear that social work was no panacea for the social problems of the time. The partialization of the problem focus, created by an agency's function, was a part of the Functional approach to social work. Today, the Functional approach may focus more on the limitations imposed by the program guidelines in which the social worker operates, rather than on an agency's function, as most social work is delivered within the guidelines, policy, and standards of a governmental program. The agency delivering this program may also help shape and influence it, but the primary determinant of social work practice tends to be the program to which it is attached.

The Functional School was trying to establish social work as a profession separate from therapy and relief work. Casework is the focus, as the most refined and dominant method in social work at the time of this theory's creation, but the same principles apply to social workers in group work, community work, supervision, and social administration. It was by representing the agency and developing an identification with its purpose that the helping process could be defined as separate from therapy and relief. Taft compared function, with its expression in agency policy, structure, and guidelines, to the scientist's experimental process, with its hypothesis, problem, and experiment, which impose limitations on nature (Taft, 1942). Agency function provides the protective and limiting elements that enable the client 'not to know, but to discover whether this is the answer to his need' (Taft, 1942, p. 108). Unlike therapy, which excludes exterior reality to focus on the client developing their self, Taft saw casework as dealing with reality in the helping relationship. This made Functional social work deeply relevant to the times. Taft was steering social casework between the unreality of therapy, with its obsessive focus on self, and the mind-numbing routine of relief work.

---

Reflective Exercise 2.1: The personal challenge of working in child protection

In her book *Social Casework with Children*, Taft states that the student social worker is faced with a dilemma they need to clarify personally. According to Taft, the student either:

- 'Can never accept the rightness of taking a child from their home, and cannot identify with the agency's function', and/or

- 'Denies, because she cannot bear it, the pain and inevitable trauma inherent even in the most thoughtful, considerate taking over of a child from his own parents' (Taft, 1940, p. 3).

**Question:**
- Do you think there is a personal dimension to the social worker coming to terms with the child protection role?

# The 'greatest conflict in social work'

The context of the development of the Functional School in the United States was the mass unemployment created by the Great Depression between 1929 and 1940, social work's continued focus on its poor status and standing in the community, and the adoption of the Richmond medical diagnostic model of practice together with an embracing of Freudian ideas. The Freudian Diagnostic School of casework had already become established and was considered 'scientific' in mental health in the 1920s. During this period, a rank and file movement of social workers was formed that aimed to challenge the narrow casework focus of the dominant professional social work elite. The rapid expansion of social workers into the profession and their employment in governmental agencies also created a fear of loss of professional standards among the dominant professional social work elite. The Functional School emerged from the interest in psychoanalysis and its application in social work through Otto Rank's influence and his eventual rejection of the psychoanalytic approach. Functional social work was allied to the rank and file social workers, who were attracted to the democratization of the casework relationship the Functional School espoused (Ehrenreich, 1985).

It is hard for the social workers of today to appreciate the division within social work that occurred at this time. The profession was split between the minority 'Functionalists' and the majority 'diagnostics'. The division was fundamental, ideological, and practice-based. It even affected people's job prospects (Reynolds, 1963). It may appear to us today as a remote and irrelevant conflict, but perhaps one way in which it lingers can be seen by highlighting the essential contrasts between the two schools of social work and how they still shape practice today (see Table 2.1, below). The Diagnostic School eventually won the battle, and social work in the United States has continued to aspire to a more individualized, instrumental, clinical private practice model rather than to the more egalitarian, helping relationship model espoused by the Functional School (Pozzuto and Arnd-Caddigan, 2008). Over time, each school adapted to the criticisms of the other and refined their models. Popular new, 'fresh' models of casework emerged, such as in Helen Perlman's *Social Casework: A Problem Solving Process* in 1957, which attempted to use elements from both schools in new ways.

**Table 2.1** Contrasting approaches of the Diagnostic and Functional Schools, 1930–50

| Topic | Functional Approach | Diagnostic Approach |
|---|---|---|
| Primary assumption about humanity | Humans are mainly creative beings, capable of making choices and living more creatively, even people suffering neurosis. | Humans have a dark irrational side that needs to be professionally controlled, managed, and treated to maintain a healthy outlook. |
| Mechanism for Change | The client, and the function of the social work program, sets the limits of change. | The worker is the primary vehicle of change on the client through their insight and skill in analysis and treatment. |
| Process of Change Model | The helping relationship is the key to all change. Setting time limits helps to focus work. Outcomes are unpredictable. | Assessment, development of insight, and transference are techniques aimed at having the ego replace the id through treatment. Detailed planning for diagnosis and treatment is required. |
| Key Elements | Short-term treatment focusing on the here and now. Partializing of problems to address only the most pressing within the agency function of social work. | Long-term therapeutic intervention, based on in-depth investigation of the client's life history, and intensive, indeterminate treatment. Treatment and responsibility for the whole person. |
| Client-worker relationship | Equal relationship focused on client expressing their will as a positive outcome. Resistance to help seen as a positive exercise of will. Minimal use of technique in favour of active acceptance and growth experiences. Limitations are imposed by function and time. | The worker knows best, as only client involvement is allowed. Transference used to manipulate the irrational client into adjusting to the reality and rationality of their world. Insight used to help client understand and find new directions. Other techniques designed to strengthen the ego over the id and the harsh super-ego. |

*Continued*

**Table 2.1** Continued

| Diagnosis | De-emphasized, focus on uniqueness of each case, description of actual client and intervention process in detail with minimal analysis. | Crucial, precise diagnosis is used in the medical model; treatment follows and scientific methods are claimed. |
|---|---|---|
| Agency | Function of agency (expressed in policy, structure, and procedures) determines the purpose of social work intervention and treatment (including rules, time limits, etc.). | Agency is a setting only for professional intervention, which is determined by the social worker. There are no limits on the social worker's therapeutic capacity. Setting is respected as a place for therapy. |

The final functional social work text, Ruth Smalley's *Theory for Social Work Practice*, published in 1967, attempts to consolidate a generic Functional approach, but it represents the demise of this school as a separate movement in social work. Perhaps the short term, goal-oriented focus of this approach is also partly represented today by the still popular Task-centred approach, first introduced into social work in the 1970s by Reid and Epstein and based on their research into the effectiveness of time limited interventions in social casework. Meanwhile, new psychoanalytical clinical social work texts continue to be published to this day and are informed by the post-Freudian, psychodynamic, relationship-based theories that developed post-World War Two.

The Functional School did not look back to the limitations of the Mary Richmond 'social diagnostic' period and ask the question: 'Why was the everyday practice of social work excluded from your definition of casework?' The Functionalists had already been swept up in the fascination with the psychodynamic wave. It is easy, from a historical viewpoint, to be critical of their fascination. At that time, insight into the inner dynamics of personality was seen as finally offering a solution to the casework dilemmas that social work faced.

Bertha Reynolds (1963), a leading social worker on the left, has described the release of Virginia Robinson's functional social work book *A Changing Psychology in Social Casework* in 1930 as having the effect of an 'earthquake on social work' (p. 120). What was so earth-shattering about this book? What is striking about the book is how carefully and gradually

Robinson explains her case. In fact, Otto Rank is not mentioned in the first 122 pages in a work that is 185 pages in length. Robinson carefully describes the historical development of casework and gives priority to Mary Richmond's work, *Social Diagnosis*. In her analysis of this work, Robinson highlights Richmond's emphasis on the psychological factors in casework as the key to getting at the situational aspects of the problem. Robinson's description of the influence of Richmond's text on social work practice at the time indicates its pervasive influence on social work training. However, Richmond's text largely omits to address considerations of treatment, limiting its prescription for practice to social diagnosis. This has encouraged social work schools to develop specializations in particular practice areas, such as hospitals, foster care, education, etc., where the generic approach to social diagnosis could be given some additional detail for prescribed actions. However, social workers at the time did not know why they succeeded or failed with clients, nor did they feel in control of the intervention process. Robinson (1930) describes a typical experience:

> All the caseworker knows for certain, as she loses herself in the human experience, is that something very real and very significant is happening here. At times she may feel she plays very little part in these lives that act themselves out so dramatically before her, at others she may realize that, in some strange way, her entrance has made a vital difference in their situation, but very seldom does she feel that she is in conscious control of the effect she is exerting upon these personalities and their reactions. (p. 111)

In the final one-third of the book, Robinson goes on to critique the Freudian approach to social casework in which the caseworker decides the treatment approach based upon their more expert knowledge of the situation, even allowing a degree of client participation in this pre-arranged plan in order to obtain their cooperation. She explains how Otto Rank reshaped psychoanalytic theory by introducing Will Therapy into the analytic situation, which actively accepted the negative expression of will in therapy, a phenomenon often described as resistance. Two elements were seen as crucial in the worker–client relationship for this active acceptance to take place. One element was the worker's acceptance of the client's attitudes, another was the client's acceptance of the necessary limitations imposed by the relationship based on time, purpose, and function.

Robinson gives a clear example of how the active acceptance of the expression of client will can be used therapeutically through the example of a client coming late to an appointment. A non-acceptance approach, aimed at re-education, would advise the client for this 'not to happen again'. A passive acceptance would involve offering a sympathetic response, such as 'too bad you had such a hard time'. An active acceptance would look at the client's conscious effort to avoid the meeting by being late and even open up the client to their deeper unconscious avoidance by asking: 'Did you not want to come today?' In the psychodynamic approach, this question could be seen as a form of interpretation in which the therapist uses insight to interpret a client's behaviour. Will Therapy uses the insight gained from psychoanalytic training but limits the interpretation to the current behaviour and minimizes references to past experiences or childhood traumas.

Bertha Reynolds, in her 1963 biography, explains that Robinson's work gave a direct focus to the client–worker relationship as the key element in addressing the issues in the case, and further, she provided this view with a substantial theory to back it up. History taking had become obsessive under Richmond's social diagnosis model and the influence of psychoanalytic thought, and this was de-emphasized in favour of building the client–worker relationship. The client was moved centre stage rather than the 'social worker bearing therapeutic gifts', and the challenge was the building up of client strengths and actively accepting negative will expressions, with a view to redirecting these towards some unlived potential in the life of the client. In the period of 1939–52, the Diagnostic and Functional Schools fought out their war of attrition in the social work field. Reynolds (1963) labels the Functional School 'idealistic' and ends up supporting the Diagnostic School because it had the potential to become more 'scientific' over time, providing Freud's generalizations about human nature were revised (pp. 285–287). Reynolds' view of the conflict, written with the benefit of hindsight, concurs with other historical accounts of why the Functional School was eventually overtaken by the Diagnostic in the 1950s–60s. Other views attribute the rejection of the Functional School to the threat it posed to social work's professional status. Further developments in post-Freudian thought with Winnicott (Applegate and Bonovitz, 1995), Klein (Brown, 1971), and others developing ego psychology helped advance psychodynamic thought away from its pathologically deterministic focus, and in the 1950s Rankian ideas were absorbed into client-centred therapies and other experientially based therapies. There was little acknowledgement of the influence of Otto Rank on these developments until fairly recently.

The Functional School continued to advocate for itself well into the 1960s, with Ruth Smalley's *Theory for Social Work Practice* in 1967, and a certain rewriting of history took place in the way in which this theory was reframed for the times. For example, Smalley maintains that the Functional School always maintained a focus on the social in contrast to the Diagnostic School. She admits that each school learnt to absorb the key criticisms of the other. The question becomes: Why maintain the separation?

Having provided the key elements of this story in social work's history, a further question needs to be asked: Why is this story important and relevant to the existential social worker today? It is said that losers in battles rarely get to write history. Otto Rank was a loser in that sense and was written out of psychoanalytic history by the dominant Diagnostic Freudian School. His expulsion from the Freudian faction in psychiatry enabled his association with social workers to flourish. The Freudians' loss was our gain. Rank remained deeply immersed in psychoanalytic theory and built his own theories on this base. So why is he being embraced here as a key figure in the development of an existential approach to social work practice?

## Rank's contribution to social work

We have Jessie Taft to thank for Rank's contribution to social work. Even when she claimed that Rank had nothing to do with the naming of Functional social work practice, we can see that Rank's approach to therapy inspired her to give social casework a unique and separate status to therapy and not to see casework as merely some lesser form of therapy. Like the Rankian-imposed time limits to therapy (actually attributed to Freud, by Rank, and pragmatically required because of his touring schedules), the Functional name was a pragmatic label thought up by Taft to distinguish social casework from therapy and to give it special status as a uniquely social work method. In this naming, Taft reflected her academic background in the philosophy of George Herbert Mead, a leader in the development of pragmatism in America.

Taft was applying all she had learnt from Rank on the creative process to her creation of a unique role for functional casework. What Taft had learnt from Rank was to pay attention to creative potential in the client, but also to the limitations and accepted realities of any circumstance. Rank came to regard neurotic behaviour as frustrated creative energy, in comparison to the average person who is happy with their circumstances in life and the artist whom Rank considered to be a person with a strong ego. According to Rank, the neurotic is a frustrated artist, a person 'who cannot or will not accept herself' (cited in Stein, 2010, p. 118). Rank's focus on the present and de-emphasis on the past reflects his experience with neurotic obsession with the past, which he felt Freudian therapy encouraged. Only in the present can 'thinking and feeling, consciousness and willing occur' (Rank, 1936, p. 38). Rank believed that all the symptoms were present in the room and needed to be addressed in the present through the relationship with the therapist.

As an example of Rank's (1936) continuing relevance, here he describes how the neurotic person is led to a voluntary acceptance of themselves and their responsibility by facing up to the present: 'The desire to be rid of the present which forces a flight into the past or future by means of thinking or day dreaming, rests actually on the process of comparing which plays the greatest role in psychic life' (p. 46).

Rank describes the way to address inhibitions and fixations through the 'voluntary affirmation of the obligatory' (Taft, 1958, p. 279). By this, Rank means that the artist and the neurotic must 'deliberately appropriate that which happens or is given in the form of individual creation' (Taft, 1958, pp. 279–280). Rank links this view to Freud's Oedipus complex, which in Greek mythology refers to the 'deliberate affirmation of the existence forced upon us by fate' (Taft, 1958, p. 280).

Rank described his therapy as constructive because it did not alter the individual but tried to develop them, so that the person could accept themselves as they are. Rank (1936) was explicit about his use of philosophical understandings: 'Psychotherapy does not need to be ashamed of its philosophical character, if only it is in a position to give the sufferer the philosophy that he needs, faith in himself' (p. 96).

By 'will' Rank (1935) meant:

> An autonomous organization to control primarily the impulsive self; this organization, however, represents the total personality with its constructive capacity not only for ruling, developing and changing the surrounding world but for *re-creating* its true self. (p. 253)

Rank believed that the will begins as negative, with the infant's refusal to obey the parent. This is also played out in the helping relationship and the 'unbelievable difficulty with which any human being, even the weakest, brings himself to take help' (Taft, cited in Robinson, 1962, p. 307).

Rank thought that there were always two wills battling it out in any helping relationship. It is this battle of wills that distinguishes Rank's approach to therapy from the non-directive, client-centred approach developed by Carl Rogers. The central actor in therapy, to Rank, was the client rather than the worker providing insight and guidance. The worker is there, but more in an assistant role to the client. This required more discipline on the part of the worker, who had to facilitate rather than engineer the growth of the client: 'To become willing not to know everything about the patient in advance, to enter into the dynamic interplay of the therapeutic process without trying to predict or control the outcome is as exacting and responsible a discipline as exists in the world today' (Taft, cited in Robinson, 1962, p. 309).

Rank considered Freud's greatest discovery to be transference of feelings from the client to the worker because of the worker's active acceptance of the client. Transference will later contribute to Winnicott's concept of the 'holding environment', which is created by the 'good enough' parent or therapist who enables healing and recovery to take place (Applegate and Bonovitz, 1995, pp. 83–119). For Rank, the emphasis in transference was not on the activation of relationship feelings from the past onto the present, but on the current and present meaning of the relationship. Rank was once asked by an audience about his view of one of Taft's cases, in which she allowed a provocative child to stand by an open window with the risk that the child might jump out the open window: Are there any limits to what a therapist can do? His response was that the therapist can do whatever she wants, 'providing she takes responsibility for and helpfully deals with what it precipitates in the client' (Rank, cited in Lieberman, 1985, p. 37).

This is an insightful comment, not just because he backed Taft's willingness to take a calculated risk, but primarily because breaking down ego defences, through building trust and challenging the client, has the potential to leave the client defenceless and vulnerable. Personality change requires that therapists also take responsibility for the rebuilding process.

Functional social work accepted the limits and fullness of the functional role assigned to the social worker by the agency. Casework was not compared to therapy. Genuine growth could happen in casework because the client, in creative interplay with the caseworker, through the relationship and the limits of function, achieved some definite self-created goals.

## Criticisms and limitations of the Functional School of social work

What is missing from the Functional School's critique is any sense that social work rarely attempts personality change in its everyday practice, and that there was never a re-examination of the definition of social work inherited from Mary Richmond. The Functionalists accepted her definition of social casework, which diminished what social casework actually does in practice, which is to focus on problem solving, client advocacy, and linking clients to resources. The fascination with psychoanalysis and its impact obscured from view the actual lived experience of social workers and their clients. The client–worker relationship in casework became the major focus.

This narrow focus was apparent to outside observers of social work at the time. Barbara Wootton, a former magistrate, in reviewing the operation of social work in the United Kingdom in the early 1950s when 22,000 social workers were employed there, was highly critical of the influence of Freudian psychology on social work. While she did not appear to appreciate the battle between the two schools of thought in social work, she spoke of the 'erection of a fantastically pretentious facade and a tendency to emphasize certain aspects of social work out of all proportion to their real significance, while playing down others that are potentially at least as valuable' (Wootton, 1959, p. 271). She lays the problem at the door of Mary Richmond, the founder of social casework, not with the later psychologically informed social work theorists, where the 'claims to powers, which verge on omniscience and omnipotence' (Wootton, 1959, p. 271) are first expressed, and 'caseworkers see themselves as a species of social doctors' (p. 273).

In Wootton's view, social work had become obsessed with relationship to the detriment and devaluing of the sorting out of practical concerns that most clients actually present to social workers when seeking assistance. She highlighted a significant practice issue, which was psycho-dynamically informed social casework's 'refusal to accept at face value the emergencies which cause people to seek the aid of a social work agency' (Wootton, 1959, p. 277), and the duty 'to penetrate what is called the presenting problem to something deeper that is supposed to lie underneath' (p. 277).

It is difficult to determine the extent to which social work's adoption of psychoanalytic thought affected actual practice, as distinct from social work writing, at the time (Yelloly, 1980). Wootton (1959) argues that social workers were 'sensible, practical people who conduct[ed] their business on a reasonable matter of fact basis' (p. 279).

We also know that '[p]sycho-therapeutic work, if undertaken at all, [was], for most, a peripheral rather than a central feature of practice' (Yelloly, 1980, p. 3).

However, research suggests that the concerns expressed by Wootton had affected everyday social work practice to the detriment of social work's goals. A famous study, published in 1970, by John Mayer and Noel Timms, titled *The Client Speaks*, researched the level of satisfaction about and attitudes towards social work help offered by a family support association in London to sixty-one working class families. The study found a significant gap between the lived experience of the client in their interaction with the social worker and the modus operandi of the insight-directed social worker, who was informed by psychodynamic theory. As Mayer and Timms (1970) state:

> There is almost a Kafkaesque quality about these worker–client interactions. To exaggerate only slightly, each of the parties assumed that the other shared certain of his underlying conceptions about behaviour and the ways in which it might be altered. Then, unaware of the inappropriateness of his extrapolations, each found special reasons to account for the other's conduct. (p. 77)

In contrast to the insight-orientated social workers, who left clients confused, satisfied clients received 'supportive-directive' therapy, in which they:

> were given ample opportunity to unburden themselves; they were emotionally supported by the workers interests and concern; they were offered various suggestions and advice and they were 'enlightened' in ways that were apparently perceived as comprehensible. (Mayer and Timms, 1970, p. 138)

The Mayer and Timms study is not suggesting that supportive–directive therapy had necessarily been influenced by the Functional School of social work, though in his 1964 book, *Social Casework*, Timms did use a Functionalist perspective to help distinguish social casework from psychotherapy. Timms (1964) writes: 'The most important aspect of agency function is that it constitutes the meeting place of social worker and client. It is what brings them together and gives meaning and sustenance to their continued contact' (p. 8).

Following the 1970 study, Timms and Timms (1977) provided one of the first philosophical approaches to social work that was informed by empirical research, particularly on clients' experiences of casework. Twenty years later, in 1997, Noel Timms wrote an article on the Functional School of social work, which had by that time virtually disappeared from social work training. He argued for its continued relevance on the basis of its attempt to liberate social work from psychodynamic thought as a kind of second-class therapy and to give it a special status based on its Functional capacity.

Other critics have argued, more commonly, that the Functional School was naïve and limited in its failure to appreciate the potentially oppressive nature of many social agencies' functions, policies, and procedures (Hamilton, 1951). The Functionalists were aware of these criticisms. They argued that social workers were, precisely by virtue of their solid identification and understanding of agency function, most able to play a part in shaping that function to better meet client needs. The Diagnostic School also roundly critiqued the potential failure of the Functionalists to address unmet client need because of their acknowledged partialization of problem definition (Hamilton, 1951). These bitter criticisms are a matter of public record and should not deter this book's efforts to resurrect the Functional School's existential social work practice from the historical record, and to give it, at last, the status it deserves. The Functionalists' expression of existential social work was limited by the challenges, opportunities, and horizons of the time. Alan Keith-Lucas argues that the political theory implicit in the Functional School's form of casework was more democratic, positive, and strength-based and less judgmental and oppressive than the alternative model, which resulted in many abuses of human rights in the name of 'adaptation to reality' – such as psychoanalytic informed social work with unmarried mothers (Keith-Lucas, 1953).

The founders of the Functional School had discovered something special in their association with Otto Rank, who had stimulated their unique gifts for social work; because of his influence they sought to apply creativity in social work. The positive role played by resistance in therapy, as an expression of the client's will, was the key to using the so-called negative and limiting agency function, which, supposedly, acted as a break on social casework's therapeutic potential. Timms (1997) argues that Taft turned the potential 'negative', limiting agency function into a positive form of authentic social casework. It was precisely these limitations that provided the capacity for the client to 'free themselves from previous influence, so that their decisions about help could be recognized as authentic and genuine' (p. 735). Chapter 6 of this book deals further with the role of creativity in existential social work practice.

---

Reflective Exercise 2.2: Who is responsible for what?

Taft (1940) argued that one of the key challenges in working with children and adolescents is being clear about the responsibilities of the social worker and the responsibilities of the child or adolescent client, 'which they may be slow to admit or shoulder, but which they will not fail to defend, however negatively, if the worker usurps [them]' (p. 4). The same principle applies to work with adults.

**Questions:**

- Do you think helping clients assume their responsibility for things is important?

- How do you divide responsibilities between clients and social workers?

---

# Rank's lasting impact on existential social work practice

In the final chapter of Rank's 1932 book *Art and Artist*, he discusses the value of renunciation over a sense of deprivation, a process in which the creative person accepts the limitations of any form of creative expression in favour of personality development and their actual life and work. While reviewers have suggested that Rank was reflecting his own dilemma between creative works of psychology and his psychotherapeutic practice and the demands of life, I believe his argument is more subtle. It is based on his understanding of how great artists overcome the feeling of deprivation from life, in their focus on creative endeavours, through a deeply held conviction and willed renunciation in favour of their art work. Something of this renunciation is reflected in Taft's creation of the Functional School. She was, first, a highly successful and published child therapist and a trained psychologist before she came to social work. She was also keenly aware of the flaws and limitations of her use of the term 'Functional' to reflect what she was intending by this term. Much of the subsequent discussion on Functional social work has focused on the limitations of the functional element of the model, and Functionalists have attempted to adapt the term, to address the criticisms of it, and to widen its meaning to take in contemporary practice. Timms (1997) identifies this when he quotes Taft as stating:

> The task of the Functionalists was not to discover how therapy could be introduced into social work via casework, but to find what was truly indigenous to casework as such, as an authentic helping medium. Agency function provided this medium. (p. 729)

The attempt failed, but the intention was to create a unique identity for social casework. Rank read Kierkegaard and Nietzsche, and concurred that anxiety and guilt were existential givens to human life and existed prior to other instinctual content. The process of individuation involved separation from birth to death, and the will or fear to life and death are at play in every step of the journey of life. The neurotic-as-failed-artist, in Rank's conceptualization, becomes guilt ridden and unable to balance and commit to the responsibility to accept their freedom and limitations and to create new life in the process. Rank felt that the neurotic person has the same drive to create; 'I attempt to show, in the neurotic, the superhuman divine spark' (Rank, cited in May, 1967, p. 231).

How did Rank achieve this? He hardly mentions a single counselling technique, preferring to describe his approach as 'a philosophy of helping' (cited in Karpe, 1953, p. 56). Rank argued against the use of such techniques in his form of relationship therapy and prided himself on having no technique, and on being the 'first practitioner of therapy as a performing art' (Kramer, 1995, p. 78). Perhaps we get a small glimpse into his approach from Carl Rogers (1980), the founder of client-centred therapy, who acknowledged his influence on the development of his therapeutic approach. Rogers attended seminars run by Rank and employed social workers trained in Rankian relationship therapy. Rogers (1980) states that he learned much from one of these social workers. As he was developing his new approach to therapy, this Rankian-trained social worker:

> helped me to learn that the most effective approach was to listen for the feelings, the emotions, whose pattern could be discerned through the client's words. I believe she was the one who suggested that the best response was to 'reflect' these feelings back to the client – 'reflect', becoming in time a word that made me cringe. But, at the time, it improved my work as a therapist, and I was grateful. (p. 138)

From our twenty-first century perspective, this anecdote might seem a pithy but obvious insight into the expression of empathy for a client, but this was probably one of the first times these ideas were being expressed, and their influence over counselling practice and social work has been profound. Rogers built his three core conditions for the birth of a new personality from client-centred therapy on these Rankian ideas. These were that the helper must be:

> fully present in the here and now with no pretence of emotional distance, no professional façade[, …] communicate unconditional positive regard for the uniqueness – the sheer separateness and difference – of the other person and, thirdly, must express genuine empathetic understanding for the client. (Kramer, 1995, pp. 87–88)

I think Rank expressed this understanding, not just in the words he spoke to his patients in therapy, but in his conceptual understanding of the artistic challenge in becoming the person you are meant to be, the willing acceptance of both individuation and union with society, or, in his words, the 'voluntary affirmation of the obligatory'.

Rank was one of the first existential therapists to influence social work. He created a conceptual philosophical understanding of how people positively resist and receive help. He practiced therapy, and made use of his imagination, to grasp the viewpoint of the client in his attempt to understand the unique vision of the client, and then challenged the client to use this vision within the realities of their current existence. Jessie Taft applied this approach to social work as an organizational profession within the realities of agency function and structure, which are the context in which the creative potential of the social worker–client relationship can emerge.

So, what is this imagination, and how can it be applied in the everyday practice of social work? Sometimes there is a tendency to view the imagination as something that is reserved to artists and creative people but is not really necessary for ordinary people, like social workers, doing fairly mundane jobs, even if they are helping others. At these times, useful food for thought can sometimes be found by looking outside social work, at literary types who are examining the ordinary benefits to any profession that come from having a lively and educated imagination. Northrop Frye, in his book *The Educated Imagination*, examines some of the social utility of imagination. The well-trained imagination is used in normal conversation in our social life when we combine our thoughts and feelings about topics, in how we say things, in the words we choose to use in conversation, in saying 'the right thing at the right time', in responding to someone in a difficult mood or situation, in framing our message, and in discovering, for ourselves, the vision of the society we want to live in and in applying that vision to our current society and its espoused myths (Frye, 1964).

We use our imaginations to make sense of our and others' experiences. We try to find the words to express what is said, what is left unspoken, and what is merely hinted at. The philosophy of existence, or existentialism, states that our existences matter more than other eternal or immutable truths. Existences are expressed in stories or narratives, some real, others imagined, like Mark Twain's Huckleberry Finn, with whom Otto Rank so identified that he signed his personal letters to Jessie Taft, 'Huck', thereby expressing, through this identification, something about himself as a pioneering pathfinder.

When a social worker writes a court report, they are not simply writing an account of what exists or took place. They are framing an argument to an audience, trying to reveal what has been learned in the process of involvement with a client. In writing a court report, you take responsibility for its conclusions, conclusions based on judgements about events, experiences, conversations, and other relevant pieces of evidence. The social work writer is trying to reveal something they have discovered about the case in the process of searching for truths. Because of tight deadlines, the social worker may start their report a bit 'inauthentically', following the set process and 'getting the facts down' as if it were just a matter of the report corresponding to the facts of the case. The worker may follow pre-existing and pre-scribed ways of describing a situation, because this is easier than attempting to draw out the unique features of the case. They may even use some conceptual framework that helps to explain what happened and why the person acted or responded in the way they did. But eventually, if they look closely enough, and apply their imagination to what they have observed and discovered, something unique and real is unveiled about the particular circumstance, what Kierkegaard described as the 'unsurpassable opaqueness of the lived experience' (Kierkegaard, cited in Sartre, 1963, p. 9 n.6). This is an example of the creative application of the imagination in social work practice to produce a report that brings to light the reality of a situation.

# Conclusion

Rank and the Functional School of social work brought existential concepts and thought into social work practice. This begins in the effort made by the social worker to engage the client in a relationship. Without genuine engagement, it is very unlikely that anything of real value will happen; there will be pseudo-engagement in the delivery of services for a variety of reasons. Real change can take place when we engage both our emotions and intellect and learn from experience more than simply receiving insight from others. Rank's focus on the present, the new, and the unique over the past and the future highlights his existential emphasis on perceiving the helping situation as a genuinely creative experience that requires the therapist to adapt to the client rather than vice versa. His setting of time limits and an end to therapy is consistent with the existential givens of life and was followed by the pioneer functional social workers when they creatively adapted his theory to their work. Rank also embraced existential philosophy through Nietzsche and Kierkegaard and, through this experience, developed his willing acceptance of the givens of life, including its finale in death.

Existential theory grew from Husserl's phenomenology and the assertion that consciousness is intentional: 'All consciousness is consciousness of something' (Sartre, 2010, p. 43). Rank reintroduced the focus on the will in the helping relationship and reminded us of the intentional character of our being-in-the-world, or as Sartre (2010) put it: 'It is not in some lonely refuge that we shall discover ourselves, but on the road, in the town, in the crowd, as a thing among things, and as a human being among human beings' (pp. 45–46).

Above all, Rank helped his clients who were saying 'no' to their lives to learn to embrace creatively who they were and wanted to be. This was what the Functional School of social work set out to do for social work – to allow it to appreciate what it is and to make it come alive to its creative potential within the functional limits of its capacity.

## KEY POINTS FROM CHAPTER 2

1   The Functional School of social work is the first expression of existential social work practice.
2   By accepting the limits and parameters of program function, a creative focus on the present is encouraged, which engages people in the process of assessment and intervention.
3   The assumptions and principles of the existential Functional approach seem more suited to most social work in the twenty-first century.
4   The exclusive focus on the worker–client relationship in the Functional approach failed to address the diversity of practice interventions used every day by direct service social workers.

# 3

# EXISTENTIAL SOCIAL WORK COMES OF AGE

Social work writer Noel Timms (2014), in an interview, described the 'course of a life' as resembling 'the meandering flow of a river, which every now and again breaks into existential floodplains' (p. 750). In the 1960s and 1970s, the period examined in this chapter, existential floodplains developed within social work. Social work writers began explicitly applying existential thought within social work and identified themselves as existential social workers for the first time. Since the late 1960s and to the present day, existential thinking has been present in social work in the influence of a variety of existential therapies, in the application of existential philosophies to social work, and in the identification of existential issues clients face, including their making sense of their involvement within human services systems.

In this chapter, I explore the first social workers who identified as existential social work writers and the 'fellow travellers' who use existential thought and combine it with other approaches. I also explore one existential and phenomenological thinker who has been largely ignored by existential social work to date. A practice example is provided to show ways in which raising existential issues in practice can help a client face their personal challenges. In this review of existential social work writing, I describe the key developments of this first flowering. Finally, I make some suggestions about what needs to happen now if existential social work is to progress into the twenty-first century.

As with Albert Camus and other famous existential writers, it is not uncommon for existential thinkers in social work to reject identification with existential thought (Barnes, 1997). Partly this is due to existential thought being primarily identified with key atheistic French writers, Jean Paul Sartre and Simone de Beauvoir (Aho, 2014). Other existential thinkers seem to have felt obliged to distance themselves from these very popular

**Table 3.1** Classification of Existential Social Work Writers

| Existential Social Workers | Social Workers using Existential Theory |
|---|---|
| Donald Krill | Howard Goldstein (Cognitive Humanist) |
| Neil Thompson | Malcolm Payne (Humanist) |
| Jim Lantz | Ruth Parkes (Kantian) |
| John Stretch | Elizabeth Randall (Eclectic) |
| Kirk Bradford | |
| David Weiss | |

adopters of the label. I suggest that there is a basic division of existential thinkers in social work into two categories: those who embrace an existential or existentialist approach and those who incorporate existential thought in their overall approach to social work practice (Table 3.1).

There are also social workers who adhere to some form of existential therapy, such as logotherapy, which originated with Viktor Frankl. Jim Lantz was one such person, a prolific existential social work writer and family therapist. He was also strongly influenced by other key existential thinkers, such as Gabriel Marcel (Lantz, 1994a, 1994b, 1994c, 1998, 2000, 2001). Existential therapy has grown more popular over the years, and sometimes existential social work writers make little distinction between the two, leading to confusion – social work as a practice is more than just therapy. There is overlap between existential social work and existential therapy, and it is important to acknowledge the growing influence of existential therapies in their contribution to existential social work practice.

Irving Yalom (1998), arguably the world's most famous existential therapist and writer, has certainly influenced social workers, along with many other professions, that practice group work and psychotherapy. He forms part of the large contingent of existential humanist thinkers, primarily in the United States, who have built upon psychodynamic thought and incorporate existential issues. While the existential humanist school of thought in therapy appears to be popular, it operates no separate school of therapy and has, until recently, discouraged separate technical training, unlike every other school of therapy, all of which have special techniques unique to their approach. Existential therapies do take different approaches to practice, and existential approaches to therapy remain highly popular, despite finding little support in tertiary education institutions. Perhaps this focus on existential theory as foundational rather than prescriptive of practice has enabled key influential teachers and writers of mainstream psychotherapy texts, such as Gerald Corey (2009), to maintain an overall commitment to an existential approach to therapy while embracing other approaches within their own integrative frameworks. This theme of existential thought being a meta-theory also occurs in Neil Thompson's (2010) approach to existentialism and social work practice, which I discuss later in the chapter.

The influence of existential therapy on social work has been mainly limited to the provision of clinical private practice social work. Payne (2005) locates existentialism within the spiritual approaches to social work practice, which does tend to marginalize existential thought to the broader social work field. A major theme in the history of existential social work has been the supplementation of existential thinking with other sources of inspiration, such as humanism (to create 'existential–humanist thought'), incorporating spiritual writers like Simone Weil (1987, 2001) in the case of Ruth Wilkes (1981), and other popular spiritual writings of the time, such as those on Zen Buddhism for Donald Krill (1978). Howard Goldstein (1974) originally advocated for a unitary approach to all social work methods and later embraced an explicit existential humanist framework, supplementing it with cognitive theory. Before I examine some of these existentially informed social work writers, I will address the beginnings of explicit existential social work thought in journal articles by less well-known writers.

# The beginnings of explicit 'existential social work'

The first journal articles and lesser known existential social work publications focused on existential thought and social casework. In these articles, the themes of avoiding reductive deterministic theories were highlighted instead of the concrete existence of human life. This is partly in response to the dominance of Freudian thought during social work's early development. Existentialism's emphasis on free choice and the resulting responsibility and on the search for a more authentic existence are major early themes. The early existential social work articles concur with Kierkegaard's view, outlined in his work *The Concept of Dread*, in which he asserts that normal anxiety needs to be embraced, not avoided, as it stimulates growth in the individual (Kierkegaard, 1980). Emphasis is placed on the social worker–client relationship, reflecting Martin Buber's respectful 'I–Thou' relationship, which treats the other as another person of equal value and uniqueness, in contrast to the 'I–It' relationship, which treats the other in a non-personal, thing-like, or instrumental manner (Cooper, 2003, p. 20, 2012, pp. 36–37). Concern is expressed about existential thought's potential to be a cultish theory, although its failure to find a leading figure, such as Freud, was seen as potentially positive. The disadvantage of there being no leader is that people choose their favourite existential writer(s) on the basis of personal preference rather than the actual usefulness of the work.

In one of the first texts, *Existentialism and Casework* (1969), Kirk Bradford argues that the existential approach is humanistic and challenges the medical model of practice, which assumes that the client needs to be cured of problems by the expert professional social worker, who has all the answers. He refers to the work of Truax and Carkhuff (1967), two early researchers of counselling theories and models who summed up their findings with the three essential ingredients required of any system of counselling. These were:

- First, the counsellor's qualities as the 'genuine article' (authentic, mature, congruent, etc.). We might also say 'someone who is trustworthy and knows what they are talking about';

- Second, the counsellor's ability to demonstrate accurate empathy; and

- Third, the counsellor's ability to provide a warm, non-possessive, safe container in which therapy or social casework can take place, something akin to Winnicott's (1986) 'holding environment' concept, a safe space in which to explore problems.

From the very beginning of social work being informed by existential thought, we find existential ideas incorporated alongside humanistic thinking. Carl Rogers (1980), the founder of the humanistic school of psychotherapy, built his approach on extensive research on counselling processes and outcomes, in which the 'necessary and sufficient conditions of the therapist's therapeutic effectiveness' were:

1 *Congruence and genuineness*: in existential terms, someone who is authentic, someone who lives what they talk;

2 *Unconditional positive regard*: in social work terminology today, the capacity to demonstrate and convey non-judgemental attitudes, although even Rogers had to qualify this condition with very immature, 'regressed' clients, who responded better to a more conditional, parent-type relationship; and, finally,

3 *Accurate empathetic understanding*: the ability to accurately convey and understand the client's feelings and experiences.

By implication, congruence for the existential social worker might mean that they have read existential thinkers like Sartre, Camus, and de Beauvoir and have applied this thinking to their own lives to be able to convey a sense of authenticity. Sometimes there is the sense that existential social work requires that the social worker first heal *themselves* through existential thought. This view harks back to the earliest western philosophical traditions, in which philosophy was thought to be a way of life and not just a conceptual framework. The existentialists were reconnecting with the origins of western thought, making philosophy relevant again to real-world issues in the twentieth century, and providing new ways of living based on values like authenticity, freedom and responsibility, and lived experience. By the time existential social workers were writing the first journal articles explicitly applying existential theory to social work, humanistic thought – focused on the human person, primarily through Carl Rogers and the client-centred therapy movement – had been thoroughly integrated into existential social work practice.

## John Stretch and crisis in social work

In 1967, John Stretch, in one of the first articles ever written on existentialism in social work practice, asserted that existential thought would help social work embrace the inherent crisis nature of social work practice, even for the prevention of social problems. Contrary to popular belief, Sartre, in his early philosophy, was far more focused on contingency than freedom. Contingency is the idea that anything can happen. *Nausea*, his first novel, is rife with attempts to make sense of our contingent world. Contingency is one of the three elements that challenge our capacity for freedom, the others being causality (the view that we are driven or our actions deter-mined by external and internal drives, such as scarcity and hunger, and by impulses and unconscious thoughts) and tragedy. Tragedy is the view that everything eventually ends in failure, loss, death, and nothingness and thus leads to a loss of meaning.

In a 1974 article, Stretch asserted that existential thought would save social work by providing a framework that would root its efforts at pre-venting social problems in crisis management of current issues. This view arises from existentialism's denial of the possibility of social utopia and its acceptance of the inherent crisis nature of our world. Stretch contrasts social with critical existential thought. Social work's embrace of the social encounter via casework, group work, and social action is testament to a form of social existential advocacy of partial fulfilment through others.

Critical existential thought (referring to 'crisis' and not to critical social work as a theoretical approach) acknowledges that crisis is perennial. Ontic, or worldly, anxiety provides the foundation for social work's contin-ued need to assist humanity in practical, helping ways and in humanity's search for meaning in this context. This is where existential social work is contrasted with client-centred therapy and with the idealistic movement and its goal of self-actualization. Existential social work insisted on the dark-ness of concrete reality – there is to be no social utopia. However, the early pioneers of existential thought in social work, like Stretch and Krill, shared an over-optimistic and ambitious view of existential philosophy's potential to be some kind of panacea for social work's woes, rather than just one choice of framework amongst many equally valid and useful perspectives.

## David Weiss, 'compathy', and Martin Buber

In 1975, David Weiss wrote one of the first existential social work texts, *Existential Human Relations*. He was not writing exclusively for social work-ers, but for human relations workers more broadly. Yet social work seems to have been his main pre-occupation. Weiss centres existential social work within humanism and defines an existential approach as one that is 'committed to healing and revealing' (Weiss, 1974, pp. 17–25). But what does he mean by healing and revealing?

Martin Buber (1970) is Weiss' central inspiration throughout the text when describing the essential transition necessary for client fulfilment: the transition from an 'I–It' relationship to an 'I–Thou' relationship. Weiss also describes another relationship, even more fundamental than the 'I–It', and that is the 'I–Neuter', which describes someone operating on an existing biological basis – someone affected by apathy, fatigue, exhaustion, numbness, or withdrawal, for example. Social workers come across people experiencing these conditions. These are a subcategory of the 'I–It' relationship. As I have stated above, 'I–It' relationships exist wherever someone treats other human beings as objects or focuses solely on objects, as an addict focuses on a particular substance or activity, rather than on another person.

It is also possible for a professional social work relationship to assume elements of an 'I–It' relationship to the client, particularly when interviews are prescribed by procedures and program guidelines. For example, I can perform an interview with a client in my role in intake, and by going through only the set questions and motions I can treat that client as an object rather than as a unique individual. Current objective case-recording requirements can inadvertently support this tendency in practice. I could repress any involvement of myself, remain impersonal, and use whatever diagnostic tools are available to describe the client's situation 'objectively'. There seem to be degrees of 'I–It' and 'I–Thou' relationships. A social worker applying a category to a client needs to be careful to avoid what Neil Thompson (2010) has described as a reductive approach, which oversimplifies and falsely uses one element of a client's situation to explain them in their entirety. We all use categories or conceptual analyses to make sense of the assessment process, but an existential approach argues that we are always more than any categorization into which we might fit.

An 'I–Thou' interview, by contrast, requires that I enter a genuine dialogue with the client, based on our mutual respect as unique human beings, present and available to each other now, able to share our thoughts, concerns, vulnerabilities, and comments in a developing atmosphere of mutual trust. It also means I am aware that I am involved in this interview, and my presence helps to shape the interview, as does the purpose and agency setting. In existential social work there can be no objective assessment. I will explore this issue further in the next chapter on existential social work assessment and intervention.

Weiss states that I need to be at-one with myself and at-home with my professional job for the other person involved to be able to enter fully into this 'I–Thou' relationship. This does not mean I am not critical of policy or practice, but rather that I can be present with the client and offer them the best service given those policies and practices. Weiss stresses that our societies, social groups, even nation states, tend to reinforce the development of 'I–It' relationships. There is a tendency to simply get people to conform, to enact roles, which leads to the repression of the development of a genuine self. When a man states, in a men's group, that all he wants from his partner is sex and food, he is treating her in this 'I–It' manner. When a social worker 'hides behind' the rules and administers a service impersonally, he or she is treating the client as an object, not as a human person. Of course, these two examples are significantly different in that the former is abusive while the latter might be described as bureaucratic; such distinctions still need to be made within the 'I–It' relationship world. The social worker needs to affirm the client's humanity in applying the service rules and guidelines and to heal the person by allowing the person to reveal their true self. How do you, the social worker, do that?

Weiss (1974) is not suggesting that the social worker throw away his or her guidelines, classification systems, interview schedules, and all the other useful tools that have been developed by the profession, fields of service, and individual agencies or services. These are still useful as they help the social worker create order out of chaos and avoid forgetting crucial aspects of the process. But do we allow these tools to prescribe all our practice? The social worker cannot ignore program tools and obligations. Team managers and leaders expect social workers to follow these rules and procedures to the letter and to understand their rationale and importance for program structures and agency procedures.

What Weiss is suggesting is that the existential social worker is a 'part of, yet above agency structure and services' in aiming to perceive the otherness or difference or uniqueness of the other person in the room. The system doesn't really require this of the social worker, but it is precisely this perception that heals as it reveals. Having an 'I–Thou' relationship involves moving beyond sympathy (a feeling for someone) to empathy (aiming to feel what the other person feels), and, beyond empathy, to 'compathy', which involves encountering the other via co-existence, confirming the other's right to be an individual as a unique and unrepeatable human person. It is this genuinely dialogic process, which respects the limitations of the capacity of even accurate empathy to understand the other person's point of view, that allows the other person to bring forth their own self.

An example of genuine engagement from my practice: a man objected to providing his current partner's name for a safety contact, which is a requirement of involvement in the men's group program that I facilitate. He had an already strained relationship with the program, and this was my second interview on the matter. He arrived early for his appointment. I knew he was busy that day, and even though other work-ers advised me against doing this man any favours, I decided to alter my schedule and see him early. He refused to provide the requested details, arguing that we were being invasive of his new personal life. Without forcing him, I was able to use my flexibility in seeing him early to explain how certain requirements of the program were not negotiable, while other conditions could be flexible, such as accommodating his early arrival that day. He eventually provided the details. In that interaction, I made my decision quickly because it seemed the right thing to do. I accepted the concerns of my colleagues that my flexibility could play into the man's ego-centrism, but I remember thinking that engaging difficult men is part of my responsibilities, and providing this safety con-tact information, in his circumstances, was not negotiable. Being flexible about time was useful in engaging with this man, and it may be in other circumstances as well.

## Donald Krill: The American existential social work writer

Donald Krill (1978) is considered *the* existential social work voice in Amer-ica. He has been writing on the subject sporadically for forty-five years. Krill uses a much broader range of writings from new age spiritual thought than other thinkers, including works by spiritual writer Krishnamurti, as well as Zen and Christian texts, such as those of Thomas Merton, and many others to supplement and enhance existential thought. In one of his first articles, Krill (1969) explained his approach succinctly:

> Existentialism should not be considered a completed philosophical system, but rather a series of emphasized realities that can be adapted to other forms of philosophy and religious belief depending on the background and thought of the individual therapist. (p. 49)

Krill's existential social work approach gives primacy to certain themes, like alienation. Krill (1969) outlines his approach to existential practice in social work as follows:

1　Helping a client perceive their own self-deceptions, false beliefs, and discourses that are driving their problematic lives (Krill describes this as the disillusionment process);

2　Identifying the client's capacity to take responsibility and make choices that address the issues identified in step 1 (Krill calls this freedom of choice);

3　Making sense of the process by meaning-making, particularly of those negative experiences that don't make sense for the client or where their meaning is hindering the client's progress and ability to find meaning in suffering;

4　Seeing dialogue as the only way to solve social problems – no ultimate solutions, no one has the total answer (Krill calls this 'necessity in dialogue'); and finally

5　Commitment to action based on all of the above.

Krill was a pioneer of existential thought being applied to social work. Krill embraces existential therapy as social work and makes little distinction between them. He recognizes that social work is more than therapy. For example, in social action activities, Krill contrasts the naïve social activist with absurd social activism and has misgivings about more manipulative revolutionary tactics such as Saul Alinski's (1971), which legitimize scapegoating. Krill advocates an absurd social activism, based on Camus's approach.

The naïve social activist is involved in the transactional analysis triangle of rescuer, victim, and persecutor (Karpman, 1968). For example, children in residential care may be seen as victims of abuse by residential staff who persecute them, and the social activist's role is to rescue these children by removing all of them from residential care. The absurd social activist, according to Krill, avoids this triangle game by engaging in detached observation rather than passionate involvement.

Taking Camus (2000) as his inspiration, Krill is right to emphasize limitations and moderation as key existential virtues in social activism. Justice is relative, according to Camus's 'absurd rebel' stance, but the rebel is still passionately involved in the conflict in standing up against injustice. He recognizes these contradictions but puts human limitations before the absolutist reasoning of the terrorist or freedom fighter (depending on your political viewpoint) or before the status quo-defending against the rebellious.

Camus preferred story-telling to philosophy. In his story 'The Guest' (1958), a teacher at an isolated school is confronted with the task of transferring an Arab man, brought to his school by the police, to a distant court where he is to be tried for murder. The context is the Algerian revolution, and everyone is expected to take sides. The school teacher values his work with the local Arab community, which involves teaching and providing for their welfare needs. Despite not wanting this 'mandatory' task imposed upon him by the police, he embarks with the Arab on the journey, but refusing to take sides, the teacher sets him free. As the teacher leaves, he looks back and sees the accused man complying with the order of the authorities by walking towards the court, presumably to keep the teacher from getting into trouble. Upon his return to the school, the teacher finds a message: 'You turned in our brother, you will pay!' (p. 29).

In Camus's story, both sides, the police and the Algerian community, are using violence. The teacher (or social worker) is looking after human needs as best he can, but he cannot avoid being drawn into the conflict. He acknowledges his complicity, and Camus uses the concept of calculated culpability to explain his reasoned choice, the choice of the lesser evil or harm. For Camus (2000), intervention in trying to improve social conditions is potentially, or actually, harmful. We must choose the least detrimental option; it cannot be dissolved into the good. Even in moderation, social action involves getting one's hands dirty. I believe Camus's story of the school teacher–welfare worker has direct relevance to social work in searching for a humane third way between two violent adversaries.

Donald Krill continued to be the lone voice of existential social work practice in the United States right up until 2014. Like Camus's (1972) account of the myth of Sisyphus, it appears to have been an up-hill battle, but just as in Camus's version of the story, we have to imagine that Sisyphus is happy (p. 315).

# Neil Thompson and anti-oppressive existential social work

The existential social work of Neil Thompson provides a comprehensive critical existentialist philosophy for social work. In his first publication, Thompson (1992) outlined his philosophy, which is based on the period in Sartre's post-World War Two phase in which Marxist social and political theory became prominent. Thompson criticizes Sartre for his undifferentiated lumping together of matter, or the material world. Machines, buildings, nature, and even animals are all considered to be contained within the concept of being-in-itself. Humanity, in its self-consciousness, is described as a being-for-itself. Sartre was a man susceptible to extreme changes, and Thompson also criticizes his abandonment of existentialism for Marxism, for his uncritical acceptance of Marxist views on culture as derived from the economic base, and for his advocacy of revolutionary violence as a necessity.

What Thompson finds valuable for social work in Sartre is his existential sociology, combining ontology, phenomenology, ethics, and social theory. Sartre's philosophy maintains the importance of the individual's commitment to social action and of the dialectical process of social change brought about by social movements, the creation of social institutions, and their critique from the point of view of the oppressed. Here Thompson has found the theory and tools, such as Sartre's progressive regressive method of existential biography, to critique the dominant theories used in social work. He uses Sartre's existential sociology to challenge psychoanalytic theory, moving it towards existential psychoanalysis and existential therapy. Behaviourism, symbolic interactionism, systems theory (which includes ecological approaches and family therapy), and radical social work are all reviewed and found to be limited and to have been subsumed within the more satisfactory meta-theory of Thompson's existential social work.

Mainstream or traditional social work practice comes under criticism mainly for its lack of a political dimension of practice. It is Thompson's critique of radical social work that enables him to position his framework as an alternative approach, which embraces a social–political or critical social work perspective while also acknowledging the dialectical character of social work as an agent both of social change and of social control. The important point for Thompson is the vital role of social change for the social worker who must choose sides. To quote from his 1992 book, *Existentialism and Social Work*: 'There is no middle ground. Intervention either adds to oppression (or at least condones it) or it goes some small way towards easing or breaking such oppression' (p. 169).

Thompson acknowledges that state employment or funding does place limits on social work's social change function. Social work's social control function also engenders mistrust, further limiting the social worker's capacity to contribute to social change. Nevertheless, taking sides on all forms of oppression forms the basis of Thompson's anti-discriminatory model of social work practice. Social work clients want assistance to alleviate their immediate problems, which usually means helping them to adjust to the existing system. This process involves interventions designed to provide relief, and, in that sense, social workers are meeting human needs and helping people to adjust to the status quo. Our duties involve a substantial degree of social control, which can put us into conflict with our clients and require negotiation and conflict resolution skills. Clients experiencing oppression can also be oppressing members of their own families. The social worker is often in a position where he or she is balancing the risks and needs of complex situations, where the presenting oppressed client is oppressing others, including the social worker as a representative of 'the system'. The social worker's task is to deal with these multiple oppressions while maintaining a working relationship with the hostile client.

Social work aims to do more than social control, symptom relief, and social adjustment – social change is also a critical and fundamental aim. Most social change in social work is aimed at addressing oppression and tackling social problems, but social work can rarely do this on its own. It requires the co-operation of other, more powerful elites, along with social movements, to create fertile conditions for social action. It is not so much a question of taking sides as of building an irreversible impetus for social change, which I will discuss in Chapter 5. Thompson acknowledges that he got the idea of taking sides from Freire's (1972) educational political philosophy (Thompson, 1992). Another way of describing the transformative process that social work should aim for is as helping our clients live the fullest life possible. Neil Thompson describes how social workers need to recognize and help their clients to see the internal and external constraints created by free human praxis that society and social constructs place upon them. These constraints are not set in stone.

I came to Neil Thompson through his anti-discriminatory practice work, when I had begun teaching community workers. His PCS (personal, cultural, structural) model of oppression analysis helped students to imagine the person in front of them as experiencing multiple levels of oppression (Thompson, 2006). PCS analysis helped students to better understand how oppression affected their clients' circumstances and to reduce worker oppression of clients stemming from the workers' individual personality issues, including their own liking or disliking of the client.

Thompson (2000) is very good at providing general practice guidelines to existentialist social work practice. For example, he suggests that existentialist social workers should:

> help people recognize those areas of their lives in which they have a degree of control, seek to influence the range of options available, distinguish the subjective and objective elements in assessments and interventions, boost confidence and self-esteem, take seriously the challenge of our own authenticity, and always work in a shared partnership in helping and in encouraging collective responses to social problems. (pp. 206–211)

Thompson is a prolific writer of human services books, and these books enable new teachers of human services workers to deliver comprehensive lessons on most subjects. What made Neil Thompson's existentialist social work so useful was the clarity and succinctness of his writing. Sartre is a verbose and sometimes confusing writer. In contrast, Thompson, the United Kingdom's most distinguished existentialist social work thinker, explains his viewpoint in a straight-forward manner, linking it to other theories and practices that are compatible with his existential meta-theory.

Thompson (2010) also challenged other critical approaches, arguing social work informed by, for example, postmodern approaches to be inherently flawed. I, in contrast to his rejection of even 'weak' forms of critical postmodern social work, view existential therapies' embrace of postmodern thought as being complementary and even as adding useful and additional thought and practice. Thompson's rejection of the playfulness of some postmodern thought does not sit comfortably with Sartre's acceptance of playfulness and his rejection of serious essentialist thinking. Postmodern thought has brought tangible benefits to social work practice: for example, in the work of psychotherapist Alan Jenkins (1990, 2009), of social worker and family therapist Michael White (2011), and of others from the Dulwich Centre in applying narrative therapies in a range of services areas, including family violence. Social workers can benefit from both postmodern and existential thought, particularly in co-creating alternative meaning-making and sense-making processes of intervention and in challenging oppressive practices. An important skill that social workers use on a daily basis is to help clients make sense of their involvement in the service system so they can feel empowered and make the best use of what is on offer. Helping clients to see how certain discourses can limit and degrade people's lives is a valuable and beneficial use of postmodern thought in everyday social work practice. It helps externalize and objectify a false ideology that is oppressing their lives. In some situations, clients can be blind to the oppressive discourses that sanction them causing suffering for themselves, and others.

I believe that existential social work should adopt a humbler attitude to theoretical perspectives that provide useful alternative ideas and strategies. I acknowledge the existing positive contributions of Thompson (1992, 2010), Krill (1978), Lantz (2000), and others to the development of existential social work, which should be comfortable offering itself as one perspective among many alternatives that individuals can compare, examine, and choose to apply in their social work. As I have argued above, postmodern social constructive theory, such as narrative work, is compatible with an existential approach to social work practice. It seems that existential social work thought can be combined with a wide range of other theoretical approaches, such as cognitive, systems, poststructural, and feminist theories. The crucial point, from an existential viewpoint, is not to view any theory, including the existentialist, as the total answer. There is always more to reality than any one theory or combination of theories.

## Why some mainstream social work values still matter in existential social work

Thompson (1992) is critical of mainstream or traditional values such as the client's right to self-determination because these values don't have critical use. I disagree with Thompson's dismissal of mainstream social work principles like self-determination.

Below is an example from my own practice of the value of self-determination. Frequently, social workers are dealing with pre-contemplative clients, people who don't recognize that they have a problem, despite other agencies having determined that they do. They come into groups resentful and angry at their treatment. The groups are set up for clients who recognize that they have a problem, and, as a result, pre-contemplative clients often disrupt and dominate the discussion.

On one occasion such a man joined a group I was co-facilitating. He missed his orientation session and proceeded to dominate the discussion. I was required to point this out to him and to request that he desist. He didn't like it, but he stopped. In a follow-up group meeting, he joined with another man to launch an attack on me for dismissing his views.

'Storming' is part of group process. It is where the participants feel confident enough, in the group, to challenge the group facilitation. How was I to respond? I apologized to him for any disrespect he may have perceived on my part. Why did I do this? I could only think that it was how I would want him to react if he felt disrespected by someone else.

As social workers, we have an agenda in our work. We are seeking to help people change, but we have to achieve this change by giving people (sometimes, people we find personally obnoxious in behaviour or attitude) demonstrated respect and dignity, no matter how they are behaving. We are modelling respectful behaviour. We invite them to consider new ways of relating that are respectful and safe. We do not impose this on them; they can choose to reject our approach. This reflects our adherence to their right to self-determination or freedom, which is an essential part of human dignity. Perhaps I was too abrupt with this man and he deserved my apology. I may have erred, but he, too, may err in the future in his ongoing relationship with his ex-partner and mother of his children. How will he react to future perceived slights?

We have seen the downplaying of relationship-based social work as a result of risk management and other managerial strategies designed to control limited social resources and protect reputation. Recently, we have observed the commandeering of individualization and personalization by competition policy and the expansion of market forces into social policy. These ideas were mainstream social work values and practices long before they were applied as a market tool, as a way to turn clients into customers. Existentialism did not invent these values, but they are very consistent with existential philosophy. Individualization or personalization is a foundational principle of good casework practice. Similarly, a good relationship is central to all social work practice, and much intervention fails because of limited engagement with clients. How we ensure that clients, who are often mandated to receive our services, use their self-determination is critical to their development and to good social work practice. Freedom exists in every social situation in which social control is exerted. The social worker helps the client to discover freedom and to use it appropriately.

Thompson (1992) is correct that mainstream social work has failed to tackle the social change aim by attempting to force adjustment to the existing social system. The challenges of the twenty-first century for social work are about ensuring that these important existential human values are not used and shaped solely by market forces, because there is so much more to individualization, personalization, and client self-determination than mere customer choice. I will be discussing these ideas further in the next chapter on existential assessment and intervention, as well as in in Chapter 5 on team work, social policy and social movements. Treating these values as a 'dead end', as Thompson (1992, pp. 106–113) describes them, only abandons these important principles of practice to their reshaping by market forces.

## Ruth Wilkes and the need for moral philosophy in social work

Ruth Wilkes, in *Social Work with Underprivileged Groups* (1981), is concerned with challenging the idea, currently dominant in social work, that our purpose is to change people. She argues that this managerial approach devalues client groups for whom change is not the focus, such as the elderly, and those suffering from chronic diseases or who are facing death.

But she also says that all social work practice needs to value difference, look beyond abberant behaviour to understand the person behind the difficult individual, and stand for change that is self-directed as far as possible, even in statutorily prescribed or limited situations.

I have added Wilkes to this small group of existentially informed social workers because her work is inspired by a philosophical approach that combines Kant, Kierkegaard, Simone Weil, and Gabriel Marcel. She is attracted to the mystical realism of Weil and rejects the limited, atheistic existential thought of Sartre with its talk of consciousness as nothingness and of the inevitable conflict in relationships. Wilkes adopts a false either-or dichotomy in which geniune helping does not attempt to change others but to understand them, and where disrespectful social work is geared towards making changes with clients because it is doing good for them (i.e. 'we know better') or towards helping others who are negatively affected by their harmful behaviour. Wilkes' work reminds me that the social worker's first task, before deciding how to intervene, is to try to understand a client. This requires that we try to see things from their lived experience, even though we interpret this experience through our professional lens.

To illustrate her position, Wilkes offers the example of a very independent 87-year-old woman who was hospitalized after a fall. Various formal and informal helpers persuaded the social worker that this lady would be best off in a nursing home, despite her determination to live independently. The change-focused social worker in her case example sided with the prevailing view without doing her own independent assessment and coming to her own conclusion. But what is missing from Wilkes' analysis is the possibility that these change agents may be right. The elderly woman may have been better off in care, even after her preferences were given their due. Wilkes is arguing for a moral position in social work under which we would 'first do no harm'.

In a social work assessment, all appropriate options need to be considered, and the least detrimental option may turn out to be institutional care. And what about self-determination in this scenario? Wilkes comments that no one tried to become part of the elderly women's situation and to see the situation from her lived experience or from the perspective of her preferences. Respecting self-determination means genuinely making an effort to understand the client's viewpoint, not that we must adopt it in all circumstances, but that we do give it weight and consideration.

What is important about Wilkes is not so much her key arguments, which are flawed, but that her view reflects a current attitude within social work.

I worked for many years with Jesuit Social Services (JSS), a Catholic welfare agency in Australia. Their motto is 'standing in solidarity', with the poor, marginalized, neglected, unwanted, and difficult people who society and other services found too hard to deal with. It is important to note that this approach is based on Catholic social teaching and absolute moral values. In this view, it is more important to 'stand with' the poor than to change them or their circumstances. The 'stand with' comes first, before the change, which, when it comes, must be self-directed. This principle shapes the service response of the JSS, which aims to value the person of the client above all other considerations.

Building upon a Christian vision, Wilkes is attemping to use Kant, existential thought, and the work of Simone Weil to re-assert this absolute moral philosophy in social work. Existential thought rejects nihilism, embraces the human person, and requires us to decide as if we were making our decision for all humanity – a Kantian perspective built on a Judeo–Christian ethos that values all human life.

Versions of this Judeo–Christian vision have shaped social services, through many service agencies created by Christian communities and organizations, since the beginning of social work. Their practice continues in the present and into the foreseeable future. Ruth Wilkes' work reminds us of the ethical position of standing against oppression, with those who are oppressed. But as we saw with Albert Camus and Neil Thompson above, life tends to be more complicated than taking one of two sides, and social workers are required to balance multiple objectives in their work.

Even our most oppressed clients expect us to help them in addition to valuing them for themselves. Wilkes reminds existential social workers that ethical concerns are central to the existential approach and shape the way practice is conducted. Social work clients are frequently the least respected, most despised, and most difficult people for society and other service systems to deal with and assist. How we work with them is as important as the things we want to achieve with them.

## Lantz, Marcel, and Frankl in family therapy and social work

Lantz adopted Gabrielle Marcel's existential philosophy along with logotherapy to produce a body of existential social work practice in family therapy and other fields. As a family therapist, Lantz (2000) maintained 'the desire to experience meaning is the primary and basic motivation for most human marital and family behaviour' (p. 5). Using Frankl's theories, Lantz argues that an existential vacuum results when people fail to address a lack of meaning in their lives. The purpose of therapy is to help shrink the existential vacuum thereby reducing the symptoms of this disease, which other therapies tend to treat directly. Lantz used recollection to help families recover the meaning in their lives and empathetic availability to teach a new approach to the self that is other-centred and filled with love and charity towards family members. Lantz applied Marcel's work on problem and mystery to families. He called the two processes primary reflection, to problem-solve and reduce problems, and secondary reflection, to discover wholeness and mystery and the unity of experience as making sense of lived experience.

Lantz challenged the use of abstraction by both clients and workers, as well as the use of technological skills or what he described as 'techno-mania', in which treatment employs a range of helping techniques drawn from different schools of thought. Where people focus on things and on controlling others in the family, Lantz (2000) calls it 'marital or family possession' (p. 38). This represents the sense of 'having' rather than 'being in' a relationship. Having possessions cannot be avoided, but Lantz is addressing the dangers associated with an attitude of power and control over things and others.

Lantz expressed disillusionment with the loss of spirit and soul in the family therapy movement. He was critical of the 'shifty radical construc-tionists' (2000, pp. 103–104) who claimed that all reality is socially con-structed. He praised their willingness to respect the client's narrative but decried their claim that love, commitment, fidelity, meaning, and intimacy are simply constructed and can be changed. At the other end of the family therapy spectrum, Lantz believed that the 'controlling technomaniacs' (pp. 105–107), or strategic family therapists, used technical strategies to make changes to family systems, like technicians fixing a machine.

Lantz was particularly attracted to Marcel because of his concrete, or incarnational, introduction of the holy into family life. An example of this was his use of secondary reflection on values, spiritual realities, and poten-tials in the family through the 'shoebox exercise'. This exercise involved family members revealing the thoughts that they had been afraid to share with each other in the past. Like Otto Rank, Lantz welcomed a family's resistance to change and viewed it as their positive effort to develop their own freedom and to find a way out of their dilemmas, thereby leading to growth. Surprises and attempts to develop their own solutions are not discouraged in this approach, but equally the therapist is actively challenging and promoting change through experiential work and reflective activities.

This battle of opinions is highly valued in existential therapies, with the therapist guiding, but not directing, the outcomes. Lantz also advocated the use of cognitive theory in existential practice through Socratic dialogue, analysing thinking processes that contribute to feeling states and actively changing these thinking patterns, beliefs, and self-talk (Lantz, 1996). Lantz considered Marcel's philosophy to be consistent with the use of cognitive theory in social work treatment. He used primary and secondary reflection on unmeasurable meanings and for discovery through participation and encounter, through concrete experiential activities instead of abstract insight approaches (Lantz, 2000).

Lantz used Marcel's work to create a unique approach to the evaluation of existential therapy, via what he called the participation report. This report addressed the ways in which the therapist and the client engaged with each other, what reflective processes were used, and how they communicated their results. Various qualitative approaches were recommended, with change coming from a variety of potential sources, not just through the therapist's interventions. In standard experimental designs, the therapist's interventions are assumed to be the source of change. Lantz developed numerous experiential and art-based approaches to therapy, including the use of testimony, as described by Marcel in his application of existential therapy.

It was Marcel's existential philosophy that helped Lantz restrain his own tendencies to be a 'shifty radical constructionist' and a 'technomaniac' strategic family therapist. Lantz (2000) recognized that the key to his social work practice in family therapy and in other methods was Marcel's focus on the 'manifestations of change that serve and follow the spiritual realities and potentials of marital and family life' (p. 108). Lantz has provided a comprehensive and detailed clinical elaboration of existential social work practice in short-term crisis work, cross-cultural practice, work with diverse populations, such as victims, as well as military work, and family therapy and practice.

Throughout the twentieth century, certain existential thinkers, such as Sartre, Marcel, de Beauvoir, Merleau-Ponty, and Heidegger, gained notoriety and attention whilst other existential and phenomenological writers were largely ignored by social work. This is now changing, and, into the twenty-first century, access to other existential writing is reshaping the breadth and depth of existential thought. I now wish to turn my attention to one of these writers, whose ideas may have a significant effect on social work practice in the future.

## Edith Stein and empathy

At the beginning of the phenomenological movement, before she became a Christian, Edith Stein wrote seminal works on empathy and created a powerful alternative critique to Heidegger's existential analysis. The oppression of Jews and women ensured that her thought was marginalized, but since her beatification as a Catholic saint, all her writings have been published. They display a remarkable alternative existential analysis of the human person, of communities, societies, the role of the state, and the meaning of being. Contrary to Heidegger's existential analysis, Stein argues that our first experience is 'being with' others in family and community. Development is an essential aspect of human beings, something Heidegger rarely mentions, yet it is so important to social work practice.

The human person is the bearer of all the existentials or elements of existence, which includes the body, the mind, and the soul or spirit, which provides for the infinite being of the person. In all communities there are leading lights, humans who take responsibility and form and shape their communities. Heidegger ignores human fulfilment as a phenomenon and denies that human beings can learn anything from others' experience of the dying process, for example. Stein thinks Heidegger places too much emphasis on the future project of humanity, thereby missing the fullness of existing in the present moment. Being present is the way of being fulfilled. For Stein, what gives human life fullness is joy, love, and all the other qualities associated with the spirit. While praising his achievement in *Being and Time*, Stein thinks that Heidegger cut himself off from being, by limiting himself to the human understanding of being. His being is 'unredeemed being' (Stein, 2007, p. 81). Although he was completely unaware of her critique, the later Heidegger coincidentally changed in ways that address some elements of these criticisms.

How is it, Stein asks about our motivation, that we accomplish unpredictable, surprising things?

How do we make unexpected changes in our lives? How do we charge up the battery of the human heart? How do we maintain our life-power, drawing upon sources of energy that seem to be infinitely renewable?

Stein's work on empathy argued that this ability was essential to our personal growth and development. Below is a case example in which an existential social worker demonstrates empathy for a middle-aged man with an addiction to pornography. She is able to name the addiction for him as an existential issue, which helps the client to understand the inauthenticity or, in Sartre's terminology, the 'bad faith' operating within his life. The social worker was also growing in her ability to empathize with her client's existential challenge.

---

### Case Example 3.1: Naming a problem as existential

A 45-year-old Caucasian male of middle-class background had been educated at an all-boys' school before entering a Defence Force Academy at 18 where he trained as a professional soldier, graduating as an officer and serving until he was 33. He is now employed as a consultant in his profession, is highly paid, and is very successful. He describes himself as being socially competent and very achievement-oriented, being a keen athlete and skilled musician. He married soon after his discharge and has one child, a girl, age five. He describes his wife as being very outgoing (far more so than he is), also a highly skilled professional, and highly independent. He describes himself as 'having everything'.

He was referred by his doctor to a social worker to address issues around his habitual viewing of pornographic videos. He is afraid that this may jeopardize his marriage. He also sees it as morally abhorrent behaviour – as a manifestation of his moral weakness. His viewing of such videos and magazines began soon after entering the academy, though he recalls that his father used to read 'girlie magazines'. He likes women, although he had not been particularly sexually active prior to his marriage, with his wife initiating the courting. He enjoys regular sexual intercourse with his wife, however it does not provide him with the 'thrill' he gets from the videos.

What the female social worker did with this client was to adopt a position of non-judgemental curiosity towards this troubled man. She wanted to know about these two separate worlds that he had created for himself, one respectable and safe, the other shameful and exciting. She learns about this other, hidden world, its details and how he objectifies the women it depicts. She began to understand that his hidden world was eating up his sense of self, creating an existential crisis for him, and she named it as such, stimluating his curiosity about the meaning of the term 'existential'.

As a group of social workers listened to the description of her practice with this client, so troubled by his addiction, one of the other female social workers commented that the man's social worker had 'wrecked it for him', which caused a burst of applause from the group – this was exactly what had happened.

Perhaps she did not set out to do this. But her willingness to share the client's world with him, her genuine curiosity and non-judgemental approach, had enabled the client to expose this world to the light of focused, joint co-attention of two adults, sharing their exploration of its meaning to him. This was a new world to the social worker, which she had not previously explored. She could have adopted a cognitive behavioural approach of suggesting strategies to alleviate the addictive or obsessional behaviour that was troubling him. Instead she was able to engage this man at a deeper level, where his sense of his identity was being challenged, creating in him an existential crisis. She was able to highlight how inconguent his behaviour was with his feelings for women, for his wife, and for himself. She shone a light on it by being curious. She exposed the 'I–It' nature of the activity and how inconsistent this was with the genuine intimacy he sought. She was able to discuss the possible real lives of the women in the pornographic images with him. She was able to explore his empathy for their experience, and through this exploration he gradually ended this obsession and grew out of that world.

**Questions for reflection:**

● What kinds of problem can be existential issues in social work?

● Do you think it is important to name existential issues in social work practice?

In its second century, social work faces more diverse cultural communities than it did in its first. Existential social work thought has tended to be Eurocentric. Interestingly, existential social workers working with Australian indigenous people, for example, feel that there is an affinity between the existential and indigenous worldviews, particularly in the emphasis placed on being in existential thought, rather than always doing or having, and on the Dreaming or spirit world of the ancestors' being-in-the-world. Australian indigenous people seem to understand existential thought culturally and to live it.

Similarly, black existential thought is thriving in the Americas, and there is a long history of existential thinkers addressing the issues of colonialism and neo-colonialism. The roots of African-American existential thought predate the modern existential era and represent an independent development of the core concepts. There seem to be elements of existential thinking within all cultures, and part of the social worker's task is to learn about these cultural beliefs and to help people of those cultures to tap into their positive roots to make sense of today's challenges. Below is an example of what this might mean in practice.

---

Case Example 3.2: Social work with refugees with culturally complex trauma

A girl with cerebral palsy is born into a Pakistani refugee family living in Australia. A social worker with a disability support agency discovers that the family interpret their daughter's disability through their cultural and religious framework as an evil and a curse. The father becomes emotionally disengaged from his wife and from their four-year-old daughter. The mother experiences her life as painful and her nurturing and protection of her daughter is the price she must pay for the curse and its affliction on her and her family. The family experience deep shame, and they struggle to engage with services, seeking to withdraw. They hope and pray for a miracle cure. The agency becomes aware of evidence of financial and emotional abuse being perpetrated by the father on his wife and daughter.

The social worker organizes English classes for the mother to assist her in connecting with the local migrant services. Safety planning is provided to address the family violence and abuse issues, as the mother clearly expresses her wish for the family to remain intact. The social worker expresses empathy for the feeling within the family of being 'stuck, in a hopeless situation and unable to shift', which she attributes to the multiple traumas this family has experienced and continues to suffer.

▶

The social worker connects the family to the local refugee community from Pakistan. This experience helps the father and the family to soften their attitudes to their daughter's disability, but the social worker states that the father tends to accept their advice 'begrudgingly'. The social worker sees her task as being to help the father and family make sense of their daughter's disability and of their other experiences in a more constructive and accepting manner. She becomes aware that the humane, western, scientific view of their daughter's disability could also be experienced, by the family, as a source of added oppression of their own cultural perspective. Rather than imposing this view upon them, she sees her task as being one of chipping away at their self-loathing and of their wish for their daughter to be dead.

This involves working with the parents in a way that acknowledges and respects their views, addresses the multiple traumas and impacts on the family, and helps them to see a way forward into a future where there is less shame and growing respect for their daughter's life with disability.

**Questions:**

- Do we have a right to impose modern western values on people of other cultures?

- What are some strengths of other cultures' values that could be embraced in social work?

- What lessons does this case example offer about oppressive practices in social work, cultural relativism, and pathways to co-discovery, as well as in unearthing values of compassion, and what it means to live a meaningful and vital life?

# Conclusion

The existential floodplains of the late 1960s stimulated the growth of existential social work theory. Since then, existential thought and therapy have continued to grow and mature to a point where the existential approach currently thrives across the globe in a variety of forms. In this chapter, I have examined some of the key pioneers of explicit existential social work practice and those who have amalgamated existential thinking with other approaches such as humanism and narrative thought. There is significant diversity within existential social work, reflecting the absence in existential thought of a central, Freud-like figure, and its tendency to be malleable and adaptable to a range of interpretations. The initial existential social work writers were ambitious in suggesting that existential thought was a panacea for all of social work's woes. Later writers argued for existentialism as an overarching meta-theory for social work, but without much success. In the twenty-first century, when existential risks and issues are prominent, there appears to be much potential for its development in social work practice.

Today, existential approaches are a choice amongst many other approaches to social work practice. Every time a social worker helps a client make sense of an experience he or she is bringing a sense of meaning making into the practice for the client. The social worker is using an existential approach often without their conscious knowledge. The world is discovering new depths in existential and phenomenological thought at a time when it needs more understanding and acceptance of difference, purpose, and meaning.

## KEY POINTS FROM CHAPTER 3

1  The first explicit existential social work writing combined existential thought with humanist counselling approaches.

2  The appeal of existential thought to social work was its more realistic approach to contingency, crisis, evil, and other unexpected or negative experiences, rather than the exclusive focus on self-actualization found in client-centred counselling approaches.

3  The new values espoused by existential writings – of freedom, authenticity, and taking responsibility for choices – helped existential social workers to challenge clients deceived by unexamined or false ideas and beliefs that were shaping their lives.

4  Existential social work rejects utopian thought that fails to address social work's role in society as both a social control and change agent and in the search for the least detrimental option to affect positive change.

5  Existential social work helps clients to name issues as existential.

6  Existentialism has a Eurocentric focus. Existential social work has been surprisingly capable of adaptation and combination with many other approaches, such as the ecological, as expressed in indigenous cultures, with the embrace of mainstream and critical social work, and with postmodern thought.

# 4

## EXISTENTIAL SOCIAL WORK ASSESSMENT AND INTERVENTION

## Introduction

Social work texts face some level of program prescription regarding assessment and intervention in most human services fields. Computerized case management systems, and the presence of detailed and regularly updated government-endorsed guidelines and policy frameworks in most high-risk areas of practice, mean that social work texts face a perpetual test of relevance. In this chapter, an existential approach to social work assessment and intervention is proposed that focuses on the elements that remain crucial to the service encounter. The existential approach builds upon traditional social work practice and experience in valuing the unique personal circumstance of each client. The uniqueness of these situations needs to be discovered mutually with the client as part of the transformation process of discovery. Current social work approaches to assessment and intervention can be divided into the modern and postmodern, and the strengths and limitations of these approaches are explored in this chapter. The existential approach embraces modern and postmodern elements whilst aiming for a practice that is present and available to the unique and personal aspects of the given situation.

Below, two case examples from the published literature are presented to help illuminate key aspects of existential social work assessment and intervention.

## R. D. Laing's work with the Clarks

In 1968, existential psychiatrist R. D. Laing (1971) gave a lecture to social workers challenging standard practices in mental health when it came to diagnosis or assessment using a case study of the Clark family (pp. 21–42).

Laing was asked for a second opinion on David Clark, a 9-year-old boy with a possible diagnosis of schizophrenia. Instead of making an office appointment, Laing wrote to David's mother, inviting her to contact him. When she phoned, he arranged a home visit with colleagues, in the evening, when most members of the family would be home. Laing wanted to get a quick, overall sense of the family.

Other people or institutions, such as courts, police, families, or agencies, begin to define the situation before social workers meet their client. In high-risk situations, social workers cannot afford to ignore these appraisals. An understanding of the key details of the referral can be enormously helpful in the initial engagement with the client. Even before meeting the client, the social worker can begin to work out the unique aspects of the situation. In David's case, Laing didn't ignore these details, but neither did he assume that they were accurate.

During the home visit, Laing discovered that the boy was modelling his behaviour after his mother. His mother followed in the footsteps of her father (David's grandfather), who, at David's age, had ignored the normal social demands, such as attending school, to enjoy practical activities, like helping workmen on building sites. David's grandmother kept telling his mother that she should have 'beaten it out of David' (Laing, 1971, p. 28), as he had done to her. Laing discovered an intergenerational drama, in which David was playing the part that his grandfather had once played in the family. Laing's assessment was that the boy was in danger of falling into the self-fulfilling prophecy of the 'schizophrenia' label if he continued to be treated as the problem. He recommended that the mother and grandmother be assisted to better cope with David's ways and that clinical treatment of David cease.

What interests me about Laing (1971) is not whether his prescriptions were correct, it is his conclusion that 'the situation has to be discovered' (p. 33). By this, Laing means that assessment and intervention is a process of discovery for us and for the client. It is a process of seeing through the problem definitions of others, to what we consider is really going on with the client. Laing is not suggesting that his perspective is objective, only that our aim needs to be one of discovery with the client.

Before Laing had made his home visit, David had received three months of weekly therapy from a psychiatrist, and his mother had been having a fortnightly 'talk' with a psychiatric social worker. The child psychiatrist had not seen the mother and the social worker had not met the boy, and neither had met any other members of the family or knew anything about the intergenerational drama, let alone seen them interacting in their home environment. This reflects the normal practice of the times. Laing's intervention enabled the mother to discover *for herself* the intergenerational link between her son's difficult behaviours and her history as a child of the same age, and his grandfather's similar social behaviour.

Assessment begins as soon as a social worker encounters a situation, and the way they see that situation changes it. Here Laing captures the essence of the existential approach to assessment and treatment. It is an experience with the client that should include the way words are spoken, the concrete lived experiences of the human person, and how the client's body movements reflect their social situation. Laing's example does not prove the value of home visits for assessment. The programs that social workers operate in tend to prescribe how assessments and interventions are to be conducted. Most social workers don't have Laing's professional prestige and manoeuvrability, but we can still adopt an openness to assessment and intervention as a joint discovery process.

## Yalom learns from an early Freud case study

Today we live in a world in which recorded case notes and written assessments are provided to clients and can be subject to subpoena at any time. Agencies provide detailed guidelines to all staff. Social workers are required to be objective and to avoid personal reflections or making any form of judgement and must provide evidence for their views, such as verbatim accounts of the client's words. In this next example, we return to a time when everything was recorded, no matter how insignificant. In existential psychotherapist Irving Yalom's 1980 book on existential psychotherapy, he begins by making an analogy between psychotherapy and cooking. Yalom (1980) believes that it is often what he calls 'the throw-ins' by the chef during cooking that make cooking the dish successful, not the original recipe (pp. 3–5). What the social worker does with a client also involves an element of this spontaneity. However, this cooking metaphor is paradoxical. Culinary failure is a common experience, often because of not accurately following recipes that have been meticulously tested. Perhaps the requirement to 'follow the practice guidelines' has its place in high-quality social work practice.

To back up his claim about throw-ins in therapy, Yalom explores Sigmund Freud's first successful case of psychoanalysis. Yalom examines Freud's case history of Elizabeth Von R., because it contains many details that were written out of later cases. When a new theory becomes an orthodoxy, these details are viewed as extraneous to the purpose of the intervention or experiment (Yalom, 1980, p. 4). In the embryonic days of psychoanalysis, we see Freud acting something like a social worker might with a 24-year-old female patient, referred by a medical practitioner because of a two-year history of leg pains and difficulty walking, which the referring doctor suspected to be a case of hysteria (psychosomatic illness). Freud saw Elizabeth over a two-year period, from 1892 to 1894. Yalom documents the following 'add-ons' to therapy included in Freud's case history of Elizabeth.

Freud directed Elizabeth to visit her sister's grave, encouraged her to attend a party where an old flame might be present, took a friendly interest in her family's current circumstances, and interviewed her mother and 'begged' her to be supportive of her daughter and to encourage her daughter to unburden herself of her worries and to freely communicate with her. Freud established the unreality of Elizabeth's fantasy of one day marrying her dead sister's husband (her brother-in-law) and encouraged her to face the existential given of the uncertainty of the future with calmness, as a current-day existential therapist might do. Finally, Freud consoled Elizabeth that she was not responsible for her erotic feelings towards her brother-in-law, and that the repression of these feelings, which caused them to manifest as physical symptoms, only demonstrated her high moral character. After successful termination of the therapeutic relationship, Freud obtained an invitation to attend a private ball where he enjoyed seeing his former client 'whirl past in a lively dance', and he remained in touch with the family to find out that she had later successfully married (Yalom, 1980, p. 4).

Yalom is right to refer his readers to Freud's early case histories, because they are meticulous recordings of both the patient's circumstances and of his failed and successful interventions. They reveal more than just the add-ons listed above: in Elizabeth's case, Freud admits to an inability to improve upon the referring doctor's initial diagnosis of hysteria. He commences four weeks of 'pretence treatment' (Freud and Breuer, 2001, p. 138) that involves various physical therapies, and to Elizabeth's question of whether she should force herself to walk, Freud provides an emphatically positive response (p. 138). The results of this approach are minimal, and so commences Freud's exploration of the problem, which he describes as like 'excavating a buried city' (p. 139), trying to establish the causal links between the events of her illness and the physical symptoms.

In this case, Freud also documents one of the first ever psycho-social histories of a patient's family. We learn that Elizabeth is the youngest of three daughters and her father's favourite, whom he describes as 'cheeky and cocksure' (p. 140) and would have difficulty fulfilling the standard expectations for attracting a husband. Elizabeth was ambitious and wanted a musical career, but her father had heart problems and required two years' nursing by Elizabeth, which included her sleeping in his room in the time before his death. Freud states that this experience formed the beginning of her illness, but it was two years after his death when Elizabeth's real problems began and that she is first described as the invalid of the family. Freud documents the gradual social isolation of the family, including Elizabeth spending seven weeks nursing her mother in a darkened room because of her mother's eye problems. Following this decline, one of Elizabeth's married sisters died from heart problems, and this resulted in eighteen months of seclusion for Elizabeth while she cared for her mother.

Freud was disappointed by this story of 'commonplace emotional upheavals' (Freud and Breuer, 2001, p. 144) because he was trying to discover a missing link between physical symptoms and an emotional cause, given a lack of any physical reason for them. He tried hypnosis and failed. He attempted a head pressure technique, which he had experienced previous success with, by pressing his hand on the patient's forehead and removing it, while, under his instruction, the patient was to tell him what came into consciousness at that moment. Using this technique, Elizabeth recalled her attraction to a young suitor. Feeling that he was making progress, Freud insisted even more on her recollecting memories through this technique.

Elizabeth began taking on her therapist's agenda, and remembered that her father used to rest his legs on the general area of her leg pains when she was replacing his bandages. Freud noted, at this point, that her pains had begun to 'join in the conversations' (Freud and Breuer, 2001, p. 148) by coming on during his analysis. He learned that contemporary events stimulate memories in the patient, and this observation explains his suggestions to Elizabeth to visit her sister's grave and to attend the party that her old flame or suitor might attend.

Freud notes how his patient uses reflection to reinforce her illness, adding to her woes, as well as the fact that her use of symbolic metaphors like 'standing alone' (Freud and Breuer, 2001, p. 152) have begun to creep into the analysis. He notes her resistance to his technique. He discovers that she resists because she is critical of her trivial thoughts or finds them displeasing or unacceptable. Freud insists on her full co-operation with his technique and threatens that refusal to comply could mean no cure (p. 154).

Finally, as in a good detective novel, Freud discovers the hidden secret when the brother-in-law arrives unexpectedly at his office, and Elizabeth becomes aware of his presence. Freud witnesses her reaction of sudden severe pain and realizes that she had repressed her love and desire for him upon the death of her sister, because it was too shocking for her, and that this thought was thus converted into hysterical pain. Freud confronts her with this truth, which has a shattering impact on her. She denies it and his consoling begins, combined with his interpretation to help her understand what has happened to her. But Freud is also aware that to 'mitigate her sufferings' (Freud and Breuer, 2001, p. 157), multiple interventions will be required and hence arrives at the psycho-social interventions itemized above.

Yalom does not mention the set-backs that Freud recorded, which resulted from his add-on interventions. Elizabeth's recovery was anything but smooth. She became furious at Freud's betrayal and disclosure to her mother of her secret erotic passion for her brother-in-law. Her pains became severe and she isolated herself, leading her mother to describe the treatment as a 'complete failure' (Freud and Breuer, 2001, p. 160). Elizabeth refuses to see or have anything to do with Freud, and her mother seeks Freud's advice. Freud is convinced that he has achieved a breakthrough with Elizabeth and that her return to previous patterns of behaviour is a temporary set-back, to be expected as part of the change process. He declines to comment further and is proved correct in two months (p. 160).

In this short summary of Freud's detailed discussion of Elizabeth's case, Freud apologizes that his case history 'reads like a short story', rather than having the 'serious stamp of science' (Freud and Breuer, 2001, p. 160), but he finds that only detailed descriptions, like those more common in imaginative writing, are adequate for the case material. His purpose was to prove that his theories were sound. He wanted us to be persuaded by the connections that he had made between psychic repressions and physical symptoms, which were astonishing to people at the time.

Even Freud's failures, like those experienced by Elizabeth von R., are fascinating for his detailed analysis of them, which is rare in practice today. He is open about his poor abilities in hypnosis, for example. He cannot diagnose Elizabeth himself, and so accepts the referring doctor's tentative diagnosis and begins what he describes as a pretence treatment, which has only marginal effect.

Yalom is correct to welcome Freud's willingness to be open and frank about his actual practice. Isn't it also the case that social work is required to commence treatment or intervention before assessment has really begun? How different is Freud's from the practice described in social work assessment textbooks? Freud is aware of the impact of his positive attitudes on the patient's progress. He documents these things, such as the interest he shows in her, the understanding of her situation, and his hopes for her recovery, but they are all designed, in Freud's mind, to elicit secrets from the patient. Paradoxically, he seems oblivious to the impact of his breach of privacy with Elizabeth's mother on his relationship with Elizabeth. Elizabeth never visited Freud again, even though she promised to. Her cure includes this qualification by Freud: 'She still suffered occasionally from slight pains' (Freud and Breuer, 2001, p. 160).

He acknowledged that Elizabeth had glimpses of the central plot line of her case history, and that she was erotically attracted to her brother-in-law before, during, and after the death of her sister, and that this thought was 'totally unacceptable to her' (Freud and Breuer, 2001, p. 165). He documents the disclosure by Elizabeth of a lightning-flash realization upon viewing the recently deceased body of her sister: 'Now he is free again and I can be his wife' (pp. 156–167). Freud acknowledges that Elizabeth's case is only a 'partial conversion' (p. 167), and he qualifies his research findings, just as a good practitioner–researcher should. An existential psychoanalytic reading of this case history would focus on these conscious aspects and on the intentions of the therapist.

Freud constructed his assessment around his intention to uncover Elizabeth's secrets. In doing so, he influenced the patient to be an active participant in this uncovering process, in her disclosure first of her suitor and then of the position of her father's bandaged leg on her pained thigh. Further, she began to embrace his agenda in searching for meanings in the symbolic intensification of her sufferings, which Freud acknowledged reinforced her illness. Reading his case history over 125 years later, one cannot but be impressed by his dedication and faith and his firmness and resolve in finding the truth, all carried out in a genuinely caring practice, beyond the call of duty. In Elizabeth's case, his conviction proved correct and even survived their damaged professional relationship.

What can social work learn from this detailed case history? Assessment and intervention is a messy business in practice, often partial and overlapping as client and social worker search together for meaning and truths. Honesty in documenting successes and failures is also vital to progress in the profession. Freud learned to adapt his practice techniques when hypnosis didn't work for him as a therapist, and his skill in observation and bold interventions is on display in this history, as is his maturity in providing direction to his client when needed. The professional needs to guard against bias and examine their assumptions about practice. Freud was directing his client's attention towards exposing her secret emotional life. Social workers need to be aware of how they influence their clients to come up with what we want from them. This is not to say that Freud made up Elizabeth's situation and implanted it in her mind by suggestion. As he stated in the case history, the symptoms were often on display in the room and in the corridor outside.

In social work today, reflection on this case would highlight the oppressive gender power relationship, displayed by Freud in his arrogant rejection of Elizabeth's views and wishes. Freud's practice was a private clinic and not subject to the structures and restrictions that most social work operates within. This example shows how Freud's intentions shaped his practice, as well as his attitudes to the participants and to what he discovered. The professional's intentions cannot be exempted from the assessment and intervention process.

## Existential social work assessment and intervention

Current social work assessment and intervention approaches can be usefully separated into those that adopt a modernist, 'objective' approach and those that adopt a postmodern, constructivist approach. Either approach can include a variety of critical or mainstream conservative views on social work practice. Postmodern approaches assert that all assessments and interventions are subject to criticism. The existential social work approach concurs that all approaches to assessment and intervention are constructed. Both modern and postmodern approaches are built upon traditional or historical social work practice, not simply on evidence-based practice, as is the modern view (O'Hare, 2009). The existential realities of actual social work practice often go overlooked by modern, critical, and postmodern approaches. An existential social work approach to assessment and intervention seeks to help clients cope within the oppressions of the existing system, as well as to work with clients and others to change these oppressive conditions.

## The modernist approach to assessment and intervention

A recent example of the modernist approach can be found in Thomas O'Hare's *Essential Skills of Social Work Practice* (2009). O'Hare describes a multi-dimensional functional (MDF) assessment process. He contrasts his approach with the 'theoretical orthodoxy, tradition, postmodern ideology and other forces in the profession that reject empirical testing' (p. vii). He proposes that all decision making around assessment and intervention is evidence-based practice, built on 'controlled clinical research' (p. 108). The multi-dimensional nature of assessment is uncontroversial in this view and builds upon the traditional psycho-social models, which ignore political dimensions of practice issues. For example, domestic violence is described as psycho-social, thus ignoring all of the political or spiritual dimensions to family violence. Psychiatric diagnoses are considered essential when dealing with serious mental illness, but no examination of the limitations and flaws in the medical model of practice is evident. O'Hare's model shares the strengths and limitations of the functional approach to social issues. Thompson (1992) has critiqued O'Hare's approach from an existential social work perspective, arguing that it is based on a consensus model of society using a positivist view of social issues.

There are many other recent social work texts that fit into the modernist approach to assessment. Bloom and Fischer (1982) began with a devastating critique of social casework in the 1970s and has followed the clinical evidence-based approach to social work practice, which fits well with a private practice clinical model but is difficult to apply usefully in many other practice arenas. Pamela Trevithick's *Social Work Skills and Knowledge, A Practice Handbook* (2012) also fits evidence-based methods into the broad category of the modernist psycho-social approach to social work assessment and intervention. Her method is informed by her preference for a psycho-analytic relational-based social work. She combines this mainstream social work view with a structural critical and systematic perspective that includes an anti-oppressive focus for practice (Trevithick, 2012).

The main strength of the modernist approach is that it provides the social worker with useful ways to produce more accurate assessments and interventions. The limitations include that their texts read like scientific manuals, describing a systematic and analytic approach that, if followed, will result in accurate, 'objective' social work assessments. The problem is that social work practice is rarely, if ever, this systematic or objective. As Gordon Hamilton (1951) stated more than 70 years ago, social work assessment and intervention is more like a living event than an episode (p. 2).

Below is a case example illustrating how assessment and intervention are often intertwined in practice, and that these processes are confronted with uncertainty and the contingent.

---

Case Example 4.1: 'The boy who burned down part of his own sporting facility'

I was facilitating a group conference for a boy charged with arson on part of a sporting facility that he attended. The team coach refused to be involved in the group conference but agreed to support the process and to allow other coaches in the club to attend. The children's court referred the boy to the conference, and my role as the group conference facilitator was to assess, brief, and prepare the participants for the group conference (including the police, the boy's legal representative, the boy and his family and supporters, the victims and their support network, and other relevant professionals); to facilitate the actual large group conference; and to provide a report to the court of the process and its outcomes.

This involved approximately four weeks of very intensive work. As group conference convenor, I was briefing people about the conference, finding out more about the situation as the planning for the conference developed, and helping to determine who should be at the conference, what had happened to cause this offence, what the issues were that needed to be addressed in the conference to prevent the boy from re-offending, and, finally, how he could make amends to the community for the devastation caused to the victims.

On the day of the conference I sat in my car preparing myself by meditating. Nothing more could be done at that stage. I always arrive very early to prepare the room, deal with any last-minute issues, and allow myself the spiritual space to create, for myself, a deep inner calm before I enter the room. Just before ending my meditation, I received a call from a clinician, three weeks after I had contacted them. They disclosed to me a pre-school history of fire-lighting by the boy. This placed his current offence in a completely different light.

As I commenced the conference, the team coach walked into the room and announced that he wanted to say something. He explained why he would not be attending, and that he supported the group conference and the attendance of many of the other coaches.

The group conference was a success. Many of the coaches used the conference like a debriefing session after the trauma of the fire. At court, a few days after the conference, I remember feeling very relieved that my court report was detailed enough for the Chief Magistrate to order the boy to complete a brief probation period. The group conference process was meant to be a diversion from probation, but in this case a probation order was necessary as a precautionary measure, given the serious nature of the offence and what we had learned about family dysfunction and the boy's history of fire-lighting. All of these things we discovered in just a short period of assessment and intervention.

**Question:**

● How does assessment and intervention actually take place in most social work settings?

Saltiel (2016), in an ethnographic study of two child protection social work teams in Northern England, made similar findings: that social workers faced 'unreliable or incomplete information, poorly defined and fluid situations, pressures of time and heavy workloads, which favour quick, intuitive decision-making' (p. 2114). While not rejecting the usefulness of elements of the modernist empirical approach to social work, the actual lived experience of social work assessment and intervention suggests that the social worker plays a more active part in shaping these processes in their social work world, which reflects their immediate team, field of service, program and agency requirements, and 'the way business is conducted' in their workplace. Saltiel observed social workers using their communication skills to engage with callers and to form alliances offering professional advice that enabled more information to be obtained, but no recording of these vital processes took place as they were considered routine. In the engagement process, anonymous callers disclosed their identities because trust was being built, and better pictures of what was really going on were being developed. In uncovering possible abuse, the social workers cross-checked information from a range of sources instead of relying solely on medical or clinical evidence. All work of this kind is done in the context of a high-pressure environment in which just processing the number of constant new referrals can be overwhelming.

## Is traditional social work theory still useful?

I have already mentioned that all models of social work assessment and intervention are built upon a history of traditional psycho-social social work theory and practice, not simply the latest evidence-based practice. Traditional, historical social work texts are rarely explored in social work courses. Practitioners of social work still have their favourites, which they refer to at times for inspiration. Felix Biestek's *The Casework Relationship* (1957) analysed seven principles of casework practice. His concept of individualization is foundational in the history of casework. Current social policy adopts this principle in developing new approaches to service delivery. Biestek acknowledges the source of his clarification of first principles to be the existential Functional School, specifically Virginia Robinson and her classic book *A Changing Psychology in Social Case Work* (1930). In Biestek's first text and his later book *Client Self-Determination in Social Work* (1978), Biestek attests to the first principle of social work being individualization, or valuing the unique nature of the individual, social group, or community in which the social worker is practicing. Each client in each situation has unique qualities, and it is these that need to be recognized and given their due attention in social work.

What is missing from Biestek's 1957 analysis is any criticism of the cultural and structural conditions by which clients of social work agencies are oppressed. His 1957 work aims simply for a better adjustment between the client and the environment and imposes no requirement on the environment to change. However, in his later book, mentioned above, Biestek examines the fifty-year history of the use of the concept of client self-determination and describes how the 1960s social movements focused attention on the need to change the unjust, oppressive social environment when it is denying rights, and, more generally, when positive change can be made. Social work had been transformed by the emergence and experience of new types of practice, such as group work, community organization, and social action, and casework needed to change to reflect this. By defining self-determination as the 'second most important value' (1978, p. 183), Biestek was also reaffirming social work's primary value to be the inherent worth of the human person. It is quite possible to disagree with Biestek's preference and approach, but at least there is clarity in this prioritization.

Thompson's (1992) critique of traditional social work is that it is only superficially similar to existential social work practice. Social work needs to empower clients, and anti-oppressive practice is its primary goal. Even the social worker–client relationship is secondary to the political goal of standing in solidarity with clients through the partial relief of oppression and the enhancement of their authenticity, which Thompson defines as acceptance of their freedom and responsibility. By implication, Thompson gives priority to empowerment or self-determination over individualization.

Thompson takes account of the social work context with multiple accountabilities and responsibilities through which clients can be oppressing other clients. In these circumstances, it is difficult for a solidarity perspective to provide much direction for practice. Thompson (1992) describes Biestek's concept of self-determination as 'merely a handy tool and a dead end' (p. 111). When you are dealing with mandated clients with hostile or oppositional attitudes to social work assessment and intervention, clarity around what is and is not negotiable is very helpful. In a sense, the social worker creates more self-determination for the client in finding out how much room there is to negotiate and in using as much of that room as possible. James Barber (1991) wrote very succinctly on the importance of negotiation skills and clarity in casework in recognizing conflict, and he did so well before the many more recent texts on social work with involuntary clients were published (pp. 42–60).

Biestek describes only an enlightenment view of self-determination, which cannot distinguish between egoistic freedom and genuine self-determination, which is other-directed. Hegel realized that the enlightenment, modernist view of self-determination was limited by its finite aim. To be genuinely self-determining the person must find transcendence in something greater than themselves, such as another person, their children, a project, or some purpose. A person can seek transcendence in a purpose that has harmful intent but that does not lead to genuine transcendence. Hegel realized that genuine self-determination could only come when a moment of our lives has a meaning beyond itself (Wallace, 2005). In some way, this going beyond our egoistic needs embraces a role beyond our finite existence and thus touches the infinite. When a person is giving back to a cause that has helped her, it feels like she is genuinely self-determining. This view of self-determination is linked to Hegel's concept of true infinity, in which the finite existence of our lives is interconnected with the infinite. Self-determination remains a crucial value in social work practice, providing our understanding incorporates this deeper existential meaning. Going beyond ourselves can be as important and as simple as an abusive man putting the safety of his family before his need for relationship (Griffiths, 2016).

Gisela Konopka (2005), one of the founders of social group work, argued for the same view of the importance of self-determination in an article critiquing some of group work's more questionable fads. She writes:

> One of education's hardest jobs is to increase the capacity of people to think for themselves, to learn even to refuse rewards, for instance, if this contradicts their convictions, thinking, concerns. Where would social movements be if people only worked for rewards? (p. 22)

Using existential philosophers to explain social work concepts can seem otherworldly. Below are two case examples in which the genuine concept of self-determination was useful in social work practice. As I stated in the previous chapter, Jim Lantz (1994a, b, c) applied Gabrielle Marcel's concept of problem and mystery in his family therapy work. I have adapted those ideas to work in any social work service. Second, Virginal Satir, a social worker and family therapist, shared some of her ways of working in really difficult situations and with really difficult clients using her spiritually inspired approach to practice.

## Reflective Exercise 4.1: Two ways to bring the infinite concept of self-determination into daily social work practice

*1 – Applying Gabriel Marcel's distinction between the problem and the mystery*

Unless social workers explicitly use a strength-based approach, most social work is focused on problems and problem-solving. Instead of always focusing on the problem (in a group you are running, an interview you are conducting, etc.), ask yourself: *What is the mystery here?*

Mystery in this context does not mean mysterious, but exploring the non-problematic, including how you as a social worker participate in the event. This includes:

- Your presence in the situation (being-in-the-world). How present are you to what is actually taking place? How does your presence shape what is taking place?

- Your presence also includes the reality that you happen to be here in this job, seeing this client, in this field, and there are deep reasons why you are doing this work at this point in your life.

- Others' presence in the situation. (What makes them truly *other persons* to you?)

- Absence – What is not appearing in the conversation, missing, that is in some way helping to shape the conversation? What, if anything, is totally absent from the conversation? (For example, in a men's behaviour change program, what is often absent is the presence and voice of the men's children and female partners.)

- Significance of what is happening – The deeper reality, feeling, or meaning of what is happening. (A resistant man in denial about his family violence arguing at length about how the police and courts have erred can be reminded 'nevertheless you are here with me now, contemplating doing a men's behaviour change program'. This results in him acknowledging that things need to change if he were ever allowed contact with his family. It is not an admission of his violence but something that provides room for further exploration.)

Virginia Satir was a pioneer existential social worker in family therapy. She shares in her 1967 and 1976 texts key techniques that worked for her in her daily practice working with high-risk people who had been rejected by other, medically trained therapists, because they were considered 'untreatable'. Satir suggests:

- First, work to be as congruent in yourself and in your life as possible. Know, deep down, that you are spirit (which is total goodness and light), that you have endless energy sources to draw upon, and thus that all your thoughts, feelings, and behaviours need to be aimed at progressing this energy in your world.

▶

- Second, work with the spirit energy in the room. This translates into approaching people with the knowledge that they are always more than their:

  1. Worst behaviours

  2. Worst feelings of self-hatred and disgust

  3. Worst event or disasters, problems, tragedies, or any other defining incident

  4. Limited, finite, life span.

- Third, be alert to meta-communication – of what is being said by the non-verbal, body expression, interaction, and how it differs from the verbal, stated, official version of communication. Further, be able to share these observations in non-confrontational ways that help people make sense of their incongruence.

**Exercise:**

- Think how you might be able to apply Marcel's idea of mystery and Satir's notion of spirit in your social work practice.

In the next section, I explore how it is possible to combine mainstream social work values, like real self-determination as explained above, with both a functional and a critical perspective on social work practice.

# The contribution of structural and critical social work practice

Structural and critical social work practice contains a very diverse range of views and perspectives. Payne (2005) provides an overview of these views and some critical reflections on the strengths and limitations of this perspective. Thompson's existentialist, anti-oppressive theoretical perspective is an example of a critical existentialist view of social work. One of the more common criticisms of approaches like Thompson's are the limitations of the model when applied to direct practice in social work, although more recent work has addressed this issue (Sakamoto and Pitner, 2005; Herz and Johansson, 2012). However, even the earliest writers in this approach specifically addressed social workers working in direct service areas. Moreau (1979), one of the founders of structural critical social work, has argued that intervention to help people address their immediate issues involving family violence must also provide opportunities for people to identify the institutional and political dimensions of the problem. Moreau states that addressing everyday social work concerns is important, such as by acknowledging people's feelings, attitudes, and ideas and helping them gain a better understanding of, and finding a better way of dealing with, others.

But equally important is the need to address oppression in mediating structures and how the clients themselves contribute to the oppression of others, as well as the need for the social worker to provide immediate, concrete help to relieve their client's stress. According to Moreau, the primary aim must be the development of critical consciousness in clients when fundamental changes are made. For example, men in patriarchal societies are frequently unaware of, or simply assume that, their privileges are normal. Family violence is embedded in a society in which male privilege is seen as part of a male's normal entitlement.

It can be a very powerful experience for many men to realize how many of the things they take for granted are aspects of their male privilege. Just being safe walking down the street and not being accosted by others is an example of a privilege that very few women experience. The structural or critical approach asserts that real transformation occurs when a critical consciousness is created in workers and in clients of their own oppression and oppressive practices. While most people today agree on the equality of the genders, my experience has been that many of the men arriving in behaviour-change programs consider themselves to be victims of an unfair system that oppresses them. The challenge of this kind of work is in accepting these expressions of resentment and frustration without condoning the opinions that underlie them and in building trust in the group process that will gradually help them to consider new ways of examining their predicaments. The critical or structural view is correct about the need to challenge current oppressive practices and to develop critical consciousness, but the question is how do the social workers help their clients to get to that point?

The functionalist model, in contrast, is focused on helping people fit in and adjust to society as it is. Sometimes people do want help with fitting in, but what if the system is treating them unfairly or they are being oppressive of themselves or of their families? Sometimes clients don't want to fit in, or they want to fail. They blame the system for all their problems and aren't interested in receiving the help provided by the social worker.

A structural social worker may concur with the client that the system is to blame for their problems, and that social work cannot help them. My experience has been that most clients are not happy living in oppressive situations or contributing to other people's oppression – when this circumstance is pointed out to them in a respectful, accepting manner. In other words, most people desire genuine help from services that will improve their lives. This includes helping them with their immediate issues and seeking transformative change through which lasting results can be achieved.

Below is an example of how a structural functional approach to family therapy can identify ways to help families that can contribute to improving their overall functioning in society (Bloom, 1993; Coull et al., 1982).

---

Case Example 4.2: My experience of the existential in functionalism and social work practice

I began my postgraduate social work career in 1979 in public welfare. Back then, I was in a generic social worker position, which meant I was responsible for child protection, child welfare, probation, and adult and juvenile parole cases. The Regional Director had just completed a Master's Degree thesis under the supervision of Len Tierney, using family functioning profiles to assess the role of the family in the re-socialization of young offenders on probation.

The family functioning profile was based on the research work of Ludwig L. Geismar (Bloom, 1993). It measured family and community functioning before and after intervention. I discovered that Geismar had developed his approach after being a researcher with Alice Overton. Overton was instrumental in the 1950s in the St Paul Project in Minnesota, which provided preventative social work service to what used to be called 'multi-problem families', or what Dr Tierney described as 'excluded families' in his PhD dissertation by the same name. Tierney's dissertation was based on his work with 56 excluded families over a 16-year period (Tierney, 1976).

I wrote an 18-page assessment family functioning profile on a family using Overton and Tinker's *Casework Notebook* as my guide. What I learned from this experience is that you can intervene in one functional area of a family's life (e.g. financial advice and counselling through referral to a family support service), and that this intervention could have positive ramifications for other areas of family functioning, in improving the marital relationship, say, and, indirectly, the upbringing of the children.

▶

Overton's book was probably the most valuable tool in public welfare for its time, because it dealt with the issues of client resistance and of their not wanting 'the welfare' in their lives. In each section of family functioning, the *attitudes and feelings* of the client were as important as the so-called objective facts of the situation (to use the language of the era) (Overton and Tinker, 1959).

These clients were different, challenging, difficult to engage, and struggled to make use of, or have access to, formal systems such as education or employment. It was a question of social work intervention trying to make a difference in their lives. What areas of their lives could be improved by better involvement with other services? Some excluded families don't want to be poorly functioning. They are usually in survival mode most of the time. By gradually building trust and confidence in the worker, the family can begin to engage in a more constructive manner with other mainstream service systems – at least that's the theory.

Today there is more evidence that very poor communities with better formal and informal support services do much better than other similarly poor communities with a more disorganized and smaller family and community services infrastructure. Jesuit Social Services in Australia pioneered this study by comparing geographical areas of similar disadvantage and assessing the benefits of improved services to outcomes between those areas (Vinson, 2007).

**Questions:**

- Does improving families' and communities' functioning make a difference?

- How does helping families with immediate practice issues help build confidence and trust in you as their social worker?

- Why are attitudes and feelings more important than facts in assessment and interventions?

# The postmodern social work approaches to assessment and intervention

The postmodern assessment and intervention approaches coalesce around the socially constructed nature of process. Postmodern approaches claim that there is no objectively correct assessment and intervention process, and so the process must examine the way people make sense of what happens not from the point of view of a professional observer but from the perspective of a participant professional mutually making sense with their clients of a socially constructed situation. We are all immersed in discourses of various kinds, but some discourses are more powerful than others. Institutional discourses, such as the market economy, or the medical discourse in health settings, are examples of discourses that strongly influence and shape social work practice.

These dominant discourses are ways of framing reality, but they can be dislodged from their dominant position by naming them so that they can be examined as language and then dismantled. For example, dominant masculinity can be a discourse that abusive and violent men unquestioningly embrace. Part of challenging their abuse and violence can include exploring their unearned privilege and the negative consequences for them and their families of their continued adherence to this version of masculinity. Alan Jenkins (1990) has used a postmodern, narrative approach in working with male violence that is based on de-centring discourse-based excuses men use by asking the question: 'What is stopping you from being non-violent?'

The postmodern approach seems to be more aware that most social workers today are employed in services in which all processes are thoroughly prescribed. Wilson, Ruch, Lymbery and Cooper's *Social Work, An Introduction to Contemporary Practice* (2008) adopts a relational postmodern approach to social work assessment, arguing for the constructed nature of all assessment processes. They also highlight the extensive institutional foundation and prescription of assessment and pre-occupation with risk management, and the risk that this can become a bureaucratic exercise of unthinkingly following procedures, guidelines, and checklists. The postmodern perspective also challenges the 'expert' model of assessment and embraces anti-oppressive practice in its focus on the power relationships in assessment, as well as the need to emphasize service user perspectives and to create a more collaborative, partnership-based approach to the process.

While postmodern approaches have brought a welcome critique of the claims to objectivity of modern social work assessment and intervention processes, there have also been some issues for which theory has driven practice and in which the inconvenient empirical facts of situations have been ignored – a detailed example of this is provided below. In their efforts to deconstruct mainstream and modern approaches to practice, postmodern writers can remain unaware of their own preferences. Healy (2005) critiques neo-classical discourse without mentioning the inefficiencies of bureaucratic economic models, as if only market models are deeply flawed. No mention is made of the reason competition is dominant as a driver of economic and social policy across all sectors – which is partly because bureaucratic models of service delivery can result in poor allocation of resources and inefficient service delivery.

One of the last monopoly bureaucracies is the court system. Many court practices exist for the efficiency of the system itself, not to suit the people that use it on a daily basis. In Australia, people attending court must arrive before 10am, even though their case may not be heard until 4pm. Their hearing may even be delayed to a new date. No business, subject to competition policy, would survive in the marketplace if it provided such a service. Of course, the court system could not be put out to tender, and it is becoming subject to improved management practices, and to new ideas, such as specialist courts and therapeutic jurisprudence. In their daily lived experience, social workers and other professionals working within the courts, as well as people attending court, experience the impact of the monopoly that courts have on the justice system.

On my first day at work as a child welfare social worker, I had the experience of being given numerous case files of wards of the state, all piled up on a desk. Many of these children were residing in central institutions, yet no-one had looked at their files for months. This reflected a period of welfare history in which the bureaucratic administrative model of practice was dominant. In this system, social workers had more authority and administrative discretion. For a range of reasons, children experienced much longer periods of residence in central institutions. Later the harms to clients caused by this approach swung the pendulum across to the justice model of service delivery, under which rights were enshrined in legislation, administrative discretion was curtailed, and more power to make major decisions was transferred to the courts. Delivery of welfare services is now subject to quasi-market mechanisms, but you will not find much discussion, in the postmodern texts at least, of the inadequacies and inefficiencies of the social welfare administrative discourse model of practice, which the equally flawed competitive market system has replaced.

While discourse analysis is a useful tool in challenging dominant discourses, postmodern approaches can exaggerate the potential for instability in systems and can mislead social workers by implying that everything is simply text. Healy quotes Rojek approvingly in his assertion of the 'changeable conditional character of social work' (cited in Healy, 2005, p. 9). Rojek claims: 'There is nothing fundamental or inevitable about the form of social work. Social work is just that: a form' (cited in Healy, 2005, p. 9). While social work is practiced in different ways in diverse settings, it is shaped by its history, and its future will be shaped by the actions of the profession today and by the new challenges our society faces. It is misleading to suggest that social work can simply reshape itself in any way it chooses. For example, in Australia, since I began practicing over 30 years ago, social work has lost influence in corrections to psychology, while in child protection it remains significant but is not in an exclusive position. Why did social work lose its influence in corrections? Some of the possible reasons include that the profession was more focused on other areas of practice, such as community work, social action, therapy, and clinical work, which it felt were more appropriate to its modus operandi. In corrections, social work had a strong focus on rehabilitation, which fell out of favour with the 'tough on crime and criminals' political agenda and the consequent separation of adult corrections from other welfare service delivery. Psychology, with its narrower focus on delivery of therapeutic programs, is given preference within a system focused primarily on security.

Postmodern approaches can be highly critical of traditional social work practice. Leslie Margolin's (1997) study of social work entitled *Under the Cover of Kindness, The Invention of Social Work* is a good example of a critique. In this book, Margolin uses postmodern theory to question the goodness motivations of social work practice. His book has been critiqued by Wakefield (1998), but Margolin's approach remains influential, and postmodern critiques of social work using Foucault have referred positively to his work (Irving, 1999).

One of Margolin's particular foci is the St Paul Project and the pioneering work of Alice Overton in providing preventative services to marginalized families. The St Paul project was a preventative initiative aimed at hard-to-reach families who initially resisted help, or one of whose members, usually the male head of the family, opposed the involvement of welfare services. Margolin constructs a version of the facts to demonstrate that social work's core mission is to justify its own existence through its breakthrough case studies of helping people who initially resisted that help. He bases a story on Raymond, age 8, a boy whose case study was included in an article written by Alice Overton in 1953, titled 'Serving Families Who Don't Want Help'. Margolin doesn't refer to the first case example in Overton's article, Ken, age 10, who truants from school and, when he attends, prefers to wander around with the janitor.

Overton's program was experimental, designed to test whether preventative family work can reach those most in need, who may resist help. Ken's family is well known to authorities, whose assessments are uniformly bleak, based on two years of involvement. After ten years on public assistance, the father is particularly hostile to the welfare attempts to engage him. The family consists of nine children, with both parents described as being of low IQ and the children as being neglected. Overton completes a comprehensive evaluation, based on home visits and school assessments, which reveal that the eldest son (17) is doing well in his third year in high school, the eldest daughter is also performing well, and though the four other children's behaviour at primary school is not as well-adjusted, it is also not as bad as Ken's problems.

Other positives they discover include 'a picture of family solidarity, a couple, in spite of their limitations, that had status with their children and expended great effort so that the children could achieve worthwhile goals' (Overton, 1953, p. 306), such as involvement in church and sporting activities. Overton makes the point that marginalized families can develop, over time, very negative attitudes to any authority, which is reinforced by those same authorities operating with strong negative sanctions against the defensive stance of the family member. The engagement with the social worker can be the first positive experience with authority (as represented by the social worker) for such a family. Skills learned in this interaction by the family can transfer to other authorities, such as school staff and employers.

Margolin (1997) describes Overton's second case, Raymond, as one in which the social worker met another angry and highly resistant father, whom she gradually won over by refusing to be cowed and persevering in attending to speak to the mother while showing respect for the father, resulting in the family showing dramatic improvement (p. 93). Margolin accuses social work of 'twisting the facts and mis-describing them' (p. 179). First, Margolin describes Raymond's problem as disruptive behaviour – stammering, truancy, and stealing – which, because of his age, has to be treated as a child protection matter. Margolin makes no mention of the family violence that Overton (1953) documents, including 'beating [of] the children and demanding complete silence at home', nor of the mother's fear of her husband (p. 307). To engage the father, the social worker promptly helps in obtaining a work release for the father's brother, who is in jail, assists the eldest son to obtain a part-time job, helps arrange for three of the children to go to camp, and helps with an extension of time to clear up an eligibility problem for the father relating to his public assistance.

Do these actions go some way to explaining how these positive experiences helped engage a man who was highly resistant to authority? As the relationship grows, the social worker is able to assist the father with his misconceptions about his diabetes and its impact on his body and even to challenge him about his violence towards the assistant school principal, which negatively affected his children, and the social worker also helps him to control his anger. The social worker also works with the school to improve the staff's understanding of and work with this family, resulting in an improved relationship (Overton, 1953, pp. 307–308). None of these actions is mentioned in Margolin's (1997) account, which he claimed was based on Overton's report (pp. 93–94). My purpose in documenting these flaws in the case descriptions by Margolin, a writer using postmodern discourse theory, is not to discredit the theory, such as narrative work, to social work, but to defend what has been described as traditional social work from misleading descriptions that imply that social work students would gain nothing from examining Overton's social work. So what would an existential social work approach to assessment and intervention look like?

## How existential social work assessment and intervention differs from existential therapy

Sue and Neil Thompson describe some key elements of assessment and intervention in existential social work. They write on the importance of working in partnership with the client, of seeing things through the client's lens as far as possible, on assessing within the social context of the client, which will include identifying and addressing oppressive factors, and on remembering that one of the key resources is the social worker herself (Thompson and Thompson, 2008, pp. 58–61). While social workers can gain significant benefits in their practice from learning from existential therapies along with other therapeutic approaches, it is important to clearly distinguish existential therapy from existential social work practice.

Standardized assessment procedures, using predefined typologies, categories, or diagnostic criteria as part of the assessment process, could form a significant part of an existential social work process, whereas these procedures tend to be excluded from or de-emphasized in existential therapies. Many existential therapy approaches de-emphasize assessment altogether. The infinite value and uniqueness of the person of the client is equally crucial in existential therapy and existential social work, but categories can be useful in understanding a person's situation, providing that there is recognition that the person is always more than any category can describe or contain. Common typologies used in social work practice that are compatible with an existential approach would be the transtheoretical model of behaviour change, various developmental theories, a strength-based approach to the DSM classification system, and family systems theory, which is applied every time a social worker creates a family genogram.

In existential social work, the focus is as much on the social as on the psyche of the client. While existential therapy may have an unlimited time in which to assist a client with movement towards authenticity or genuine transformation of themselves, depending upon what is mutually agreed to by the client and the therapist, existential social work tends to have more time-limited aims of achieving some goals that will help towards the authentic self, leaving the client the option of pursuing this aim via therapy at a later time. Furthermore, existential social work may have more limited aims than achieving authenticity, such as helping clients deal with immediate needs, but these aims are always sought in a way that recognizes the client's unique humanity and must include addressing of any oppressive factors that de-personalize the client. Existential social workers simply cannot afford the intensive long-term individual work required of therapy, but that doesn't mean there cannot be significant gains for the client nor that this intervention cannot be commensurate with, or act as, a preliminary and complementary intervention.

The clients of existential social work are mandated and involuntary, clients whom existential therapists are less likely to be involved with. Given policy and programmatic limitations, existential social work may not be able to be as confronting with clients as existential therapies sometimes are in challenging their defences, given that reconstruction of broken defences requires considerable time and individual focus that only therapy is able to provide. Existential social work is bounded by defined roles and procedures, contained in program documentation that clearly establishes the limits of assessment and intervention. Finally, existential social work places limits on the professional relationship and on the levels of intimacy within that relationship, which certain forms of existential therapy aim to remove. For example, one of Yalom's group work techniques in the early phase of that process is to encourage new group members to anonymously disclose a secret that they would be unwilling to share with other group members as a way to show the universality of our deepest fears and concerns. Implementing this exercise in social group work, however, which has defined aims and objectives, may be asking for an inappropriate level of intimacy from the participants.

Randall (2007) also questioned the appropriateness to social work of the 'no-limits approach to matters of self-disclosure' (p. 328) in certain approaches to existential therapies, and this reflects the different purposes and roles of social work and therapy. Below is an example from an existentially informed social worker that contrasts the broader nature of an existential approach to social work assessment and intervention with a more limited existential therapy approach. Social work, while being constrained in certain aspects of practice, does have other tools in its toolkit. This case illustrates the broader role of existential social work.

---

## Case Example 4.3: Assessment and intervention

### The referral

Jack is a 78-year-old man referred by his doctor for social work intervention or counselling because he was depressed and suffering from gender dysphoria (GID). He had been placed on antidepressants by the doctor. At the referral stage there is discussion of his depression and of the possibilities of hormone therapy.

### The assessment

Emma, the existential social worker, discovers that Jack has known she was the wrong sex since before her mother died tragically when she was a child. She subsequently experienced periods of depression and received electric shock therapy in her early years and had residential stays in psychiatric facilities. Eventually she married and lived a conservative life as a farmer. She had two sons, although she did not enjoy sex at all. One son has died due to poor health from addictions, and the other has moved far away and is not close to Jack.

▶

Jack had also had a part-time job managing the local cinema and would secretly dress as a woman and express her femininity in the projector room while films were played. Eventually Jack came out to her wife, who was, to Jack's surprise, sympathetic and supportive. Subsequently, Jack was allowed to dress as a woman at home, and even to go out dressed as she wished at night walking with her wife. It has been several years now since her wife's death, and Jack is now living in an aged community where the social life is okay. Jack dreams of becoming a woman and of seeking a relationship. She fears dressing as a woman and is too scared to go out into the community dressed as she wishes to.

Recently Jack attended the dentist and was thrilled to hear the dentist describe her jaw as feminine and to say that he would make a beautiful new set of dentures for her. This confirmed Jack's view that she had been born the wrong sex.

### The social work intervention

Emma makes visits to Jack's unit, where Jack can be herself, and has intimate discussions with her about sexuality and her life in general, which is one of real sadness and fear to be herself in public. Emma fully enters Jack's world, allowing the client to play her favourite music and to dance in her beautiful dresses.

Emma arranges with the client for a beautician to visit the unit to paint Jack's nails and to teach her how to do make up and groom herself.

She discusses with Jack the possibility of creating a small group of her most supportive friends as a circle of support where she could feel safe as herself. Jack declined this possibility. (Emma was attempting to broaden her world of support, as she was mindful of a growing dependency on her and was trying to find a possible solution to this; Jack 'really looked forward to our sessions,' Emma recorded.)

Emma helps Jack explore the internet and to put up a Facebook profile, thinking this might help her find a supportive group, but Jack is not very computer savvy.

### Reflections on the situation

Emma was careful not to impose her desires on Jack to come out as a transgender person and to remain in step with what she wanted. Emma had to accept that Jack had lived most of her life painfully, in two worlds, not belonging in either. In her practice, Emma had become interested in transgender and sexuality issues, particularly as it affected clients living in remote and rural regions, far away from major cities. She offered training to other helping practitioners in the area, with the hope of building a support network for Jack and other clients with similar issues.

Existential social work enabled Emma to adopt a broader range of strategies than a talking psychotherapeutic intervention. She introduced totally new experiences in the client's life by arranging for the beautician to visit. She accepted the current limitations of the client's ambiguous relationship to her female gender identification. She visited the client in her home, enabling the client to use her as a primary resource, where the client could be her true identity, at least during Emma's visits.

Emma wasn't entirely successful with Jack in the client's rejection of the idea of creating a small support group of her friends, but Emma hasn't given up. She is building her network, exploring internet options, and, maybe, even helping Jack to create her own online story.

**Questions:**

- Can you identify the advantages of existential social work over existential therapy?
- What are the limitations of existential social work?

# Conclusion

Existential social work builds upon the efforts of previous generations of social workers in constructing methods and general underlying principles and in evolving approaches to engaging and helping individuals, groups, and communities. I started this chapter with two examples from twentieth-century thinkers, Laing and Yalom, who helped shape social work practice.

R. D. Laing, in speaking to social workers, was helping to create an existential approach to assessment and intervention by showing how gaining a lived experience of a family can help us discover how the intergenerational pattern shapes that family. In Laing's example, a young boy was being labelled as mentally ill. Laing discovered this with the family and helped to avert the danger of a narrow focus on set procedures in mental health.

Yalom provided us with an early psycho-social case study of Freud to demonstrate that, in real practice, there is much more going on, and that it is impossible to know what will make the difference. Indeed he suspects that what is of most benefit is the personal input of the helper, rather than the set processes. However, examining the actual case study by Freud showed that the helper's agenda also shaped the assessment, and that events surrounding the intervention, both inside and outside the assessment room, also played their part. The results of even this successful case were mixed and were only partially explained by Freud's theory, as Freud himself acknowledged. The existential social work approach acknowledges the active role of the social worker in shaping assessment and intervention.

The current context of social work assessment and intervention was explored through the two competing frameworks, with modernists building on traditional psycho-social assessments – and claiming evidence-based, objective methods – and postmodernists claiming that all assessments and interventions are socially constructed and thus being highly critical of modernist claims to objectivity and freedom from bias. Many of these latter approaches adopt overtly political perspectives, including the anti-discriminatory practice perspective that Thompson advocates (Thompson, 2006). I noted how this approach judges all interventions on the basis of whether they add to or challenge oppression in all its forms, asserting that there can be no neutral ground even when the situation is complicated, with oppressed clients oppressing other people, such as their family members. Thompson has criticized relationship-based social work interventions for placing the professional relationship with the client above political considerations of the kind mentioned.

I have argued the merits of some of the traditional social work approaches, which value the uniqueness of the individual, group, or community you are working with above all else. But these traditional approaches failed to address the oppression within the wider system that acts to depersonalize the client – an existential approach must address the oppression factor within the social situation as well.

When you examine any field of service in which social workers practice, the existential perspective requires that this be done from within the world in which the social worker and client are meeting. The social worker brings to the encounter:

- Their presence and availability to the other person(s);

- Their ability to empathize and engage with the other in a non-judgemental manner;

- Their preparation and knowledge of the individual client, but also of their particular and universal needs (through knowledge of the problems, classification systems, and other tools in this field of service);

- The ability to manage the self-determination needs of the client through clarity in the negotiable and non-negotiable elements of the process; and

- Help in making sense for the client of the various processes of intervention.

The existential social worker follows the policies, the frameworks of practice, and procedures; uses the right tools and refers to the case manuals; and, more importantly, adheres to their supervisors' and team approaches when working in a government-regulated and funded agency. But what the existential social worker also brings to the encounter is themselves, their communication skills, and their understanding of the professional social work role, which provides more intervention options than therapy.

The client also brings their unique situation to the table. Often they do not understand the workings of the system. Their attitude may be hostile and antagonistic to intervention. These are the real challenges of practice. Sometimes these challenges are impossible to overcome, resulting in failures to assess and engage the client. While the social worker comes to the assessment and intervention with an agenda, so does the client. The client's agenda can be different from, and even opposed to, the social worker's agenda. It is in these highly challenging situations that professional and program purpose become vital in helping to resolve the conflict, as does the existential social worker's ability to make use of conflict resolution strategies as described above.

While our aim is to understand and assist the unique person in the situation in front of us, we also exist within a field of service, an agency, and a program that has a limited focus, aims, and boundaries, within which the client's issues and needs may or may not fall. Resources are also limited, and part of our professional responsibility, which we share with our field of service, agency, and program, is managing this scarcity and need in the fairest way possible. Thus, in the real, finite world of social work practice, part of running a successful assessment and intervention program is, paradoxically, recognizing the reality that there will always be failures, people who don't fit the guidelines, or who are not appropriate for the existing program and who would not benefit from participation in the program at this stage of their lives. Camus (2000) espoused this need for moderation and acceptance of limitations in the finite world more than any other existential writer.

The limitations of our existing programs should be our inspiration to never forget the other element of assessment and intervention stressed in critical perspectives and by Gisela Konopka: existential social work's need to change oppressive practices, to challenge existing systems, and to improve our programs so that more clients can benefit. In the next chapter, I examine some of the ways in which an existential approach to social change can assist direct practice.

## KEY POINTS FROM CHAPTER 4

1  Existential social work assessment and intervention aims to achieve a joint discovery process with clients.
2  As a participant in the assessment and intervention process, social workers need to be aware that their purpose and presence shape that process.
3  The modernist and postmodernist approaches to social work assessment and intervention both have strengths and limitations. An existential approach recognizes that social work processes are messy, and that while all approaches have some usefulness, none offers a complete answer.
4  Existential social work assessment and intervention has a broader focus than existential therapy. Tools of assessment are used with the knowledge that they are partially rather than totally useful.

# 5

## EXISTENTIAL SOCIAL WORK IN SOCIAL POLICY, SOCIAL MOVEMENTS, AND TEAM WORK

What do social workers need to know about social policy and social movements? Do these things really have any relevance to the day-to-day social work that practitioners face in direct service? Once again, I commence my examination from the point of view of the lived experience of the direct service social worker. When commencing work in a human services system as a social worker, it can feel as though everything is prescribed. It can feel like you are a small cog in a huge machine, but there are usually many other small and medium-sized cogs whirring away nearby. Here is where I want to begin, because, in one sense, immediate team relationships *are* more important to team work performance than social policy, or program direction or procedures.

At the same time, the apparent stability of social policy is quite deceptive. The existential idealist philosopher Hegel (2009) understood that the real, material world we look at everyday would not exist without all the ideas that created it. Think of cars, computers, desks, and chairs. In social welfare, nearly everything we assume about our complex service systems has come about through social pressure on governments by lobby groups and related social movements. Social work itself emerged as a type of social movement from within the charity organizational movement (Lubove, 1983). State social welfare services were created in response to the successful actions of social movements over many decades (Piven and Cloward, 1971, 1979). In fact, a historical perspective on social movements, and on any social welfare practice area, helps to describe the emergence of current institutional arrangements, the continuing process of dynamic change occurring, and the likely future developments (Trattner, 1974; Thompson, 2002; Marston and McDonald, 2012).

In this chapter, I examine the broad topic of social work in team work, social administration, social movements, and social policy from an existential point of view, looking particularly at social workers' lived experience in these areas. In reality, and if we stop to examine our practice, direct service work occurs in all these areas. For example, I could ask the question, 'Why am I working in this team of people?' To answer it, I would need to understand my field of service, the policy decisions made about how services have been designed and resourced, as well as the agency I work in and how it came to sanction this program and team. I would also have to link my answer to the historical dimension and to my personal journey to this work, which always includes an element of human mystery. In existential theory, mystery does not refer to the mysterious, but to the non-problematical, to the notion that I am involved in my history and world, and that I help shape that world in some way.

## Team work and existential social work

Besides our direct work with clients, everything else we do is indirect work aimed at supporting our service work. Indirect work includes all the computer- and paper-based record keeping and team work activities with immediate staff colleagues. The atmosphere and morale of the team is crucial to effective team performance. A work team can be inundated and overwhelmed with referrals of cases and with administration, but if the team has a welcoming and happy atmosphere, with everyone chipping in and helping each other out, then the huge demands of service can be made more tolerable. All the recording and administrative work that many direct service workers complain about is also a direct result of social policies and the resultant administrative procedures for the management of program and agency risk. Understanding this historical circumstance and being aware of how quickly these procedures can change can help the social worker to cope with the load.

Indirect work by team members is vital to maintaining this morale and atmosphere. The team leader plays a key leadership role, but so does every team member. It is rarely the clients or the challenge of the direct service work and more often the bureaucracy attached to that work that causes social workers to want to leave their workplace. Staff relationships and the tensions within teams are the primary sources of dissatisfaction. Conversely, almost any challenging social policy area can be handled well by a high morale and well-functioning team, including administrative and professional team members.

The consequences of this existential lived experience of social work practice for social policy is that we should give more attention to those aspects of the work that can make a significant difference to team morale and functioning. First amongst these aspects of the work is an acceptance of responsibility by the social worker for their part in the team's performance. Our work in a team can be very emotionally draining, but we have the capacity, as adults, to rise above negative responses and emotions and to address issues with a focus on benefitting overall team performance.

Here are some ways in which we can enhance team performance that are within the scope of any direct service social worker:

- Be fully present and available to others (leave your own issues behind and be available to others at work).

- Focus on your work so that tasks are completed, but also be open to occasional conversations, which enhance team morale.

- Never refuse to assist others in the team, and think beyond your own agenda to the team's objectives.

- Ask yourself, 'How important is winning this argument to me compared to the team's performance?' and then act accordingly, dropping the argument if there is little benefit.

- Work proactively to identify what can be changed to improve performance and what cannot be changed because you have no power to change it.

- Avoid focusing on what you cannot change.

- Accept other people's flaws, quirkinesses, and idiosyncrasies, and recognize that you, too, may have many annoying little habits that other team members tolerate.

- Always ask yourself, 'How important is this issue, conflict, or topic to team functioning?' If it's not important, drop it.

● If you are really struggling with someone, a question you may wish to ask is, 'What if this was the last time I spoke to this person?' Seeing them in the light of eternity can help you address the challenge of a difficult working relationship in the best possible way.

● Be cognisant of priorities and of doing what needs to be done according to team goals.

In the harsh reality of the demands and pressures of daily practice, the higher purpose of the program can easily be overlooked. For example, problem clients get significant, often daily attention, while those successfully using the program to make changes receive less. The team leader must be able to set program boundaries and place limits on client's behaviours. Team members have a special responsibility to support their team leader when the tough calls have to be made, including when clients have to be removed for violating boundaries – I am assuming, here, that the client's boundary violations are not legitimate challenges to normative and oppressive regulations, in which case the challenges are appropriate. Team leaders shouldn't feel as though the other members of the team paint them in the 'tough person' role, and this is a joint responsibility of the leader and the other team members.

While great team performance is vital, the program I operate in could not exist without the integrated family violence system. This system refers the clients and delivers services, dispositions, and program responses aimed at providing safety and protection for people affected by family violence. It also makes perpetrators accountable for family violence; this is the program's higher or primary purpose. It helps if the social worker can keep this in mind through the daily grind.

The idea that social work operates within a field of service (such as child protection, family violence, mental health, medical, schools and education, corrections, etc.), has a long history within the profession (National Association of Social Workers, 1971, pp. 1477–1481). But this concept has been challenged since the early days of the profession's attempts to provide a generic form of social work applicable to all settings. Although it is sometimes described as antiquated, I think the 'field of service' concept still has considerable value in helping social workers make sense of their practice and in linking their contribution to the aims of the overall system. Many of the problems social workers deal with, such as child protection or homelessness, are often described as 'wicked problems', because the solutions are not easily identified. Only whole-of-government and community- or system-wide solutions have any chance of making headway on these issues. But how can you, as an individual social worker, relate to a field of service?

## Making sense of your program

It takes considerable time in direct service practice to understand how a field of service like child protection or family violence works. We become skilled at the immediate tasks required in our practice area. Specialist knowledge and practice skills are acquired in order to operate in a small team, delivering one aspect of the overall service system. The digital and administrative systems for this area need to be understood and handled. Through acting in this area, we gradually become familiar with other subsystems that may be delivering services that complement what our program delivers.

When students are given their first placement, suddenly the academic work starts to make sense; as they gain practical experience they can start to form their own opinion of the theories about which they have read.

Below is an example, from my current practice working in men's behaviour change programs, of making sense, for myself, of my own practice area. The field of service is family violence. Our program exists as one part of an integrated system of family violence services, which includes the courts, the police, child protection, women's services, men's services, and correctional services – we receive referrals directly from these agencies and from the men themselves.

---

Case Example 5.1: Making sense of a program *from your own perspective*

Relevant to the family violence program that I work in, which operates men's behaviour change programs, a State Royal Commission into Family Violence has just delivered a 7-volume, 2,082-page report, containing more than 200 recommendations for the Victorian government. The only area of practice on which the Royal Commission recommended further research, by a 'Committee of Experts',

▶

was perpetrator programs (Royal Commission into Family Violence, 2016, Vol. 1, p. 69). This recommendation came about because the Commission received mixed and diverse expert opinions about the nature of the programs, how they should be operated, and their impacts. They were presented with the Duluth model, and with psycho-social approaches that use various cognitive behavioural therapy, strengths-based, and forensic approaches to target different risk levels with programs and enhancements such as the Good Lives program.

Our agency's peak body representative argued that only a political perspective would be adequate to encompass the true aim of the program, one informed by a pro-feminist stance. This perspective rejects the therapeutic approach as too pro-male, the educational view as limited, and the various psycho-social approaches mentioned above as failing to address the gendered nature of harmful behaviour (Vlais, 2014). As an existential social worker, I cannot wait for the experts to sort out this area of practice.

After more than thirty years in social work practice, I have been facilitating regular weekly men's behaviour change programs for more than four years, and have completed a special one-year graduate diploma on male family violence. It wasn't until I made time to read Irving Yalom's *Group Psychotherapy* that I began to really understand what I was doing. Yalom (2005) mentions men's batterer programs in the preface of his book, so there is no doubt that he had these programs in mind when he wrote it (p. 7). What I discovered in Yalom's work was the core technique of successful group work practice: that the facilitators pay attention to group process and to the here and now of group interaction.

I frequently have little say over what is presented to the men. The curriculum, each week's topic, the group exercises, the subjects of discussion, are prescribed by our program, and the ways these topics are handled are generally determined at team-leader level. I can contribute to the development of this material, sometimes, but I don't have the final say and am required to work with what I am provided. Like most social programs, there is often little time allocated for program development, given the pressures of day-to-day social work.

Yalom distinguishes the 'front specifics' of the program – the standards and prescription, the specialized language, guidelines, and rules of the areas of group work practice – from the core elements of the group process that are common to all group social work: these are the facilitation of group interaction and the group reflection process, in which the facilitators have a key role.

The reality is that men often bring their anti-social behaviours in some form into the group, where it can be addressed. Men speak over one another. Some men dominate the discussions, some are sullen and silent. They express their views through their body language, comments, and interactions with the facilitators and the other men. The key element in existential group work is the co-facilitation process with the only female in the room in order to create a safe, respectful learning environment. We also have a special responsibility to bring the voices of those not present into the room, the voices of the children and women affected by the men's violence and abuse.

In one sense, you have to make this area of practice your own, and this requires work on your part. You cannot rely on others to provide you with the right approach. Yalom's work was not mentioned in the year-long post-graduate course I took to qualify to facilitate male family violence groups. I had to discover his work (now in its sixth edition) for myself. Everything began to make some sense to me, and my group co-facilitation now has a framework around which I can make sense of all the requirements of the program I have to use and of my unique contribution to the work. Yalom's work on group psychotherapy helped me make sense of my contribution to this field of service, but it is by no means a panacea for practice in this area.

Discovering Yalom's text on existential group work has assisted me in gaining a personal perspective on my daily work in the program to help these men and to protect their families.

## Being part of a social movement

Family violence services, as a field of practice in social work, would not exist if it weren't for the women's movement and their lived experience of male family violence. These men's behaviour change programs didn't exist more than 35 years ago. A social movement created all the services we now describe as 'family violence services': women's refuges, men's behaviour change programs, and the myriad high-risk programs that are now being implemented. In the United States, these programs grew out of a social movement that was challenging patriarchy. Alongside this social movement came significant law reforms and new definitions of family violence that broadened the definition to include controlling behaviours. New ideas challenging men's power over women and bringing to light the lived experience of women contributed to the social movement that started to challenge the ways these problems were then being ignored or poorly addressed. An existential approach to social policy, team work, social administration, and social movements focuses on the people being served by the programs, not on the organizations and methods of delivery (Dixon, 2010). In the case of male family violence, this begins with the lived experience of women and children affected by that violence.

Social movements tend to be written out of social welfare policy texts. You gain the impression that governments analyse and develop policy, allocate resources, and determine delivery systems by themselves, occasionally consulting stakeholders and interest groups, and as a subtask of the primary business of government determining policy directions.

In reality, all the social provisions of the welfare state and other programs have come about because people protested, and demanded and fought for action on intolerable situations. They formed action groups with other powerful interests, like unions, created unrest, and disrupted normal activities to bring attention to themselves. They demanded their rights and staged protests to win the support of the public. New ideas like public health, settlement housing, mental health services, the New Deal, feminism, restorative justice, and welfare rights energized activists and stimulated new ways of being and of doing things. Social movements play a critical role in winning over public opinion to new and better ways of living. They challenge the existing, change-resistant status quo, defenders that initially attempt to disparage and critique such movements' claims.

Often people's only exposure to social movements is seeing sometimes violent street protests, especially when that violence is between radicals and the police. While demonstrations are a part of social movements, they are made up of so much more than this most visible form of public dissent. As Neil Thompson (2002) has stated, 'professional social work is not simply an organ of the state and is therefore in a position to seek to influence the state and the political sphere more broadly' (p. 720).

My experience of participating in social movements is that it has added significantly to my understanding of social change and to my passion for the work. The restorative justice movement is the one I know intimately, and my experience in it taught me to appreciate the value of social movements, as well as the fact that we cannot expect to change the world without engaging the world in the process. Through this experience I became interested in social movement theory. After meeting his partner, Carol Perry, I became familiar with the late Bill Moyer. Moyer wrote *Doing Democracy* (2001) and designed a model for social movement called MAP, the Movement Action Plan, based on the claim that social movements go through a series of eight stages of development. Moyer was very clear about the purpose of social movements: to win over the general population to the movement's aims. To ensure that this was achieved, their strategies must be non-violent, peaceful, and democratic. Moyer saw the absorption of social movements into the institutional mainstream of services and policies as an indicator of their success and included these processes in his eight stages of successful movements.

This view contrasts with other social movement advocates, like Cloward and Piven, whose 1979 work on poor people's movements perceived bureaucratic endorsement as a sign of failure: when the social movement declines and is invariably bought off by the defenders of the status quo, co-opted by the state, and absorbed into the current system to serve the interests of the dominant group. This helps explain why successful social movements maintain a presence outside government, ready to respond to new and unmet needs in the community.

Moyer (2001) claims that there are four roles that need to be adopted for social movements to be successful: the citizen, the rebel, the change agent, and the reformer. Social workers have performed all these roles to achieve social change. Let's look at the social worker as rebel.

Moyer states that negative rebels often attach themselves to social movements. These people actually harm the cause, because they do things that draw attention to themselves and alienate the general public, such as using violence in demonstrations. Positive rebels, though, always have the end-game in mind, which is winning over public opinion to the cause because that is what political elites ultimately respond to. Here is a recent example, from Australia, in which social workers, with other health professionals at one of our most prestigious public hospitals, were able to draw positive public attention to one of Australia's most shameful public policies.

## Case Example 5.2: Is political protest an appropriate part of social work?

Direct service staff sometimes take matters into their own hands when they feel ignored by the bureaucracies in which they work. A recent example of this in Australia involved doctors and nurses at the Royal Children's Hospital in Victoria taking a stand against the federal government's policy of returning asylum-seeker children to offshore detention once they have been treated in a mainland hospital. The operational staff were pointing out that, from a clinical point of view, returning children to detention would be harmful to their health. Their action also highlighted, in a most symbolic way, the inherent tragedy of the current bipartisan status quo in Australia's border protection policies. This is an example of a symbolic action that had the potential to radically change a policy that has wreaked significant damage on Australia's reputation internationally and has harmed many extremely vulnerable people who have come to Australia by boat to seek asylum.

These members of the hospital's staff were not acting outside their operational responsibilities, and yet they had the courage and determination to take a stand. Change will not occur because of this demonstration alone, but what it symbolizes and highlights are the inherent contradictions in the federal parliament's position. Would this action have been so powerful if the social workers at the Royal Children's Hospital had taken action on their own, without the participation of the nurses and doctors? Clearly not, because what made the protest so powerful was that some of the most highly regarded doctors and nurses took part in it, medical professionals with a much higher profile than the social workers. It is important for social workers in social policy and social action to be aware that forming alliances with more influential elites or with other professionals has great potential for effecting change. The social workers could not expect to achieve the kind of results that this combined symbolic action may have on policy in the long term.

Public support for this action was obvious, which embarrassed the government. While the bipartisan policy of keeping asylum seekers in indefinite offshore detention, without access to Australia's court system, remains in place, it is interesting to speculate on the actions that may be taking place in the corridors of power to avoid any further embarrassments of this kind.

I chose to write about the rebel role because it appears, on the surface, to be the least acceptable role for social workers to perform. Social workers are more comfortable in the roles of concerned citizen, of professional change agent, or of reformer, and far more has been written about these roles for social workers.

Some problems are so important that they must be made known to the public. Social workers also need to be smart about this and not become martyrs. Here is a mainstream social work writer making the same argument:

There is much to be said for social workers who will never be satisfied with the way things are and will continue to thrive in the role that serves clients best, without having to be approved of by powerful elements in society. (Meyer, 1976, p. 12)

Finally, social movements are not focused solely on changing society. Successful social movements also aim to help their members change personally and to develop a changed consciousness. They seek to embody the change that they wish to create in society. A successful example of this approach is the Twelve-step movement, which aims to assist addicts to recover through participation in regular group meetings and individual mentoring, as well as through the development of their spiritual life and participation in the recovery movement. The Twelve-step movement saves lives. For most people in recovery from addictions, a combination of professional and self-help interventions gradually help the person create a new life without the compulsive focus of addiction. For many, participation in the Twelve-step movement is crucial to their recovery. Without the meeting to attend on a Friday or weekend night, recovery would cease. The arguments about strategies of abstinence versus harm minimization that occupy researchers fail to address the lived experience of the addict struggling to avoid a relapse after the professionals finish work. In this sense, the Twelve-step program is an existential social movement *par excellence*. I would encourage social workers to visit as observers, as I have done on countless occasions, and see for themselves how the Twelve-step program uses narrative and other self-help strategies to help people change themselves.

# Social workers as policy advisors

After gaining some experience in direct service practice, many social workers move into line management positions, as program managers and eventually as agency leaders. Another path is to move into policy work, usually available in larger governmental or private agencies and in peak social welfare bodies. In social administrative theory, these positions are referred to as 'staff' positions, as distinct from 'operational' positions, and include administrative roles like human relations, financial management, and research. Various quasi-governmental agencies that monitor service delivery systems, ombudsman bodies, for example, also provide advice to legislatures on the performance of human services systems. These positions do not hold operational responsibilities for the delivery of direct services. They are exempted from this work so that they can concentrate on developing new policy, giving policy advice to government, and on developing, improving and maintaining existing policy and programs through improved legislation, procedures, and guidelines.

These kinds of jobs require a different range of social work skills: writing skills, for example, which become important because ministers of the Crown generally require extremely clear and succinct policy advice, or the political skills involved in negotiating with key stakeholders and in maintaining support for the policy directions that are being proposed. Line management and direct service staff rely on accurate, concise, clear policy, program, and procedural guidelines. Policy advisers are required to regularly liaise with operational staff to ensure that whatever they are proposing is accurate, acceptable to the field, and appropriate from a policy perspective and not simply from an operational efficiency perspective.

Existential social work practice in social policy needs to begin with the realization that social work is a politically marginal profession. The kinds of effect that we can achieve can only come about through creating and developing social movements and working with other, more powerful professions, such as the legal, medical, and political (Keith-Lucas, 1975). Conversely, powerful professional groupings and advocacy groups can undermine social work policy objectives, as has been demonstrated throughout the history of the welfare state.

From my own experience, one of the first lessons I learned when I transferred from operations to policy work in a major governmental department was that I had to expect that much of the work I did would amount to nothing. Policy work is often used in political arenas for damage control. For example, one of my first policy responsibilities was to conduct a review of the adult youth training centre system, a system that allows some seriously immature 17–21 year olds to remain in youth detention facilities, instead of being moved to adult jails. I became involved after a major front-page story had broken: a young offender, on weekend release, had made a threat against one of his previous victims. The story ran with the headline 'Your dead meat!'

The Minister at the time needed some way to get this bad news story off the front pages of the major dailies. A review was recommended by senior bureaucrats, and I was given the job of conducting it. I spent approximately twelve months conducting the review in liaison with operational staff from all our major detention centres and wrote many draft reports with recommendations on how to improve the program. All this busywork was really a subterfuge to enable the Minister to say that a review was taking place, and that all matters would be considered thoroughly by the department. Eventually, after about eighteen months of work, the report was handed to the Minister. By this stage, documents take on lives of their own. They become the end product. In a strange way, the actual program becomes irrelevant. I eventually realized that the senior bureaucrats who had managed this program for the last twenty years had no intention of altering their adult youth training centre weekend leave program.

The purpose of my report was to manage an unfortunate incident that had developed when the operational manager of a particular youth training centre had decided to release all the young inmates on extended leave so that he could conduct desperately needed staff training. Unfortunately this strategy backfired on him, and the resulting actions of one manager had thrown the whole adult youth training centre weekend leave system into question. By authorizing the review, the Minister managed to remove the story from the front pages. When the report was finally delivered, nothing happened. Perhaps the survival of a worthwhile program after a crisis and a formal review can still be considered a valuable policy result.

My next position involved being part of the implementation of a new law, the Children and Young Persons Act 1989. The implementation team was put together from various sections of the department. I was to represent the area that provided policy direction to out-of-home care services for children and young persons. My tasks included the development of regulations for out-of-home care to accompany the Act, as well as the development of secure welfare services to provide detention care for children at substantial or low risk of harm to themselves.

This Act had come about after a significant review of child welfare in the state, called the Carney Review (1984). It brought a youth justice model to a system that had been operating on a welfare approach to service delivery. Terry Carney is a lawyer, and he strongly advocated for the view that the failures of the welfare model necessitated a modern social justice approach to the management of children in care needing protection, as well as for those committing offences. These children are now to be dealt with separately, as belonging to distinct categories: those in need of care and those who commit offences.

It is important in an existential approach to social policy to highlight failures as well as successes. One of my failures on this team was my attempt to develop regulations that would ban corporal punishment (smacking, hitting, etc.) in out-of-home care of children. A community backlash among fundamentalist Christians, who were very powerful within the foster care lobby, ensued, and the department quickly scuttled this proposal. In the youth justice area, similar regulations, which included prohibiting isolation in detention in the youth training centre system, became part of the revised legislation. This was a smart move on the part of my other colleagues in youth justice, because legislation is passed by Parliament, whereas regulations are forms of law that bureaucrats create and must be justified in the public arena through the development of a public document called a regulatory impact statement. The whole exercise is fraught with potential danger for bureaucrats, because it uses the power of the Parliament, which is the ultimate lawmaking body. Social workers in policy positions need to be highly attuned to the legal ramifications of their actions given their position.

The reality is that changing the law is an extremely difficult task and takes years of patient and dedicated work by multiple stakeholders. Below is an example of an occasion when policy work suddenly changed detailed governmental plans.

Case Example 5.3: A Minister changes a detailed governmental plan; moving Secure Welfare Services into the community

Ministers seem to appreciate graphs and figures even more than words when it comes to making key decisions. I have been asked to evaluate the possibility of moving secure welfare services, a kind of secure care residential service for young people in protective detention, out of the detention complexes for young people who are being detained in connection with criminal charges or convictions. At that stage, there was no plan to do this. I had only been asked to 'look into it as a possibility'. The existing State-wide Redevelopment (SRD) Plan for central institutions had been agreed to through complex industrial negotiations and had been in place for over ten years. It did not address the issue of moving protective clients out of the care and management of services primarily designed for offending young people, even though this was a key policy direction. It was assumed these services would be managed in the same way.

I established a set of objective criteria upon which to base a decision and then evaluated the proposed community buildings against these criteria. To my great surprise, the Minister accepted my report and, as a result, SRD planning had to be rethought. Secure Welfare Services were moved into community detention facilities, completely separate from correctional services. This was the first time I realized that my work could potentially change governmental policy. It was an awesome responsibility.

# Social administration and leadership: The program implementation process

Much less is written about policy and program implementation than about policy formulation, even though far more social work hours are focused on these tasks (Gilbert and Terrell, 2010). Policy implementation is a neglected area of analysis, and yet so many programs lose public support because of poor implementation. One common finding is that governments frequently fail to realize the scope of problems and thus do not allocate sufficient resources to fix them. Little attention is given, too, to the unintended or unanticipated consequences of the implementation of programs and policies. It is not only governments that implement programs. Community and private social agencies also aim to engage their supporters and clients to deliver high-quality support to their clients. What are some of the key skills and talents required in effective program implementation? Program leadership plays a key role in the implementation of social programs. Below is an example from my own practice.

---

### Case Example 5.4: Creating a sense of belonging: The Jim Stynes story

I was working in group conferencing, which involves young offenders meeting their victims in the context of a court-ordered meeting. Supporters of both parties are present at these conferences, including professionals such as the police and the legal representative of the young person.

The social worker's role is to assess who should attend the conference, to brief those people on the process, to facilitate the meeting, and then to prepare a report to the court on the process and its outcomes.

On this occasion, a young man (with accomplices) had committed an armed robbery against his employer, a fast-food restaurant that was part of a large chain. The young man had left school early and had a very good record with his employer, but he had missed out on a recent promotion. This caused him to feel resentment. The young man and his accomplices wore balaclavas in the armed robbery, and it was a very serious offence that would normally have warranted a custodial sentence.

In my preparation for the conference, I met with the late Jim Stynes, one of the founders of the Reach Foundation in Melbourne, Australia, a group that runs innovative youth programs that aim to help young people reach their full potential. Jim was a famous Australian Rules footballer, originally from Ireland. Jim asked to meet me personally to hear about the case and the process, then we arranged for him to meet the young man. I had met with Jim because I had heard he was going to be running a one-off program in which supporters of his organization were going to spend a night in an old jail with young people from Reach to highlight the plight of young people in care and to give their supporters an experience of custody. I thought this might be something that would benefit this young man. His offence was far more serious than Reach normally dealt with.

In cases like this, the police provide the contact details of all the victims of the crime so that they can consider whether they wish to participate in the process

---

and in what manner. The manager of the restaurant was not listed, and I questioned this. The police response was that 'he was not present during the armed robbery and has subsequently left the company and moved interstate'. I insisted on them providing his contact details, which they did. I contacted him, and as it turned out he was the crucial element of the group conference's success. All the other victims only attended the conference because their then manager was going to be present; had he not been there, they would not have participated. This demonstrates the importance of a social work assessment to the outcome of the process. With all the victims, everyone who had been affected, present, the full impact of the offence could then be explored.

Among the outcomes of the group conference was that the young man attended the Reach Foundation program.

I maintained my involvement with Jim Stynes by attending one of his charity events. At this event, it really dawned on me why he was such a successful youth program organizer. He created a genuine sense of belonging and connection, not only amongst the young people and their families, but amongst the rich and influential benefactors and *their* families who supported the Reach Foundation's work. He realized that rich people often have unmet needs, too, and he did not discriminate – often this need was to belong and to connect to a bigger family and purpose, and that is exactly what Jim created.

What Jim was doing goes back to the origins of social work in the settlement house movement; the affluent being linked back into the work of helping the poor and alienated. Both groups have needs, and these can be addressed by acting as a conduit to create opportunities for genuine community engagement. Jim Stynes' life was cut short by illness, but the Reach organization he established continues to thrive. You can read more about it here: http://www.reach.org.au/.

Leadership in program implementation also requires people who have a clear understanding of the aims of governmental policies and the ability to articulate these aims to the public and to key stakeholders. Here is an example from social work history, Jane Hoey. This social work leader steered the first US Social Security legislation into practice, giving the poor and destitute a right to a payment so that they could survive and become independent of government. With the advent of the Trump administration, this example takes on deeper significance.

Hoey was an existential public administrator *par excellence*, but not because she used existential philosophy. To my knowledge she never even mentioned it. She espoused mainstream social work values such as the importance of valuing the uniqueness of all human beings, a position consistent with existential thought. Waugh (2004) states that the existential public administrator takes responsibility for stewardship; they have a 'deeper understanding of the nation and act to preserve its past and its future even when elected officials and the public choose actions that may damage the future' (p. 435). I could have used a more recent example of social leadership, but I think that Hoey's story illustrates everything relevant to this book about existential social work leadership: a deeply committed ethical practice base, a commitment to achieving social betterment within the system using democratic means, an understanding of democracy that includes providing the means for all people to experience full participation in their society, a strong commitment to social work as a profession, and a recognition of the need for the further development of the field.

# Jane Hoey

Jane Hoey was the first director of the United States Bureau of Public Assistance (now the Social Security Administration). When she was first appointed by President Franklin D Roosevelt, she insisted that she be given a civil service classification as a professional and not a political appointment, even though she was politically well-connected. Hoey took up the post of director on 7 January 1936, when she was age 44. Her task was to implement the famous Social Security Act 1935, which was a landmark social policy that established the first entitlement, or right, to social security for people in various circumstances, including poverty or destitution. Previously, help for the poor had been handled through the charity provisions of the states or local counties. Instead of groceries, second-hand clothing, and a token, one-off grant, people entitled to support under the Act would receive a regular payment. Originally trained by Mary Richmond, Hoey held the director's position for nearly twenty years. With the election of the Republican Eisenhower to the Presidency, the position was reclassified as administrative (from professional–technical), allowing Eisenhower to place a political appointee in the role. Hoey made a statement against the politicization of the directorship by refusing to go quietly by resigning, forcing Eisenhower to formally sack her in 1953. Why is this important?

Hoey was the highest ranking female social worker in the United States at the time, and she was highly regarded. Her letter of resignation and the administration's response are available online at http://www. socialwelfarehistory.com/people/hoey-jane-m/.

In her resignation letter, Hoey argues that professional social work training and experience are required for the position, because it involves policy formulation rather than policy decision making, which remains a political function; 'There is nothing political about poverty,' Hoey writes. What did she mean by this? That human need should be addressed similarly to illness. Hoey was content to give the elected government the final say but felt that policy should rest upon solid experience of practice in helping people to help themselves.

The Social Security Act 1935 created the Aid to Families with Dependent Children (AFDC) program, which matched federal funding dollar-for-dollar to the support offered by states to up to the age of 16. This was a ground-breaking decision because it allowed payments to be made to very poor families with the aim of making people feel more independent.

In 1957, social worker Alan Keith-Lucas released a book titled *Decisions about People in Need*, which examines administrative decision making in public assistance and specifically contrasts two southern US states in terms of their administration of the AFDC program from 1950 to mid-1953, the final years of Jane Hoey's leadership of the Bureau of Public Assistance. While Keith-Lucas was careful not to say explicitly that he was comparing these two states, he found that the state that operated using a case management approach, in line with social work, had spent twice as much on AFDC as had the state in which a detailed procedural legal approach was taken. Hoey (1958) reviewed Keith-Lucas's book after leaving her job, and her review does not mention this significant increase in spending under the social worker regime; this is possibly because the book is so firm about not comparing the outcomes of the two approaches. Keith-Lucas was an early advocate of the separation of social work or rehabilitation services from payment systems in public welfare.

Hoey favoured the opposite – she wanted clients on public welfare to live the fullest life possible, and she couldn't see this coming about without the assistance of caseworkers. In her 1957 review of Keith-Lucas's book, Hoey writes that with the 1956 amendments 'Congress has decided otherwise', that caseworkers are integral to the system. She goes on to say that 'one of the limitations of [Keith-Lucas's] book is the author's desire for absolutes' (Hoey, 1958, p. 196). Congress kept services with benefits, but ultimately Keith-Lucas's view won out, when, in 1967, services were separated from benefits. The situation has not changed since. The unintended consequence of this separation has been the gradual deterioration of public confidence in any welfare model to the point where the term 'welfare' now has a pejorative meaning among people of all classes. Hoey's writings from 1938 to 1957 chart the course of her attempt to create a public safety net, using social work to legitimize the public welfare system by raising standards in service delivery for clients of the service system. In 1938, Hoey wrote against the view within social work that social workers were clinicians and thus should not concern themselves with the economic or community factors that contributed to individual problems.

Under the Social Security Act 1935, the delivery of welfare payments and services was left to the states with federal oversight. What ensured equitable treatment? Hoey's view was based on Catholic social philosophy on the true meaning of democracy; more than a form of government of free elections, democracy included the opportunity for all citizens to participate fully in society, and took in the notion of citizens giving back to their society by contributing to it. As Hoey wrote in 1947: 'The test of a government service in our democracy is not merely its efficiency or economy of operation, but the way it affects lives and carries out the ideals of the people as expressed in our constitution and the laws of the nation' (p. 6).

The state–federal relief payment and social casework provided a means for recipients to provide for their families' basic needs, as well as offering them some money to be spent as they chose, free from state interference. In 1948, Hoey had determined that casework should not be linked to financial aid, but offered as a service to help to address the total human situation so that the individual and their family could become more self-sufficient. In 1950, Hoey was still questioning whether social work had defined 'its area of competency' (p. 410). The top priority had to be the elimination of destitution in the richest nation on the planet, through a combination of 'social insurance, public assistance and payments from union welfare funds' (Hoey, 1957 p. 407). She continued to link the struggle to the US Constitution and its guarantee 'that no person shall be deprived of life without due process of law. This guarantee is meaningless without assurance of the *means to life'* (p. 410).

Hoey stressed the significant advance from 'relief in kind' that unrestricted money payments achieved for human dignity for the destitute. She strongly resisted any social work overreach into people's self-determination and argued that 'the primary purpose of public assistance is to meet need and in doing so to help recipients help themselves. The public assistance agency should not be used for other objectives' (Hoey, 1957, p. 411).

At the same time, Hoey promoted social casework in public assistance for its capacity to free people to take decisive action for themselves. It is this aspect of her focus that makes it appropriate for her approach to be labelled existential. Hoey maintained a constant focus on the ends of public administration and not just on the means (Dixon, 2010). She saw this end as the freedom aimed for in the fundamental principles of democracy, which includes fairness towards all citizens. This perspective was built upon the Catholic social philosophy of the brotherhood and sisterhood of humanity, in which democracy 'emancipates the strong from the tyranny of their strength, releasing the weak from the penalties of their weaknesses' (Kirby, 1921, p.6). Poverty was the 'failure of social justice, the protection of which is a fundamental duty of the state' (p. 6).

Hoey had no illusions about social casework's value. She maintained that, if benefits were adequate, much casework would cease to be necessary. Intensive casework was only required in a small number of cases, particularly if it prevented family breakdown, which would prove more costly to society in the future. The years leading up to her dismissal included intense media hostility to public assistance, with a focus on the immorality, dependency, and dishonesty of recipients of AFDC, even though fraud occurred in less than one percent of cases, of which many instances were government overpayments rather than intentional fraud.

In November 1953, Hoey gave an address titled 'Public Welfare, Burden or opportunity?' In it she asserts the superiority of the money payment over 'going on the county' in-kind relief system that it replaced. 'The money payment, by making people *feel* more independent, has actually helped them to *be* more independent' (Hoey, 1953, p. 378). She cites an example of public welfare as opportunity in the story of a young professor of social work who obtained permission to conduct an experiment over a three-month period during which he provided casework services to '27 of the most hopeless cases in terms of rehabilitation' (p. 379). At the end of the three months, 'three men were working, nine were looking for work, three were getting rehabilitation to prepare them for work' (p. 380), leaving twelve for whom presumably no improvement was achieved (pp. 379–380).

In the same address, Hoey provides an example in which advocates of the view that welfare is a burden on the taxpayer inadvertently worsened the cost to the taxpayer and greatly harmed a family in their policy drive to get 'able bodied mothers of school age children off welfare and into jobs' (p. 383). In forcing a mother to work with a sick husband, the end result is that the family breaks down and the child is placed in foster care with both parents in hospital; thus the public costs escalate. Ultimately social work operates in a political world. The new Republican President Eisenhower was able to remove Hoey, despite all the protests. During America's most prosperous era, poverty rapidly increased.

## The 'Common Human Needs' story

Existential social work leadership can achieve only so much if political forces in the wider community line up to usurp and destroy its policy objectives. In the example below, powerful lobby groups joined forces against welfare and health objectives to prevent public programs being developed by using an excerpt from a social work publication to assert that the publication, and thus the governmental agency, had a socialist agenda. This led to the administration being forced to ban a social work text, the only time this has occurred in social work's history. The social work profession was highly critical of the ban. This example demonstrates the power of lobby groups to destroy the social work agenda. The recent efforts in the United States by Republicans to dismantle the Affordable Care Act (known as Obamacare) reflect the alliance of interests that resists any attempt to provide universal healthcare, a service provided as a basic right in many other advanced countries.

## Case Example 5.5: The 'Common Human Needs' story

Seventy-one years ago, a social work text titled *Common Human Needs*, written by Charlotte Towle, became the only social work text ever published to be removed from sale, to have its typesetting plates destroyed by the government, and to have a direction issued against it by the federal government department that initiated the book's production that it was 'no longer to be used' in operations. How did this happen?

Jane Hoey, director of the Bureau of Public Assistance (BPA), wanted a book that would improve the casework done in state-run Social Security offices. Most of the people employed in these offices were untrained social workers, who were also poorly paid and subject to the local assessments of client worthiness and eligibility. Towle was brought in by Hoey to write a federal report that would upgrade and standardize public welfare casework skills and raise the level of service received by public assistance clients.

The text took a developmental approach to people's needs and helped workers understand the emotional aspects of receiving assistance, as well as how understanding these emotions could help the worker to assist their clients more effectively. The work was very popular and went through numerous reprints, and it helped introduce a social work-influenced individualization approach to public welfare in the United States.

As welfare came under attack, a statement in the text became the focal point of the campaign to undermine public welfare. During the first attempt to create basic publicly funded healthcare, the American Medical Association ran a successful campaign to oppose the alleged socialization of medical care: the text was publicly ridiculed in two separate campaigns waged over four years, from 1947 to 1951.

Taken out of context, these were the words used to discredit the BPA: 'Social security and public assistance programs are a basic essential for attainment of the socialized state envisaged in democratic ideology, a way of life which so far has been realized only in slight measure'.

Towle meant no more by this 'socialized state' than that a safety net of payments and services was essential for the attainment of democracy as a way of life, which had until then 'been realized only in slight measure'. Faced with a relentless campaign in the press, the BPA made the decision to ban the book.

It is important to be reminded by the above example that there are powerful interests opposed to progressive social policy initiatives. Existential social work recognizes that progressive social policy reform has enemies who will oppose reform. As in any conflict, not all battles can be won, and sometimes a strategic retreat is necessary to take the wind out of the opponents' sails.

# Innovation in social policy: The pilot program experience

When new ideas for programs are created, one way to test these ideas is a pilot program. The research component of the pilot program described below is discussed in Chapter 7 on evidence-based practice and existential social work. Below I document how this pilot program was successfully undertaken.

How do you successfully pilot a program and achieve good enough results that the larger political system embraces it, develops a legislative basis for the program, and then expands it across all areas of the state?

This is the story of a pilot project that I was involved in in Victoria, Australia. It is called the Youth Justice Group Conferencing program (YJGC). Restorative justice is now a world-wide social movement creating a new paradigm centred on healing harms and making amends rather than on correcting offending by graduated loss of liberty. Conferencing is one model that brings together those affected or involved in a facilitated group process in which they share their experiences of the harm and come to an agreement about how it should be addressed. The YJGC was a children's court program used at the pre-sentence stage for young people otherwise facing a supervisory order. It began in 1995 as a pilot program, funded entirely by philanthropic donors. Ten years later, in 2005, it became a state-wide, government-funded program with a legislative basis in the new Children, Young Persons and Families Act 2005. What enabled this program to succeed, when so many others either fail or do not progress beyond the pilot stage?

It was not smooth sailing throughout this program's ten years from pilot to state-wide implementation. As the first program co-ordinator, I was aware that two recent pilots in victim–offender mediation had failed in the pilot phase and had ended within one year because they had struggled to obtain referrals from the existing system, and because the staff had eventually lost hope and left.

There was also a pre-existing, long-standing conflict that had delayed the commencement of the program, between the initiating agency and the steering committee, which had representatives from all stakeholder groups in the existing youth justice system (such as the police, the courts, the Department of Human Services (which delivered all other state youth justice programs), and Victoria Legal Aid.

A philanthropic fund had already provided the money needed to the same agency to run the family group conferencing pilot program that was operating within the state's child protection system and had approvingly observed this program being expanded into all regions and being owned and fully funded by the state. The fund was prepared to support the youth justice program without any governmental assistance for the first three years because it wanted to see young people who had committed an offence meet their victims in a supportive environment.

At this time, the Victorian youth justice system had been in strong opposition to the pilot program because it disagreed with its philosophy and was concerned about the potential harms and harsher penalties that could result from its approach. It was also concerned at the potential for the program to net-widen and draw young people before the courts who would otherwise not receive any supervisory order. Senior policy staff within the Victorian youth justice system had published academic journal articles highly critical of the police-initiated conferencing models and of New Zealand's youth justice conferencing programs (Carroll, 1994). Youth advocates and high-profile criminologists had also published similar articles highly critical of the general push to introduce restorative justice (Alder and Wundersitz, 1995). Politicians in other states had used the introduction of this new approach as a 'getting tough on youth crime' alternative to increasing incarceration of young people. Victoria prided itself on having the smallest, most progressive youth justice system in Australia, in the context of a well-developed youth advocacy and service system that kept most young people out of the system or attempted to remove them from it quickly. The youth justice system was reluctantly forced to co-operate with the pilot – all the other stakeholders wanted to give it a try, and the private funding was guaranteed for three years.

'Project champions' play a key role in successful pilot programs. Two people were critical to this project's success. One was Tricia Harper, one of the architects of Victoria's reform of child welfare laws in the 1990s and the chair of the Steering Committee for most of that time. One of the reasons Tricia became involved in the program was that the juvenile justice reforms she was primarily responsible for had neglected the family, the community, and the victim. She saw this program as a suitable way to introduce these vital elements into the Victorian youth justice system. Jennifer Coates, the Chief Magistrate of the Children's Court at the time, became joint chair of the Steering Committee. Harper and Coates' leadership enabled the program to weather many challenges and respond quickly to opportunities and threats, such as the perennial issue of maintaining a steady flow of referrals from the courts to the program. They also provided the stability needed to cope with changes of operational staff.

Surprisingly, the Steering Committee personnel hardly changed throughout the program's first ten years. When an opportunity came for the Steering Committee to make a submission to government for draft legislation for the program, I remember how everyone on that Committee was prepared to attend daily breakfast meetings for a week in order to quickly hammer out all the details of the draft legislation. This submission enabled the Ministers involved to know that all the key stakeholders had agreed to the proposed legislation – all the key stakeholders were represented on the steering committee. In social policy areas, governments generally try to avoid open public conflict. When they know a new reform has broad key stakeholder support, they proceed confidently into parliament with their proposals. The restorative justice program touched all aspects of the justice system, including victim services, which had never engaged significantly with the youth correctional system before. It reached into communities and engaged with families, schools, extended families, community groups, and service organizations.

I remember spending my summer holiday writing the first draft of the first 'Program Description and Implementation Plan', which went through several drafts before it was finalized and published. Tricia Harper and I worked through the details, such as how we would address ethnicity, culture, and gender issues. The preparation of this document enabled all the points of contention among the key stakeholders to be resolved to everyone's satisfaction; everyone was on the same page as to 'how this program would work'.

It had a deliberate youth rights focus that ensured no young person would be worse off by choosing the restorative justice option in court.

As a voluntary, non-legislated option that asked young people to face their victims and their supporters and then to return to court for sentencing, this was a service not easily embraced by lawyers representing the young people. Some lawyers refused to use it, and others became regular referrers to the program. Magistrates either were resistant or oblivious or were enthusiastic advocates for the program. Gradually, we became better group conference convenors and gained 'court-level credibility' for the program. Some conferences succeeded spectacularly, others were more routine, and some were not very successful. There were very few that were harmful. Like most new social programs, it was a struggle, and there were steep learning curves, particularly around engaging families and victims and their supporters. Staff members were employed on the basis of their excellent youth work skills but lacked experience with victims and needed help from victims' advocacy groups to develop victim-sensitive practices. These victims' groups were very supportive, because they could see the benefits victims obtained from their various forms of participation.

All this work was conducted in an environment of constant research and evaluation of the pilot program by external and independent university researchers who attended the conferences as observers and followed up with the participants for over twelve months following their completion of the program to document the outcomes. This data was used in preparing the six independent reports published on the evaluation of the pilot program.

Receiving this level of attention provides your new program with excellent feedback on how it is working. It also means that your performance is being observed and commented on by other highly experienced social work academics and researchers. The results of this evaluation effort proved decisive in finally winning over critics to the value of the program in providing the courts with a viable new pre-sentencing option. (Details on the evaluation process are provided in Chapter 7.)

The Department of Human Services supported the funding of the program's expansion across the state, and a legislative framework enabled its wider use. Recently, the legislative base has been expanded to young people facing a detention order, enabling even more serious young offenders to be given this opportunity. No net-widening of the youth justice system has occurred in Victoria as a result of this program. The Department of

Human Services now embraces and advocates for the program at every opportunity. I have used this example partly because I was directly involved in it for a significant period of time. During this period, I remember Senior Magistrate Jennifer Coates approaching me to return to the program, because it had collapsed through staff exhaustion at one stage. The program even changed auspices under competitive tendering processes and survived the ordeal.

Group conferencing was an idea whose time had come. Victoria had to work out where the technique would fit into its existing system. The recent changes, which allow young people facing custodial sentences a chance at a conference with no legislative assurance by the court of any diversion away from detention, is an illustration of the system's continued adaptation to the benefits of using restorative justice.

For social work, conferencing provides a new direct service method alongside casework, group work, and community work, to engage people within a community of support, to help them resolve issues and come to collective decisions. The pilot program story above is a good news story for social work. It could easily have turned out differently. What makes it *existential* is that people took responsibility and took action to make things happen. They worked together collaboratively to bring about a significant change to the juvenile justice system. They were passionate in their commitment to the cause, and they stuck it out *for ten years* to see things through. They used their power, skills, and knowledge of the system to get things happening. But nothing was pre-ordained – it could all have ended in failure.

## Having a vision in social work

Increasingly, many people feel we are entering a critical period of human evolution in which certain radical change is required if humanity is going to survive and thrive into the future. In a strange juxtaposition, our modern neo-liberal democracies have much to learn from the traditional societies that have been devastated by colonialism. Are we facing a different but equally catastrophic tipping point? Are our communities facing an existential crisis?

Jonathon Lear (2006), a philosopher, became fascinated with how indigenous cultures dealt with the extinctions of their traditional ways of life using their traditional powers of visioning a future, which incorporates their traditional way of life while also embracing the opportunities available in this technologically sophisticated era. He called his book *Radical Hope*, and it tells the story of how Plenty Coup, the chief of the Native American Crow Nation, dreamed of the chickadee bird, and it told him to listen to and learn from others.

Lear's (2006) book is also directed at our current challenges: 'We live at a time of a heightened sense that civilizations are themselves vulnerable' (p. 7). In Australia, Noel Pearson, an aboriginal leader, was inspired by Lear's book to commence his own dreaming. Giving his book the same title as Lear's, in recognition of his influence, Pearson was inspired to build a new educational model aimed at maintaining and building the Australian indigenous culture within a best practice educational framework. You can watch Lear and Pearson talking about their experiences in a conference held at the University of Sydney (see https://www.youtube.com/watch?v=zMsLcg7qu2k or type into YouTube, 'Sydney Ideas – What is Recognition?').

What can having a vision mean in social work? Is it possible that our brains can deliver spontaneous, brilliant ideas through some creative process that we sometimes call dreaming or visioning? Lear references Aristotle as placing courage at the 'golden mean' between recklessness and cowardice. Lear learned from Plenty Coup that he, when facing devastation, had sought help from the spirit world to find a culturally based answer to his longing for a future for his people. What makes Coup's vision radical is that 'it was directed towards a future goodness that transcends the current ability to understand what it is' (Lear, 2006, p. 103). Lear argues that this does not require some otherworldly belief, only the recognition that there is goodness in this world that transcends our knowing. Through our innate faculty of human imagination, and our longing for a solution, we seem to have a capacity to create or be receptive to inspiration.

The symbol of the chickadee that listens to the white man's ways and learns from them has inspired the Crow Nation ever since. Plenty Coup was under no illusion about the limitations of the white man's ways, their deceptions, their lack of wisdom, and their cruelty, but through commitment to his vision of the chickadee way, he was able to realize a reasonable and realistic new future for his nation. Lear contrasts Plenty Coup's realistic and mixed future vision with the unrealistic messianic vision used by other fundamentalist Native American chiefs who wished for a return to the good old days.

Having a vision for the future is not some optional exercise. It is part of a realistic response to some of the existential challenges we currently face, such as global warming. But how do you obtain a vision? You cannot just call one up. Patience and focus is required. In my forty-year social work career I have had one vision experience that I will share as an example of facing a complex future to which the solution simply came to me out of the blue.

---

### Case Example 5.6: A practice example of the power of vision

In my first management position, I was operating a youth agency that provided after care for young adults being released from jails and youth correctional facilities. Financially, we barely raised enough money each year to survive. I remember regularly fearing not being able to pay the staff their wages, because we had no overdraft capacity. The bank required some security, such as a property with a mortgage, to provide an overdraft facility. The agency had struggled along like this for about six years since its founding. Ninety percent of our operating expenditure as a specialist youth service was covered by governmental funding, but we still managed to be without operating funds. The solution had always been to ring up the department funding our program and to cry poor; invariably a cheque would be sent to cover our immediate expenses. Previous directors had advised me to continue this practice and not to worry about it. But it seemed to me to be an unsatisfactory way to operate a high-needs-youth service. Surely we could find some way to make our finances more stable?

I had been thinking about nothing else in my spare time for weeks. I was playing with my three little children down the park when, suddenly, I received an answer. Rename the agency after a retiring, very well-known and popular Catholic prison chaplain, Father Brosnan. This idea first had to be broached with the founder of the agency, a Jesuit priest who, coincidentally, was soon to replace Father Brosnan as chaplain.

It is a very big thing to change an agency's name. The founder discussed it with the board of management, who eventually agreed to the proposal. I had to give my idea to others and allow them to embrace the idea as their vision for the agency. This was fine by me, because I was always too busy with operational matters. Gradually, over years, the idea gained momentum. Of course, as the manager, I was frequently involved in approaching philanthropic funds for donations and for promoting the idea of the Brosnan Centre Youth Service. At the opening of our new building, purchased with funds from the appeal, the then Premier of Victoria, John Cain, stood in front of a packed hall – within reach of his arch enemy at the time, trade union leader Norm Gallagher of the Builder's Labourers' Federation – to launch the renamed service. Not only did we own a building, but we ended the fundraising with a capital base of $60,000 in the trust account established for the building fund.

The days when welfare agencies could ring governmental departments and receive immediate cheques in the mail are gone. Everything is based on explicit contracts now. The Brosnan Centre Youth Service still operates today as part of Jesuit Social Services, in Melbourne, Australia.

Upon reflection, the renaming process is an obvious solution to a fundraising problem. Similarly, Plenty Coup's use of the symbolism of the chickadee can be considered an obvious strategy of co-operating with the enemy. Such a reductionist view ignores how these ideas came about. (I will be discussing in greater detail the role of creativity in social work practice in the next chapter.) Vision comes from an openness to different ways of receiving inspiration and from being open to thinking deeply about the challenges of practice.

## Conclusion

Social work operates within the wider context of a socio-economic system that has winners and (many) losers. One of social work's roles as a profession is to advocate for and improve the lives of those who are failing to benefit from the way the system is working and to challenge this system when it is failing people. We operate within human services systems created by previous generations who achieved improvements and programs through advocacy and social movements that affect governmental, and, increasingly, private enterprise, policy.

When we aim to bring about social change, it is to be expected that there will be opposition. Successful social movements win over opposition to the point that mainstream opinion embraces the implementation of the programs that have been advocated for. The most recent example in Australia is the National Disability Insurance Scheme (NDIS). There is broad agreement that the implementation of this scheme is vital to Australia's social development. It represents the most significant social reform since the introduction of Medicare, Australia's publicly funded basic healthcare system.

Every major reform has mixed results. For example, the NDIS is reshaping welfare systems through its philosophy of individualization and personalization. These social work concepts are being reframed by mainstream management approaches to service delivery. Currently, activation is the driving theory in social security provision – the idea that payments are linked to people actively seeking new skills and work opportunities. Social work itself is not immune to these changes, being affected significantly by technological developments like digital recording, and by risk management approaches that hamper efforts to provide direct services. Successful social movements also aim for personal change, and for consciousness-raising to embody the changes the advocates of the movement want in society.

I began describing how our service systems are constantly changing before our eyes, and a historical perspective is essential to fully grasp the operation of a field of service. Working in teams is where social workers first face the challenges of indirect work, and all direct service workers play a part in effective team work and in high-functioning programs. Making sense of our field of service requires the social worker to personally find their place within it.

Social work is a profession fighting for many unpopular causes, the victim, the oppressor, the marginalized, and other strugglers. Our purpose is to make sure, as far as possible, that people benefit from the fullest democratic life possible. Working with the rich and powerful as well as with the weak and powerless is important to achieving our social justice goals. Our existential vision for a better world requires that we make full use of all the positive forces in the world. We may not know our endpoint but, as Albert Camus wrote, just taking the next step can sometimes suffice.

## KEY POINTS FROM CHAPTER 5

1 Human services systems are in dynamic change and have come about through the actions of social movements.
2 Existential social workers need to develop a *personal* connection to their social movement involvement and field of service.
3 Team work is the first indirect service that social workers experience.

4 Effective existential team work requires genuine self-determination, which involves a focus on working effectively with all members for the benefit of the team as a whole.

5 The purpose of social movements is to win over the general population to the cause.

6 This can only be achieved if all a movement's strategies are non-violent and democratic.

7 In existential social policy, broad coalitions of support from the public and some powerful elites are necessary to the achievement of long-term social objectives.

8 Existential program leadership involves creating community by working with all segments, assuming stewardship of the program, and creating meaning and purpose.

9 The focus of existential program leadership in on successful implementation to improve client outcomes. Ultimate outcomes cannot be determined in advance.

10 Having a vision, especially in the light of the existential threats facing our planet, requires radical hope formed through inspiration.

# 6

## CREATIVE SOCIAL WORK AND EXISTENTIAL SOCIAL WORK

## Introduction

In this chapter, I explore what it means to be creative in social work and how an existential approach can help in maintaining creative practice. I begin with a creative act by a medical social work colleague that highlights the reality that the limitations of actual social work practice are where creativity takes place. I then examine the contribution of David Brandon, a Zen-inspired social worker, as well as the short-lived creative social work movement in the United Kingdom, where social work was explored as a literary art, and where Brandon's work continues to inspire creative writing on social work.

I argue that an existential social work approach is built on the concrete reality that we are all artists in our lives when we face our anxieties and take calculated risks. Our creativity may know no bounds, but, ethically, creative practice requires that we absorb and address the dark side of creativity and use it for purposes that enhance well-being and promote constructive outcomes.

The human services system can be designed to draw upon people's creativity, but this requires an end to seriality and the promotion of greater democracy through group work – people working to enhance individualization and a sense of concern for others. Social work has this broad focus on social action and individual help and on the dialectic of helping people to creatively make sense of their experiences.

## Case Example 6.1: The promise

A social worker in the emergency unit of a large hospital engages with a homeless woman with severe alcohol dependency. The doctors recommend her discharge after a short stay. The hospital requires that all the patient's belongings be returned to her, but this includes a number of bottles of hard liquor. The social worker objects to returning the liquor, but her opinion is ignored because it conflicts with the hospital's policy. The social worker knows that this woman will be drinking immediately after her discharge. She says to the woman, 'I want you to *promise me* you'll do one thing. When you drink, please do it where you can be seen in public'. The woman was re-admitted to emergency within 20 minutes of discharge, having collapsed drunk in a public place.

In this example, the social worker didn't throw her hands up in frustration at the hospital rules, but nor was she able to defy the hospital's policy on returning belongings to patients, despite the obvious risks in this case. She might have reflected on the social health policy that had closed down all the dedicated emergency admission and long-term units for drug and alcohol services, meaning that all cases went straight into the one emergency unit. These units can be dangerous, noisy places to work in. Security guards are routinely employed to manage the regular incidents of violence and aggression.

Within her authority as a social worker, she positions herself as a person concerned for this woman's welfare. The promise is a request of the client that she do something for her. It requires the client to act in a way that substantially reduces the chance of her dying as a result of her addiction. This was a *creative engaging act by the social worker* that the client was capable of enacting, even when intoxicated. The hospital system had to deal with her new admission. It would have proved nothing if the social worker had refused to implement hospital policy in this case. The only outcome would have been reputational damage to medical social workers for being difficult employees who don't follow rules.

**Question:**

- Do you agree with the social worker's response to this woman's situation?

# David Brandon and the creative social work movement

For a brief moment in the history of social work, in the 1970s, there was a creative social work movement, inspired primarily by David Brandon, a social worker informed by Zen Buddhist thought. I first came across Brandon through his book *Zen in the Art of Helping* (1990). Brandon approaches assisting others through his Zen Buddhist spiritual understanding of helping. His practice examples come from his social work experience, particularly with the homeless. Essentially, his approach demands that the helper be fully present in the moment and that they see without judgement, using their heart and head in spontaneous helping strategies that require as much from the helper as from the person being helped. David wrote many books, mainly on homelessness, and was also an adviser on a UK documentary called 'Cathy Come Home', directed by Ken Loach, which helped to provide improved service responses to the homeless in the United Kingdom.

In *Creative Social Work* (1979), Brandon, in collaboration with Bill Jordan, argues that creative social work is difficult to describe. It seems to come from social workers who are self-confident in their identity as a social worker and who have increased respect for clients based on a well-thought-through understanding of their field of service and of the needs of clients in that field. The movement failed to prosper, possibly because Brandon's Zen Buddhist approach was too individualized to command a large following. It also advocated an absence, or deliberate avoidance, of theory.

Brandon's spiritual approach to social work practice shares parallels with other existential approaches that involve a spiritual dimension. Basically, all these approaches ask for us to embrace a deeper attitude to our work, which involves looking at the spirit within ourselves and within the person and place. This approach includes being aware of the timeless in the present moment, which is hidden but can be discovered when we search for meaning, purpose, and learnings from our experiences. We are more than a body and a mind. The spirit is what energizes us and leaves us at death. For Brandon, this approach aims for the social worker to:

- Be a better listener, hearing 'the colour as well as the content';

- See helping as a way of living and being, rather than just a job;

- Embrace the ordinariness of our work and revel in it; and

- Become aware of how we can inadvertently hinder our clients in trying to help them, and that real change must come from the client, and that we can only assist them in making these changes, not make the changes for them.

While I don't find everything Brandon suggests appropriate, his creative approach to social work is built on a solid background of service to homeless people and advocacy for the homeless that achieved changes in societal attitudes to the problem. He discovered that his spiritual practice of Zen Buddhism had significant benefits for him as a practitioner in building a solid basis for profound creative work with clients.

## Social work as art

When practicing as a social worker, the books and theories in which you are embedded have to be left outside the interview, group, or meeting room. All that is taken into the room is yourself, your internalized understanding of social work, and, maybe, a pen to make some notes in a prescribed assessment document. How to engage, assess, understand, and intervene rely on the intuitive insights of the social worker in the moment of the process.

In the 1980s, Hugh England (1986) argued that the core skill in social work was this intuitive use by the social worker of themselves, what, in previous mainstream social work, had been called the 'disciplined or professional use of self' (p. 31). He argued that social work was more like an art than a science. It was the creative ability of the social worker drawing upon their combined skills, experience, practice wisdom, and intuitive sense for responding in the moment that best represented what social work is. His view contrasted with attempts at the time to prescribe social work practice in manuals or organizational procedures. England thought that these approaches missed the essence of social work. By adopting an artistic approach to social work, it was possible to separate good artistic social work practice from poor practice.

Since England's time, evidence-based practice has come to the field, and social work has become more prescribed and risk-averse and perhaps less willing to acknowledge the creative. Recently, Gray and Webb (2008) have revisited England's book and have argued that England was on the right track – social work is artistic, but England's approach was too subject-based. Gray and Webb suggest that creativity occurs within the social event of the meeting rather than through the creativity of the social worker.

Can social work be described aesthetically? Do we create a work of art when immersed in a client engagement process? Certainly a part of ourselves is being empathic with the client and merging with them to feel something close to their sense of their own experience. It may be more helpful to describe this interaction as the creative or learning process for both worker and client, but the worker is responsible for demonstrating and communicating the accurate empathy that provides the catalyst for creativity to take place.

## We are all artists in our lives

When I was a student in social work, I was surprised at the range of theoretical approaches in the field. If anything, students in social work today face a greater range of alternatives, within their faculties, and beyond in the literature. How do we make sense of all these diverse theories?

Dr Peter O'Connor, a practicing psychologist informed by Jungian thought, was one of my lecturers. I found Carl Jung's ideas rather remote from my practice intentions at the time, which were focused on public welfare services rather than private practice. I remember O'Connor lecturing on Soren Kierkegaard's book *The Concept of Anxiety*. When it came to reading this work, Kierkegaard seemed archaic and obsessed with sin and about as far removed from social work as any theorist could possibly be. It was reading existential therapist Rollo May's work *The Meaning of Anxiety* that helped me make sense of Kierkegaard's insight into anxiety. May's book was based on his PhD thesis, which was supervised by Paul Tillich, the existential theologian. Tillich expected May to read everything ever written on anxiety. It was Kierkegaard who provided May's insight into the subject.

When Kierkegaard is speaking of anxiety he means our normal anxiety, not something excessive or abnormal. Every human experiences anxiety.

Anxiety is linked to possibility, to the ability to say no, to choose, to decide to move in another way – in other words, to our freedom. As we grow, we take steps in freedom, and our consciousness develops, enabling us to 'confront our anxieties and move ahead, despite it' (May, 1977, p. 34). It is by facing our anxiety that we create ourselves as human beings. Every time a social worker faces a new client, there is some anxiety. The client, sitting in the waiting area, might also experience some anxiety. As May (1983) states, 'participation always involves risks' (p. 20). Anxiety is the fear of nothing, in the sense that it is the free person's realization that they are choosing, despite their concerns, to face their fear – the interview with their social worker, for example. By participating in the interview, my anxieties are dissipated. I grow as an individual by facing this anxiety, because now the interview is over and I have gained something from the experience.

According to Kierkegaard, we face our anxieties through leaps of faith into the unknown. These actions help to turn us into the person we are meant to become. This person somehow emerges from this process of facing anxiety and freedom. Kierkegaard thought that creativity was built into our essence as human persons. The human person is composed of three elements – mind, body, and spirit – and this last element enables us to discover the infinite in the moment, to choose in favour of wholeness and to reject mass thinking and negative, deadening choices or 'sin', to use his nineteenth-century theological language. I can see parallels between Kierkegaard's Christian-inspired thought on anxiety and Brandon's Zen Buddhist perspective.

In the context of social work, I think Kierkegaard's view on anxiety helps us to reconceptualize creativity within everyday life, in ourselves as professionals and in our clients' willingness to face anxiety, sharing some of our faith in the social work process and in risk engagement. Creativity is built into our freedom. It is not something special that is reserved for people we call artists.

## Ethics and creativity

Emmanuel Levinas wrote the first book on phenomenology that Sartre ever read, *The Theory of Intuition in Husserl's Phenomenology* (1995).

Levinas was there at the very beginning of the modern French existential movement in the twentieth century. In this work, Levinas, using the thought of Husserl, challenged the scientific paradigm based on naturalism, the physical sciences, which assumed that only experiential or objective knowledge is real. This approach to the physical sciences ignored the consciousness of the scientists themselves as an object of sense experience. The consciousness of the researcher affects the outcomes of their research. Their intuitions and thoughts about the subjects being studied need to be included in a broader understanding of the phenomena researched. In fact, these intuitions, held by a community of researchers, form the foundations of current scientific thought on a given subject. Inspired by Levinas' work, Sartre spent the next few years immersed in the study of phenomenology before he began to produce his own famous works.

Existential thought's darkest hour was Heidegger's support of Nazism. Levinas provided the most influential response from within existentialism. Contrary to Heidegger's focus on the primacy of being or existence, Levinas argued that our ethical bonds are constitutive of our self rather than an achievement of our pre-existing self. We wouldn't exist without others giving birth to us, helping us grow as human beings. Philosophers have tended to think in terms of a separate self, gradually building an ethical edifice. In contrast, Levinas finds this ethics built directly into our very existence in the face of the other.

The face of the other expresses our humanity, uniqueness, vulnerability, and potential for suffering. In the face or expression of the human being is the spark of the infinite potential within our finite beings. The face helps us acknowledge the personhood of the other, their wholly otherness, or distinctness from ourselves. Levinas provides a crucial ethical basis for existential social work practice.

The positive characteristic of Sartre as a philosopher was his self-critical approach to thinking against himself throughout his career as a public intellectual. In the evolution of his ethical thought, Sartre, in the third iteration of his ethics, embraced the ethical stance of Levinas (Anderson, 1993). For Levinas, and for Sartre in his final reflections on these matters, sociality comes before ontology.

## Reflective Exercise 6.1: A conference experience regarding ethics in professional behaviour

In 2015, I attended the first international conference on Existential Therapy, held in London. During one seminar led by a therapist – who acknowledged that his approach was derived from Heidegger – a leader of a delegation issued a challenge to the other seminar participants to respond to a question he had posed. The question asked was not of great significance. The delegation leader strikingly threw a significant sum of money in cash on the floor in the middle of the room and challenged anyone to come up with an answer, offering them the money as their reward.

The therapist leader of the seminar failed to respond to this insulting gesture. Many of the participants in the room were female, and this gesture, by an elderly man, was clearly disrespectful, inappropriate, and offensive. The gesture became the focus of the seminar. Almost thirty minutes went by, and still the therapist leader of the seminar had said nothing. He seemed to be following Heidegger's practice of 'letting beings be' and allowing the clearing or openness of the discourse to reveal being or existence.

Eventually I spoke up and described the action as abusive. After the seminar, some female participants thanked me for describing the action this way. Maybe others didn't agree.

The experience for me highlighted the importance of ethical behaviour in professional practice, and existential social work practice is no exception to this.

When Levinas used the human face as his foundation for placing ethics before ontology, he meant that genuine sociality or relationship requires a recognition of the unique otherness of the other person, their total uniqueness or of the infinity within their vulnerable finiteness. The gesture by the leader of the delegation in this seminar was aimed at bringing everyone partially into his domain by denying our independence from his agenda.

How we treat others affects what we discover or learn about them.

**Questions:**

- Do you think ethics comes first in philosophy?
- Is this realistic in a world in which violence and abuse happen daily?

Does creativity have a dark side? What would social work's dark or shadow side look like? Jungian writers claim that what is rejected about ourselves remains powerfully active in shaping our lives – if we bury those traits, desires, or wishes that are unattractive and disliked by our conscious minds. The suppression of this shadow leads to it becoming powerful and destructive. Each denial of the shadow increases its power.

Jungians argue that a holistic approach requires that the rejected energies of the shadow be brought into the light to be examined and given their legitimate place within our fully realized psyches. The important requirement is that the whole exercise of absorbing the shadow aspects is guided by the soul or spirit, not just by the ego. Interpreted metaphorically, the three temptations of Christ are an example of the successful integration of the shadow in Christianity's founder; he gave the temptations their due attention.

On a more mundane level, social workers experience clients whom we dislike as well as those we find more appealing. Besides our in-born and socially constructed biases, it is important to ask ourselves why these particular people produce these reactions in us. It could be that the things we despise, or intensely like, in others reflect aspects of ourselves that go unrecognized. We all admire people who have qualities we want for ourselves. Conversely, those elements we despise in others can be a reflection of things we have failed to recognize about ourselves. Being aware of all our emotions, desires, and thoughts and knowing how to integrate them into our professional self, building upon our ethical foundation, is important for practice. Existential social work is built upon a solid psycho-analytic foundation. It rejects the deterministic element of that foundation but accepts some of the insights it brings to bear upon our emotional lives. Ultimately, in existential social work, our choices and responsibilities remain ours to accept. Creative social work in the absence of a professional ethical base can be dangerous.

---

Case Example 6.2: The importance of professional boundaries

The social worker–client relationship is not a friendship. It is a professional working relationship with set aims and ways of working, within existing professional boundaries that prescribe acceptable and unacceptable behaviours. There are plenty of creative ways of engaging with and helping clients without stepping beyond the professional relationship into intimacy.

Early in my social work management career, I had to address this issue in a youth work agency. The agency valued highly their relationship with high-risk young offenders being released from jails and youth correctional facilities. I observed staff visiting these facilities and agreeing to exchange information between incarcerated young adults in different parts of the facilities. I immediately put an end to that breach of our professional responsibilities. If the authorities had discovered this practice, our agency's access to young people in jails would have been jeopardized.

**Questions:**

- Why does allowing the client to decide to be whatever their authentic self wants them to be pose ethical risks?

- Why is it vital in social work for creative practice to take place within ethical boundaries and standards?

# Sartre on how to make social work more creative

'Man is a stunted misshapen being, hardened to suffering and he lives in order to work from dawn till dusk, with these primitive technical means, on a thankless threatening earth' (Sartre, 1982, p. 126).

Social work in larger organizations can feel very uninspiring and lifeless. Sartre's comment above, which probably referred to the great majority of humanity toiling away in factories or on farms, could also be applied to office workers, and even to social work. Sartre uses dialectical thought to maintain the paradox that we are made by our world and that the human project shapes it. In Sartre's mature social ontology, human need in the context of scarcity is the driving force of history. In social work, there always seem to be more cases than can be allocated, fewer social workers than are needed to really do the job, and all of this scarcity existing within a human services system that seems to be collapsing under the weight of demand. And then there are perpetually new calls to do even more with less.

In most human services organizations in which work feels lifeless, a series of workers operating alongside each other deliver the services. Sartre compares them to a queue for a bus; a serial system. The transport system arranges people in the bus queue. Similarly, the agency resides within a human services system that sets out how its work is to be delivered. The workers seem impotent. In this system of seriality, if a social worker tries to change any part of the system, they are quietly taken aside and told to conform to the existing system or be replaced by someone else. From the Sartrean perspective, the human services system is actually a form of *'worked matter'*; it has been built up over time by various actors and designed to deliver the outcomes set by the system. Sartre uses the example of the steam engine, and the building of the coal industry and its impact on industry, and even how various associated businesses are all designed around the train line. Industry needs to be in the valleys, where the gradient allows the steam train to operate.

In a similar way, human services systems, such as the police, courts, welfare services, and health care systems, are designed and built on years of practices and technologies that have proven to deliver outcomes valued by the community. Human services systems, and organizations within them, end up having their own agendas. Individuals within those systems espouse those agendas. In a sense, these service systems create the need for social workers to operate within them, just as the steam train created the need for firemen. Social work praxis or practices become defined through this system of existing worked matter. Sartre claims that history is this struggle between creative praxis and the challenges returning to us from existing systems or inert worked matter – an apt description of our historical and built-up service systems.

Sartre's existential social thought has described how our human services systems actually create human impotence and incapacity in the way they shape the embodied practices of the human services workers who operate in them. Social workers must operate in a definite manner, according to what is expected of them by the exigencies of the existing system of worked matter. The agency, in this system, is on the side of worked matter. The hospital organizes all the staff. The steam train drives industry in the valley. Today, the side-effects of human industries, climate change, for example, produce new systems, such as emissions trading schemes, to address their impacts.

So how do we create good social work practice within a service system that positively discourages innovation and creativity? Sartre's answer is that seriality can be addressed through social movement and through the development of the group in fusion. This is not a 'fused group' but a group of people willing to come together to take action or to create a common praxis. While Sartre uses the example of the storming of the Bastille during the French Revolution, his model can also be applied to any group in which people come together to solve mutual problems through their collective agency. Gradually a group feeling develops that 'we're in this together', allowing people to forget about their own interests and work in unison for a collective end.

The social worker might be facilitating the process by ensuring everyone's safety, but the group's synergy is created from within the group. Problems can be solved rapidly. Everybody suddenly pitches in, and leadership is shared within the group. It's a wonderful experience to be in a group in fusion. After instances of such group fusion, people speak of an afterglow.

Another example of a group in fusion is a sports team performing at its peak, when all the players are contributing to the team's plan, regardless of their own individual interests or desires. There is a sense of real potency, but at the same time of the risk that it can all collapse in a second. People are freed, in this group, to create novelty and unique actions through stimulated, mutually reinforcing team effort.

Sartre argues that the group in fusion risks falling back into seriality and impotence without transforming into a pledged group. At the end of this experience of fusion, to maintain its actions and achievements the group must pledge or swear itself to the cause of implementing its plans. The pledged group makes a commitment to the cause, as occurs at the end of a successful family group conference, for example, when those in agreement discuss the outcome plan or 'what is going to be done, by whom and by when', and where next they are going to meet. They are signing on, here, to an agreed plan, and making a commitment. Unlike a revolutionary situation, where falling afoul of the pledged group might result in death or banishment, in social work, the pledged group might expect its members to agree to some accountability arrangement, to ensure that everyone completes what they pledge to do. The logic of Sartre's group process is not inevitable; rather, at any stage the risk of falling back into impotence and seriality is real, and here is where the social worker provides the impetus, and facilitation of the process, to prevent the fall back into seriality.

A successful social movement creates new social programs. In Sartre's terminology, these become entrenched in legislation and bureaucracy, becoming the worked matter or practico-inert material, the givens that the next generation of social workers have to deal with to improve existing practice.

---

### Case Example 6.3: The institutionalization of creative work

The restorative justice program piloted in Victoria, Australia, led to new legislation and a new pre-sentencing option in the Children's Court. It initially faced opposition from the relevant government department, but that department eventually embraced the program. Youth advocates were alarmed that the program would be more punitive on young people. Ten years of implementation of the pilot program proved its usefulness, but there were also many challenges, including threats to the program's survival.

With success came additional funding, a legislative base, and the potential for further expansion. But can this success actually become a barrier to further reform? There are now set ways in which the program works, prescribed by the operational guidelines for the legislation.

The government is relieved of the responsibility of genuine reform of the correctional system, which remains intact and still deals with the vast majority of young offenders in the same way. The correctional system may even be expanding and becoming more punitive.

The government can point to its 'restorative' program whenever the issue comes up. The pilot study created the program and it surpassed the old way of doing things. An unintended result, however, is that the program itself can become a barrier to further reform.

**Questions:**

- Can you see how creative change can end up becoming the worked matter that resists change?

- Why is group action, or a group in fusion, a way out of seriality?

---

Social work aims to address seriality because it lacks the ability to harness the full potential of human beings. Social work achieves this via casework with others, group work, community work, and social action.

---

Reflective Exercise 6.2: A test of seriality in your workplace

Do you feel any of the following in your social work workplace:

- Isolated

- Powerless

- Alienated

- Inert

- Atomized

- Driven by habit, convention

- That it can't change

- Passive

- A sense of working alongside others, rather than in the company of others

---

As mentioned in Chapter 1, Heidegger (1977) thought that modern technology turns resources and the world, including humans, into 'standing reserve'. By this he meant that the world becomes a resource to be used, not a river or forest to be contemplated. A coal pile exemplifies the idea of standing reserve, existing only to be used. Similarly a twenty-four-hour online bookstore enables anyone to purchase a book whenever they feel like it. Nobody can contact them to discuss a personal issue, except via email, most of which will be responded to through an automated system. There have been reactions against this standing reserve world: staff members at the Apple Store greet customers as they arrive; banks, similarly, have tried to reduce or eliminate queuing. These are reactions against dissatisfactions with the downsides of technology.

What is missing from this world is tradition, moral obligation, and opposing worldviews. The challenge to these developments comes when groups of people say:

- This can't go on,

- This is having disastrous results,

- This is scandalous,

- We need to come together to end this and develop a better system, and

- We can do this.

Through this collective experience, people join together and form groups by which action can be taken to address seriality and to develop improved systems. Sartre says we will never be finished with this struggle to improve our systems. The creative individual chooses to act and creates a group of like-minded people to challenge the existing system of worked matter that is formed into a bureaucracy. A social movement is created and challenges the existing system. This movement itself is successful and transforms itself into a bureaucracy, which needs to be reformed in turn. There is no end to this movement of creation and worked matter.

## Making sense of lived experience

As social workers, we need to recognize and acknowledge the creative work that our clients do every day in surviving and coping with the reality of their lives. We can help them identify and make sense of their experience, or acknowledge how creative they are in coming up with their own ways of making sense of things. Appendix 1 relates the story of Holocaust survivor Leon Jedwab, which illustrates how, even in the worst possible conditions, creativity plays a vital role in survival and thriving and in making sense of suffering.

In 2015, I had the good fortune of meeting Leon Jedwab at the Jewish Holocaust Centre in Melbourne. When I met him, he was 91 year old, but by the age of 15 Leon had survived five years in Nazi concentration and work camps. His story is one of implacable hope and of how he made sense of his experience. It exemplifies, for me, our creative capacities as human beings to strive and survive and to make sense of our experiences.

The Holocaust is a defining event in human history. It challenged everything that gave primacy to Western values, about the triumph of good over evil, and that God in some way mysteriously steers human history towards progress. It created a need to make sense of this human experience of pure evil, and this need persists today.

Social work includes this experience of listening, responding, and providing testimony to our client's lived experiences. Viktor Frankl (2004) writes:

> Our generation is realistic, for we have come to know man as he really is. After all, man is that being who invented the gas chamber of Auschwitz; however he is also that being who entered those gas chambers upright, with the Lord's Prayer or the Shema Yisrael in his lips. (p. 136)

Existential thought also failed the ethical test of the Holocaust. It has continued to evolve away from a focus on the individual's freedom, or an obsession with existence or being, towards the primacy of the other. Our experience is always a shared, lived one. Before we can reflect on life, before we think about life, we experience it as a result of the efforts of others. We experience the other in the care, in facial expressions, in the eyes; in the absence of the same, we experience desolation or emptiness. We all share in our and other people's suffering or in our incapacity to understand and empathize with another's experience. This direct, lived experience of other people's suffering, the prevention and alleviation of all forms of suffering or harm, is the foundation of existential ethics in social work. The direct experience of our vulnerability to suffering as human beings invokes the priority of the prevention of harm as the basis of our work. The experience of people suffering pure evil must inspire us in our continued efforts to challenge all harmful acts and systems. I hope Leon Jedwab's example helps you to see how inspiring and creative is the role of hope in his journey back to his remaining family, and in his later journey to make deeper sense of all that had happened to him.

Below is an example of how having ethical clarity creates space for creativity in social work practice.

---

## Case Example 6.4: Clarity on ethical values encourages creativity in social work

Gisela Konopka is known as one of the founders of group work. You can see her speaking at https://www.youtube.com/watch?v=yMCwf_7PD3U.

At an early age she discovered the benefits and potential evils of group work through her participation in opposition to Nazism in pre-World War II Germany. ▶

She tells the amusing story of one of her first experiences in group work with delinquent children in the clip linked above. The director of a co-educational youth residential facility used to play the banjo at dances for the young people every Saturday night. A young girl was admitted to the facility for 'dancing naked with sailors', so her admission must have been made on protective grounds.

The young Konopka was explaining to someone that she could not dance. The director overheard this remark and stated 'What? You cannot dance?' Pointing to the new girl who had just been admitted, he said, 'You shall be her teacher!'

At this facility it was assumed that the creative arts were intrinsic to life, and the professional staff were expected to be able to make use of the arts to engage the residents.

Here, Konopka also learned that group work involved professionals and clients in becoming *members* of the group itself. The professional role as leader or facilitator of the group was distinct and different from the role of participant, but they were all *members* of the group.

Her personal and professional social work history helped her in establishing an ethical basis for her practice. Konopka believed social work to be founded on two primary universal ethical values. These were:

- Individualization; the uniqueness of the individual, in every group, as distinct from their position as a member of the group; and

- Our interdependence and thus our need to learn how to help one another.

By having such ethical clarity in her social group work practice, Konopka was able to be incredibly creative in her responses to the group work process. She learned her craft from one of the founders of adult education, Edward C Lindeman, who taught her in social work. She attributes two key points to Lindeman:

- Facts are always fused with values. (Science focuses on what is, as does social work, but the latter is also concerned with what should be.)

- There are primary and secondary values, and the above two universal values are primary.

Because the foundation of her practice was so deep, Konopka (1958) could transcend the walls between social group work and therapy, as well as what she considered to be unfortunate status differences. 'Social work,' she writes:

believes in the possibility of *conscious* change, which means modifications of value systems. The concept of acceptance is one of the tools for achieving such change. Acceptance means that one does not blame a person for his behaviour or for his thinking but rather works with him as a person with innate dignity – regardless of his attitude or his potential for change. Acceptance does not mean *condoning*. The accepting person has values which at times differ from those of the client or group member. If the client or group member disregards the dignity of others, the social worker's acceptance of him often helps him change and come to respect others. (p. 182)

This statement would not exclude the possibility of removing a group member for breaches of its rules or expectations. This can be a consequence of inappropriate behaviour, and sometimes the group's needs must come before the needs of the individual member who is breaching the rules. Sometimes enforcing these boundaries against someone is the only way they can learn, accepting that the person does not have *carte blanche* for their actions. How you enforce the rules demonstrates your acceptance of the person, not of their behaviour.

# Conclusion

In this chapter, I have applied an existential approach to creativity in social work practice. The existential approach asserts that creativity is built into our everyday lives of struggle. A medical social worker responds creatively and saves a life. The creative social work movement in the United Kingdom was short-lived but inspiring in that it was built upon experienced social work practitioners trying to find better ways to engage with and help their clients.

Social work is thought of as a creative act in the disciplined use of the self and of our intuitive skills built up over time. Creativity can engage with the dark side of our humanity and of our potential for harming others. Existential social work asserts along with Levinas that ethics is first philosophy, not the artistic embrace of simply allowing things to be. Paradoxically, having clarity on ethical principles in social work creates space for genuine freedom and creative work.

## KEY POINTS FROM CHAPTER 6

1 We are creative beings in our everyday life when we face our anxieties and do our best.
2 Social workers can be creative in responding in the moment to what is needed.
3 We can become more creative by being more present to what is going on in the moment.
4 Having a clear sense of your professional role and ethical approach to practice aids in being creative in the moment.
5 Most social work takes place within bureaucratic organizations, based on set ways of operating that Sartre describes as 'worked matter'.
6 A fused group is a group of people who have created group synergy, which is one of the real sources of empowerment in the twenty-first century. Social action by a fused group can challenge existing practice. Sartre believed that any reforms introduced are converted back into worked matter, recommencing the pattern.
7 Creativity in social work comes from a strong ethical foundation with clear boundaries.

# 7

## EVIDENCE-BASED PRACTICE AND EXISTENTIAL SOCIAL WORK

## Introduction

The purpose of this chapter is to examine evidence-based practice (EBP) from an existential social work practice point of view. I explore the unique existential perspective on this topic that all research is grounded in people's lived experience in the world. I discuss the risk of scientism, which privileges a narrow kind of EBP as the only legitimate form of real knowledge. I explore the evidence that is left out of this viewpoint. There are numerous books and other publications on research methods in social work and EBP. While I don't describe those matters here, I do engage with the different research paradigms by looking at a typical family violence incident explored in a recent social work research textbook from a contemporary positivist perspective. I then consider the same incident from an existential social work practice perspective.

I examine the three worlds of program evaluation for EBP: the client world, the program delivery world, and the outcomes world. In covering these three areas, I detail the results of a research method rarely discussed in EBP, known as prospective longitudinal studies, which have significant implications for existential social work practice. In the outcomes world, I explore the experience of failure with clients in direct practice, but also in whole-of-government strategies. I discuss how an exclusive focus on outcomes can be detrimental to social work practice. Finally, I document the ten-year evaluation process of the successful juvenile justice group conferencing pilot program, detailed in Chapters 5 and 6, and look at the unanticipated costs involved in the program's success.

The core element of the existential social work perspective is the existence of social work and its intentionality in the world. Social work is an activity that is practiced with a focus and intention in the world. Social workers are encountering and using dialogue with people via casework interviews, participation in groups and community work, and social action. Both sides of the encounter, the social worker in their agency, within a program, and the clients, within their world, contribute to the dialogue and affect the outcomes.

## Lived experience as the foundation of evidenced-based practice

One way to understand the place of EBP is to envisage it as emerging from the ground of the lived experience of social workers and clients in social programs. Some forms of EBP ignore this lived experience and consider research acceptable to EBP to be the only valid form of knowledge. In existential social work, though, the lived experience of people is the primary source of our knowledge, and so-called science or EBP builds upon that base. Lived experience includes the experience of present social workers and others who have gone before us. We are historical beings, and our knowledge, skills, and experience stand upon the shoulders of others, those who have taught us and trained us on the job, whether in lecture rooms or books. The truths of our lived experiences are the powerful lessons that we learn. They include the choices that we make along the way to pursue certain paths, to read specific writers, and to look to some theories over others.

Similarly, our clients live within a different world, and doing so shapes the way they might make sense of our interventions and how they might engage, or fail to engage, with them. What clients find useful in our programs may differ from what the professional social workers think is important.

Scientism positions science as the primary method of inquiry. Existential thought embraces experiential reality as primary and accepts that we exist within this experiential reality and cannot be separated from other subjects. Existential thought is not anti-science. However, when attempts are made to measure any experience, a particular stance towards reality is adopted that will influence what is observed and measured. The stance taken will also affect the subjects that are being measured, even without their awareness.

When performance indicators (PIs) are used in social work, they inevitably give priority to those aspects of reality that are measured over other aspects. When PIs determine that an event must take place within four weeks of referral, in 90% of cases, a social worker is unlikely to delay this event for very good assessment reasons, unless good practice takes precedence over financial considerations. Over time, given the primacy of funding matters, practice will tend to be shaped by the PIs. Thus, a performance measurement has altered professional practice. This is an example in which professional social workers consciously change their practice to meet a program evaluation measure.

In existential social work, our consciousness is in the world. It is not separate from the world, existing only within our body and brain. This distinguishes the existential approach from the empirical EBP approach, which creates scales and other methods to measure external reality and then manipulates that data to create a representation of external reality. The existential social work view is that it is impossible to separate the consciousness of the EBP practitioner from the world in which she does her measurements. When this is taken into account, it is still possible to measure parts of reality. In measuring parts of reality, we change our lived experience of that reality – which contains the whole of the experience, including ourselves. Some of the most critical elements of good social work practice are actually difficult to measure and hence get less attention from EBP. Some examples of this good social work practice include engagement strategies designed especially for difficult-to-engage clients, such as doing things with them as part of the assessment process.

# What counts as evidence in evidence-based practice?

Critical theorists assert that dominant professional voices have more influence and that other marginalized voices are not heard in the evidence taken into account in EBP. While existential social workers would concur with this view, other elements of the lived experience also receive less attention in EBP approaches. Perceptual, judicative, and mathematical evidence is valued more highly than human elements.

Steinberg (2014) argues that the most significant thing missing is what is actually given to us in human experience, such as the evidence of the human heart, emotions, particularly the moral emotions like love, trust, repentance, shame, guilt, and pride. Existential social work assumes that we are interpersonal beings, inherently relational and thus not self-grounding. The norms that we live by or embrace shape our actions. We discover our meaning and purpose in life through the lack of ground within ourselves. It is only through understanding our interpersonal nature and our need to serve others that we can make sense of our lives and find a ground. Emotions and moods change things but are rarely measured in EBP. I have facilitated a conference in which a mother of a victim showed deep empathy for the struggles of the young offender's family, and this completely transformed the complexion of the conference. These experiences are rarely measured.

Being-in-the-world refers to more than just the material world. We cannot exclude being open to transcendence or the infinite, or what Gabriel Marcel called 'mystery' or the 'more than problematical'. What does it mean to have a home as opposed to living quarters? What about spiritual, moral, or ecological evidence? Can an economic decision made in a boardroom affect the living conditions of a family? What does it mean for a person to have a village of people concerned for her and a person who is crazy about her? Urie Bronfenbrenner, one of the founders of the ecological approach to human development, showed how distant decisions made in corporate boardrooms affect families' lives, how circles of influence in informal support systems affect children, and how reciprocal committed activity, by adults and children, is crucial to human development (Brendtro, 2006).

How do we measure the vertical evidence of epiphany, or the things that are given to us freely by the world, such as an amazing wilderness experience? These are examples of kinds of evidence that rarely make it into EBP. There is also the interior knowledge of the client and social worker, and of inner growth and development. In existential terms, this knowledge is *in* the world, not separate from it. There is also the knowledge gained by client and social worker in their mutual participation as they both move forward in their lives, projecting themselves towards their mutual futures. Is all this evidence valued? The danger with EBP is that it narrows the definition of evidence and values certain voices and forms of evidence over less tangible, but also highly significant, others.

I find that researchers tend to have existing theoretical perspectives that colour their results. Advocates of cognitive behavioural therapy (CBT), for example, conduct research with evidence that supports the CBT approach.

## Reflective Exercise 7.1: Kurt Wolff, and surrender and catch

Kurt Wolff (1976) was a sociologist who developed an existential technique called 'surrender and catch' to discover the ineluctable givens of a situation. The ineluctable elements are those that are unavoidable or inescapable.

The 'surrender' in surrender and catch can be described as a series of steps that require:

- Total involvement in the experience so that the subject–object distinction disappears (something like an artist being fully absorbed in their work);

- The suspension of all received notions (similar to setting aside all preconceived or everyday ideas, as in the phenomenological reduction of Husserl);

- The relevance of everything (remaining observant and aware), including of non-verbal, non-cognitive presences; and

- Identification of the risk of being hurt (providing cognitive love to the situation).

The 'catch' refers to the findings of the surrender process. The catch always takes in less than the whole experience of surrender but still contains the existential essence of the matter at hand.

Wolff argues that his idea of surrender and catch is not new, and that many existing practices, like forms of meditation, contain the same elements. What makes his idea novel is its explication of the process in sociology and of our current historical circumstances (post-1945), in which we are now capable of destroying our world. Wolff argues that these circumstances demand a more radical existential response.

Wolff's existential method resonates with my experience, particularly when facing big challenges in my direct social work practice. I have often used something like this approach and have found it very valuable.

**Question:**

- Do you think the 'surrender and catch' process can produce useful evidence?

In the next section, I compare and contrast the existential social work practice view with other existing research perspectives. Perhaps the existential approach helps to explain how researchers tend to find what they are looking for – including those researchers that hold an existential view.

# Research paradigms and viewpoints on evidence-based practice

To illustrate how our consciousness helps shape our viewpoints, I will use a family violence example, provided by Rubin and Babbie's (2014) recent social work research textbook, currently in its eighth edition. In this text, the writers compare different research paradigms and how they might shape research and its findings.

Rubin and Babbie illustrate how competing viewpoints can affect what is perceived in a common family-violence event. A husband and wife are arguing loudly. A family-violence report is made by the wife to the police. When the police arrive at the home, both parties deny that anything beyond arguing took place. 'She just fell over and injured herself,' says the husband. In the cartoon in Rubin and Babbie's book, the husband's view of the wife is of a screaming medusa, while he himself is crowned with a saint's halo. The wife's viewpoint shows the husband as a devil and she as the saint. Rubin and Babbie ask the reader to consider the view of someone observing the event. A male observer, with unexamined male chauvinist opinions, may take the husband's view. Similarly, men with unexamined male privilege may express support for the views in other males' stories that blame their partners.

Alternatively, a female observer may side with the wife's version. Rubin and Babbie put forward a critical feminist view of the same event. A social worker adopting this research paradigm would not stop at the wife's subjective view, but, using their understanding of the dynamics of family violence, would suspect possible coercive control being applied by the husband. The social worker would want to change this influence by providing an opportunity to raise the consciousness of both parties to these dynamics and to empower the wife to resist her husband's domination and oppression. Rubin and Babbie claim that a postmodern view would argue that there is no possible 'objective' view of what really happened, and that all the views are equally valid in being constructed by the participants.

Finally, Rubin and Babbie examine a hermeneutic research paradigm approach to the event, which searches for the participants' understandings and meaning-making. Such an approach may uncover a range of responses and meanings. The wife may be genuinely alarmed at the impact on her family of official intervention but also by the process of realizing how she is controlled by her husband's anger. Interviewing the husband using this approach might uncover the build-up of tension being experienced by the husband and his inability to express these negative feelings and thoughts, leading to the event in which he reacted to his wife's 'insulting remarks' with violence.

Rubin and Babbie's view can be described as 'contemporary positivism', which, while it would recognise the divergent, 'subjective' accounts, would ascertain objectively whether family violence, in the form of physical assault and verbal abuse, had occurred and whether the wife's subsequent denial comes from fear of the consequences of official investigation. An objective assessment could then be made to determine whether the wife needs protection from further family violence.

While Rubin and Babbie acknowledge the value of the contribution of postmodern, hermeneutic, and critical paradigms to research design, they argue that their contemporary positivist approach can encompass all these other approaches within a research framework that privileges objectivity based on measurement and EBP. How might an existential social work practice perspective differ from the above viewpoints?

First, an existential approach acknowledges that we operate in a world that still accepts the positivist view that it is possible to determine objectively the facts. This view is also represented in the requirement that only objectively observable information be documented in case notes; most agencies require this for legal and accountability reasons. The practitioner also examines practice from a different viewpoint than the researcher. The existential social work practitioner is focused on concrete experiences and how they shape practice.

In the context of family violence, the police investigate incidents and use standard forensic techniques, including separating the two parties and taking evidence from each individually. The courts then consider the matter and decide whether, on the balance of probabilities, family violence has taken place and whether an order is required to protect the family from further incidents. Providing criminal offences like assault have not taken place, the family violence is treated as a civil matter in which the court is required to reach a decision on a lower standard of proof than in criminal matters: on the balance of probabilities rather than beyond reasonable doubt, which is required in respect to criminal matters.

In doing so, these dominant professions (policing and law) impose their 'objective viewpoint' over other, less powerful viewpoints. Similarly, a social work professional writing 'objective case notes' is also imposing one view of what has happened on reality.

In providing services to male perpetrators of family violence, the social worker becomes involved after the matter is resolved, and the services are being provided to meet the requirements of the court; alternatively, the program is being offered to the men on a voluntary basis. An assessment needs to be conducted for the program. Nothing about the above processes prevents me, as the social worker, from taking responsibility for making an assessment. I am responsible for my assertions in this assessment. Is it the case that this event is a form of situational violence, or does it reflect intimate terrorism or a pattern of coercive control? Here, I am making use of my awareness of the different contested typologies of family violence. A critical viewpoint may assert that, even in the circumstances of so-called situational violence, men operate within a patriarchal society that privileges their status and guarantees an unequal power relationship between the genders. However, as an existential social worker, I am aware that the male client is always more than a typology can describe. There are unique features to each case, but typologies can be useful in making partial sense of a situation. I am wondering what level of responsibility this man is going to take for his contribution to the incident.

I am not an empathetic independent observer of these events. I bring my understanding of the gendered nature of male family violence into the assessment process. I bring my faith in the value of men's behaviour change programs into the interview room. My purpose is to help the man perceive the value of maintaining respect and giving priority to safety in all his decision making about relationships. This enables the male client to begin to understand why the system has excluded him from his family home for the immediate future. I am a committed professional representing an agency and a program that stands for these values. I am a witness to what he and I say, how he behaves, to his manner, mood, and body language. I am recording key elements of his responses to my questions. That doesn't make my account privileged above the client's; I am helping him make better sense of what has happened and beginning to shape how he might engage constructively with the program. I am also helping him through the process of the assessment and its requirements, so that he can trust the process and benefit from the experience. I also allow him the right to reject all that the program has to offer. I am not only dealing with what he is but also with what he can potentially become. I am not just a recorder, but a change agent. Transformation can take place in the assessment process. I am seeking to influence and understand. In this sense, the existential viewpoint concurs with the critical stance that social change is a legitimate and core aspect of social work assessment and intervention.

Existential social work practice is not just about research; it is a committed process that takes account of the real limitations of program capacity and suitability. Of course, this argument could be dismissed as simply expressing the viewpoint of the social work practitioner rather than the researcher, but the existential social work perspective begs to differ. We are all committed – the question is, to what?

## The client world

The client world is the primary determinant of a program's outcomes. In social work, our programs are under increasing pressure to deliver positive effects in shorter time frames. In Chapter 1, we learned that social casework evolved from single case studies, in which interventions took place over many years, and these interventions were aimed at personality change. You only have to look at the typical social work intervention these days, in any area of practice, to see that average length of an intervention may be only days or weeks and rarely stretches over months.

Who is the client? In involuntary or mandated programs, is it the organization that mandates the referral, is it the client who shows up at the social work office, or is it both? The literature would refer to clients as primary or secondary in these circumstances. This can be a useful device, but who, ultimately, is the client the social worker is directly helping? In family violence, is it for the safety of the victims? Are the perpetrators secondary clients? Is it just the client who presents, or do we conceptualize the client as the person in the context of his family in a community and society?

Does our theoretical approach or our intention to view the client from this perspective alter who the client is? For example, if I apply an anti-oppressive existential perspective, like Neil Thompson's PCS model, the client before me is perceived through a lens that examines oppression from a personal, cultural, and structural viewpoint. How might that affect my view of the behaviours that have brought the client to the social work interview?

The programs social workers work in have already determined who the client is for the purposes of this program. The example I used from R. D. Laing in Chapter 4, in which he discovered the three-generation history of the presenting problem because he made a home visit to the family, is worth pondering in situations where our programs might erroneously pre-determine who the client is.

One of the potential flaws in EBP research is the failure to compare clients from similar backgrounds in randomly controlled trials and other comparative methods. Risk factors that are known, from evidence, to increase the likelihood of re-offending are also often not taken into account. For example, young people entering the youth justice system in early adolescence have a much higher risk of re-offending and of receiving more punitive sentences than do young people entering the system in middle or late adolescence. The family circumstances of young offenders vary significantly, and these factors are rarely even explored in the research. Factors intrinsic to the research process also can subtly bias treatment populations versus control populations. I explore some of these biases when looking at the long evaluation of the juvenile justice group conferencing program that was undertaken from 1995 to 2010. In layperson's terms, this phenomenon can be thought of as comparing 'apples with pears'.

In Chapter 4, I also described how there are (loosely) two forms of social work assessment used today, the modern and the postmodern. The modern version claims to be objective and supported by EBP but is built upon the mainstream psycho-social model of assessment that has gradually been refined over the history of social work. The built-in assumption of this model is that social work's role is to help people adjust to the expectations placed on them by external systems, such as protective or correctional systems. The postmodern approach to assessment rejects the notion of objectivity, claiming that all means of assessment are socially constructed and that progressive approaches give voice to the marginalized. Postmodern approaches tend to denigrate traditional social work assessment methods. Previously I discussed Overton's innovative preventative work from the 1950s with hard-to-reach families and provided an example where a postmodern approach to social work history misrepresented the documented evidence on her innovative techniques. In Overton's casework notebook, she makes the point that in every area of family functioning, clients' attitudes are more important than facts. Here Overton is adopting the existential view that people's consciousness is a crucial determinant in assessment, not just their so-called objective social circumstances.

In social work, the client's world remains a mystery to us. What do I mean by that? When the social worker's assessment is completed, the social worker thinks that they understand the family, but the existential view is that there is always more to the other than any picture presents, no matter how well-constructed that picture is. Sartre spent the final decades of his life trying to prove, using existential psychoanalysis and Marxist sociology, a biographical method by which he could totally understand another single human being. In this exercise in existential biography Sartre has been criticized for his assumption that it is ever possible to fully comprehend another human being (Joblin, 1992). Within the time constraints of social work, it is far less likely that we can ever claim more than a limited understanding of another person.

As a way of beginning to understand this approach as taken in existential social work, I want to briefly examine two of the longest prospective studies ever conducted – the ability to follow people throughout their whole life in real-time is rare. These studies are called prospective in comparison to the more common, retrospective studies, which try to understand something about people by inquiring into their past from the vantage point of the present.

Long-term prospective studies of human lives are so rare because of the obvious cost and length of time required to study a large population of people in real-time. But retrospective studies, as a consequence of their relative ease of implementation, draw conclusions that prospective studies have shown to be inaccurate, for example, the idea that persistent adult offenders all have negative early childhood and adolescent experiences and histories of offending.

I am interested in what the following two prospective studies can illuminate about universal and personal elements of life courses for social work clients. Do they support an existential approach to social work practice?

## The longest prospective study in criminology

Robert Sampson and John Laub, in two works, *Crime in the Making* and *Shared Beginnings, Divergent Lives*, re-examined the longitudinal research of the famous Glueck study into 500 persistently incarcerated juvenile offenders and 500 Boston public school youths from highly impoverished and disadvantaged homes between 1930 and 1960. In the original study by the Gluecks, the two populations were controlled for age, race, and neighbourhood. Both populations were thoroughly researched throughout their adolescence (age 10–17), and then followed up at ages 25 and 32. Ninety-two percent of the participants were followed throughout the 30-year period of the study. The Gluecks were attempting to find out what made these children into persistent adult and juvenile offenders and how they differed from their non-offending peers from all-white, mainly male, impoverished neighbourhoods of Boston. For almost 18 years the Gluecks followed up these 1,000 people, until the participants had turned 32.

Sampson and Laub stumbled across the original data and decided to re-assess it using modern research tools of life course analysis. This is described as a secondary data analysis, but Sampson and Laub also conducted some primary research on the surviving population. When they released their first book, their focus was on integrating the results into a life history approach to offending that took account of the structural bases of the problem and why it did or did not persist: poverty and deprivation, informal social control or the lack of it (such as in the school and family), juvenile justice intervention outcomes (such as lengthy incarceration), as well as adult developmental history, including long-term trajectories, transitions (such as marriage), and turning points (such as military service). From an existential research perspective, Sampson and Laub's theoretical viewpoint before the research commenced grew out of their interest in proving the validity of a life history approach to understanding offending.

Their research supports a developmental approach to studying anti-social behaviours and places the main emphasis on informal social ties at all stages of development. Their research was subsequently critiqued for a failure to account satisfactorily for the personal element in offending. They decided to follow up all 500 offenders in the original study to the age of 70 and to conduct a full national death record and criminal history search. They also conducted life history interviews with 52 of the men around their 70th birthdays. This additional research makes the combined study the longest in the history of criminology. What they discovered was that current typologies and risk management approaches, in which high-risk offenders are classified, are insufficient to explain the results. Structural models that try to explain offending based on oppressive conditions cannot take account of these findings. Personal agency and situated choice play a significant part in explaining how people, over time, from highly deprived and oppressive backgrounds, make commitments that progressively shift their lives away from offending.

Why is this research applicable to existential social work? First, it reinforces the importance of an individual, personal approach, given the messiness of people's lives (as demonstrated in the contradictions found by the researchers that challenge existing typology-based approaches).

Second, it reiterates the inaccuracy of theories that explain adult lives as being determined primarily by childhood experiences or trauma. The acorn theory, in Jungian studies, that we are born with a destiny – the 'bad boys lead to bad men' theories – is simply wrong. Studying people prospectively shows that we can continue to shape our destinies throughout our lives by changing the way we respond to the challenges of life. Trauma in childhood and deprivation experiences do affect people and severely limit their potential, but they do not necessarily fully explain their life trajectories. Our clients' responses continue to shape their lives within the limitations created by childhood and adulthood experiences.

Third, the researchers found little evidence of cognitive transformations (as cognitive behavioural therapy approaches might hope for) or of redemption scripts based on sudden awakenings and 'making good'. Instead, successful desistance seemed to result from forming positive social ties to others that involved making commitments and participating meaningfully with others. This does not mean that sudden transformations don't occur or change lives, only that the researchers in this study did not come across any such events.

Fourth, they also discovered men who were committed to harming others. While the authors supported re-integration strategies for all released offenders, the personal intent of the offender still affected their outcomes. The reality is that some men choose to persist.

Fifth, in spite of this evidence of malicious intent, for even the most marginalized, nomadic adult offenders, the study found that desistence is possible if the person desires that end and the right services and connections are available. Personal will, making connections, and services do matter. You can hear Laub and Sampson talking about their research in five short clips on the occasion of receiving the Stockholm Prize in

Criminology here: https://www.youtube.com/watch?v=oqmUa9PLw8U. In their speeches, you will hear about how their research has influenced new life course studies of more diverse populations.

Our second longitudinal prospective study focuses on the Men of the Harvard Grant Study and on psychiatrist George Valliant. Social workers struggle to show empathy for people born into affluence and privilege who squander these opportunities and maintain their sense of personal entitlement. I think social work ought to have a bias in favour of the poor and marginalized, but privileged people also have difficulties that social workers are sometimes required to address. The Harvard Study of Adult Development is a longitudinal prospective study of 268 mainly white Harvard graduates from 1938 to 1941 to the present day, with over 78 men of the original cohort still being studied into their 90s. The original intention of the study was to research health.

The initial philanthropic funder, Grant, wanted to find out what made for successful careers, as he employed many managers in his retail businesses. George Valliant began working on the study in 1966 and has remained ever since, publishing many books and articles, particularly on ego defence mechanisms and their role in how people adapt to life.

When Valliant randomly sampled 100 of the cohort and examined, in detail, 30 of the most successful and 30 of the least successful men, he was able to establish an association between mature defence mechanisms, like altruism, sublimation, and suppression, and successful lives, as well as the opposite outcome for men who used what he termed 'primitive' defence mechanisms, such as blaming, denial, and acting out. The study confirms what the Gluecks' study also found: that most childhood traumas do not predict adult maturation. All members of the study faced challenges in their lives. Contrary to their so-called privileged status, some of the men grew up in abusive and neglectful families and had to overcome significant deficits. It was how they reacted to these challenges that determined their futures.

The psycho-analytic ego-psychological framework by which Valliant came to this work and which he further developed as a result of it does not have to be embraced to appreciate the depth of this research, though an existential viewpoint would argue that it shaped the research and influenced its process and outcomes. First, we all experience stress and anxiety in our lives. We use psychological defences to protect ourselves from internal and external threats. In Valliant's view, defence mechanisms are entirely unconscious. In existential thought, we are aware, to some extent, of our use of these mechanisms; the important thing is that they help us deal with reality. The more mature mechanisms are more beneficial for development. The more primitive mechanisms distort reality more and make it more likely for developmental growth to be slower.

Social work has always engaged with forms of developmental theory and that theory's application to practice. Currently, in responding to male family violence, we use the word 'smokescreen' to challenge men who use denial, blaming, storytelling, and joking to avoid taking responsibility. There are various models of developmental theory, and many of their variations in these models are less crucial than an acceptance that there are levels of maturity in childhood, adolescence, and adulthood. As social workers we need to be cognisant of this feature and how we might adapt our responses according to these levels of maturity. I have previously written about how working with immature young people requires social workers to engage with their peer group (Griffiths, 2001).

When humans are stressed, they tend to have characteristically preferred ways of coping. Typically, dealing with stress can involve either acting out the stress through action of some kind or withdrawing inside oneself and becoming more anxious. The former describes commonly extravert behaviours, which use external methods of coping, such as drug use or violence, against oneself or other people. The latter, or introverted behaviours, use passive methods like deference and shutting down emotionally. The important point here is that we all feature on this continuum of ways of dealing with anxiety and stress, and the defences we use tend to be reflective of our characteristic ways of coping.

Social workers can adapt their responses to how people react. For example, they can provide to the introvert a more intimate, counselling style of response and to the extrovert a more active, outgoing action style of response that emphasizes clarity, boundaries, expectations on behaviour, and rules. Defence mechanisms that are holding people together should be challenged, when necessary, but not necessarily torn down, unless you are prepared to put in the work needed to help build up more mature defence mechanisms. What I have done here is make a link between what these longitudinal researchers have discovered and an existential approach that embraces the lived experience of clients, as well as the ability of social work intervention to help shape informal supports for clients and to influence the personal responses of some clients to life's challenges.

While these two long-term prospective studies have some limitations around the populations they chose to research, it is still an open question as to whether some of the key findings are not more universal to humanity than the gender, social class, and period in history studied. The positive outcome is that both studies have now inspired many other long-term prospective studies with more diverse populations, and the results of this additional research may help to confirm the universality or otherwise of the findings outlined above.

None of the research discussed is inconsistent with the current focus in social work on childhood trauma, its impact on neurological development, and on healing this trauma as part of recovery from its impact. The value of the longitudinal prospective studies is that they show that people can respond to their traumas and live very constructive lives, despite their never completely overcoming their trauma-induced vulnerabilities. Somehow, some people learn to live with their traumas and to grow as people using their other talents and strengths, which often come from their connections to others. Unfortunately, though, some people don't cope, and their responses to life's new challenges remain stilted and rigid. These findings are certainly not linked to an existential theoretical viewpoint; both studies operated from preconceived theoretical frameworks and conducted their research within those frameworks.

# The program world

Does social work actually make a difference in people's lives? What are the impacts of our programs? What are their costs and benefits for all participants? How much of our program do people actually receive? Do we understand how our programs are meant to work, their logic? Are clients getting the same program or different ones, depending on who is delivering them (what is, in the terminology of the literature, our 'program integrity')?

In Chapter 5, I discussed the importance of team work in program delivery and of having a sense of the field of service that you operate in, as well as how social movements have shaped this area of practice. I provided some examples of social policy work and some examples of program implementation issues. Finally, I looked at the role of social vision in program development.

When you look at the program world in social work today, you first get a sense of the overwhelming number of people who pass through some form of social program. Most people are receiving virtually no actual service as their cases are merely being 'risk managed' according to the limited resources that are available to address such large numbers.

While the steps of the program may be understood, there is less understanding of how clients are changed by the interventions provided. Knowing how a program actually works is a crucial element in the existential social work approach to EBP. It is striking to see programs being evaluated by people with little understanding of how the programs actually work, in respect to their component parts and to how they work together in the lived experience of the program.

I have already referred, in Chapter 5, to the Royal Commission into Family Violence in Victoria and to the competing models of programs for perpetrators of family violence presented, leading to the Commission's decision to recommend that 'further investigation be conducted by a committee'. From my experience in observing men's behaviour change programs in rural and urban settings, it was apparent that the programs were significantly different depending on where they were run. How can you evaluate the impact of a program if the technology used is actually different from other programs with the same name?

What effect do the people delivering a program have on its outcomes? Given the finite resources available, and the lack of program direction from the broader field of service, it's surprising that *anything* can have an impact. My experience is that the people delivering the programs at the coalface try their best to deliver quality – to the clients in the program, these frontline workers *are* the program.

## The outcomes world

Governments and the public demand to know: is all this money having any impact? We live in a world in which everything has a monetary value, and consequently people want to know what impact their money is having on the complex problems social workers are required to deal with. In this section, I question whether a focus on outcomes alone can be a distraction from delivery of good service. I address the issue we all face in social work, which is dealing with failure in policy and in direct service. Finally, I examine what a successful evaluation process looks like in practice and what some of the program costs to success are.

While it is futile for social work not to focus on the impact of interventions, an exclusive focus on outcomes is actually not very helpful. Why? One of social work's first ethical principles is to accept people as they are. People are often referred to social work programs because others have found them extremely difficult. Our first task is engagement with this person, and failure in this precludes any progress on other objectives of intervention.

We are all good at covering things up, including failure to genuinely engage clients. Consider how many actions we take in social work to cover our tracks. Services can be delivered without genuine engagement. Men in groups learn quickly what is required of them and how to superficially comply. I have seen how this happens first hand, when a banking approach was adopted in an educational program in which the facilitators had the wisdom and saw themselves as transferring their wisdom to the participants. Instead of presence, you end up with pretence. How we approach our work does make a difference to clients' involvement in the program.

When I put my effort as a social worker into making the group the most engaging and creative experience it can be, I am focusing on what I can control, which is my level of effort and skill in creating experiences for the members to learn from the process. I cannot control how each individual member of the group will react to these activities; the results, in other words, are beyond my control. And many other factors also come into play.

Moreover, an existential approach requires that we respect the choices our clients make to refuse our help, pay lip service to our transformative efforts, or simply ignore our good-faith attempts. As the example below demonstrates, social work, despite our best efforts, is not always productive. One of the reasons for this can be that the client is a participant in the process, and their particularities may work against any successful outcome. How many times have we failed to fully seize the opportunities that have been placed in front of us? Don't the clients also have the right to reject our help and to refuse our efforts? Outcomes are partly determined by clients, not only by social workers and programs.

## Dealing with failure

Dealing with failure is a common lived experience in social work practice. We cannot help everyone. We are limited as professionals. Our agencies and programs have boundaries and limitations designed to create realistic expectations, rules of engagement, and participation, and sometimes clients do not change one iota.

In individual sessions, a client remains steadfast in their resistance to every effort of mine to shift them from their use of denial, blaming, and criticisms of others, the system, and everybody but themselves. How should I end this? Perhaps I can say to him, 'throughout this process you have attended all appointments,' (at least, there was compliance in this area), and 'Despite all my efforts I have failed to really help you, but the positive from this is that you have rejected the help offered and have chosen your own way forward, which is your prerogative. I wish you all the best for the future.' Otto Rank saw client resistance as a positive experience, a demonstration of client willpower. Sometimes the sanest response is to accept our failure in such cases and to end our involvement, noting the positives, not glossing over the truth of rejection, and wishing them well.

Consider the opposite scenario. A thoroughly involved and engaged client makes substantial personal changes while on your program in response to your efforts. After the program is completed, in a fit of sudden rage, he violently attacks his family.

We simply don't have a crystal ball with which to see into the future. Outcomes from programs are ultimately not under our control. Our focus as social workers should be on the thing we can control, which is the delivery of the best programs we can create. It is here that EBP can assist, alongside tradition, testimony, practice wisdom, critical reflection, and, above all, a sense of openness to the social work world in which you operate. For example, in the integrated family-violence system in Victoria, a common risk assessment tool was developed. Three elements are considered crucial to determining risk within this framework; the victim's own assessment of her risk, the evidence-based risk factors associated with high levels of risk, and professional judgement. All three elements are essential and equally important to the framework (Department of Human Services, 2012).

Failures don't only occur in frontline social work practice. Entire governmental strategies can fail. Whole programs can have unanticipated and unintended consequences. Below is an example of a whole-of-government strategy that failed to achieve the primary objective to strengthen the criminal justice response to sexual assault.

## Case Example 7.1: A whole-of-government strategy failure

The Victorian government's Sexual Assault Reform Strategy (SARS) was a $42.2 million, whole-of-government approach designed to transform the criminal justice system's response to sexual assault and was managed by a policy unit within the Department of Justice (DoJ). The reform commenced in 2006 across a range of governmental portfolios (justice, human services, corrections, courts, victim services, women's services, and police). A $1 million evaluation of the strategy was tendered out, and three reports were delivered between August 2008 and January 2011.

As project manager for the evaluation, my job was to manage the contract process, to help service two co-ordinating committees, and to help the contracted evaluators deliver their reports. By the time I started, all the projects contained in the strategy were largely determined, and the evaluation process had been contracted out to the successful tenderer.

The purpose of the evaluation was to determine how all the initiatives functioned *as a whole* to support the overall aim of the SARS strategy, which was to strengthen the criminal justice response to sexual assault. While the individual initiatives proved to be very successful in providing better services to victims, and co-ordinated services at that, the strategy *as a whole* proved unsuccessful in all the key indicators set by the DoJ.

The context of the SARS strategy was a determined refusal within the DoJ to countenance any consideration of alternative pathways to dealing with any form of sexual assault. Initiatives on alternative pathways originating from a pro-feminist women's policy unit within the Department of Premier and Cabinet were stopped. Senior judges' voices sympathetic to and advocating for alternative pathways were ignored. The focus was put exclusively upon using the existing adversarial criminal justice system response and on improving the experiences of all victims using the system, thereby increasing rates of reporting of sexual assaults, reducing attrition of cases moving through the system, and making resolution of cases more timely by seeking guilty pleas and convictions for sexual assault.

The evaluation found:

● Little change, but also some marked declines, in reporting rates for sexual assault;

- A significant decline in guilty pleas, resulting in extremely high numbers of alleged offenders ending up in higher courts, forcing victims to undergo cross-examination by defence lawyers;

- Higher rates of attrition (cases being withdrawn);

- A decline in conviction rates in the higher courts for sexual offences;

- Fewer guilty pleas being entered in the lower courts, but, as a consequence of the reforms, more cases being referred to the higher courts; and

- Much longer time periods for resolution of sexual assault matters.

How did this happen? As a result of the legislative and programmatic changes introduced under SARS, the number of defendants willing to plead guilty declined by one half. The final evaluation report was unable to pinpoint the reasons for this but speculated that it might be due to:

- The strong possibility of acquittal in sexual offence cases – which increased from 50% to 67% in higher courts under the SARS reforms;

- Mandatory addition to a sex offender register for those found guilty, a major disincentive to entering a guilty plea; and

- Demonization of all sex offenders, amongst other reasons.

What is not listed in the final evaluation report as a reason for the failure of SARS is the department's own failure to consider the limitations of the adversarial criminal justice system in sexual assault matters or the possibility of including alternative pathways within that system as a way of addressing some of these limitations.

The SARS strategy had no way other than sound legislative drafting of controlling defence lawyers' responses to their reforms, which, by and large, were to advise their clients not to plead guilty under almost any circumstances. A significant part of the evaluation strategy involved interviewing 86 victims, many judicial officers, and others, including police and social workers, involved in the new reforms. The final evaluation report presents the views of these victims, stakeholders, and judicial officers, including advocating for the use of alternative pathways for some sexual assault matters. Other judicial officers expressed contrary views, endorsing the existing criminal justice response.

Despite the above, the final evaluation report claims that the SARS initiative was a successful one, basing this view primarily on the systems put in place to provide better and more integrated services to victims of sexual assault throughout the process, from reporting to resolution.

There has been an improvement in the experience of victims as a result of the individual initiatives associated with the SARS reforms. The evaluation of SARS was focused on the system's impacts, *as a whole*. The results tell us a different story of the program's unanticipated failure to date. Perhaps more time is required to fully assess the final impacts. SARS was perceived, by some defence lawyers, as a more intentionally punitive response to sexual assault.

In section 5.5 of the final report, relating to reporting rates, it is stated that 'some of the mythology about the experience of reporting a sexual assault remains alive and well'. In the light of the account above, would you describe victims' experiences of the criminal justice system as consistent with that mythology?

**Questions:**

- What types of behaviours are defined as sexual offences in the criminal law?

- For example, can sexting, in some circumstances, be classed as a sexual offence?

- What are the benefits and limitations of the criminal justice response to sexual assault?

- Why are criminal justice systems underused, insensitive to victims, ineffective at prosecuting cases, and, sometimes, even harmful to victims of sexual assault?

- Should all sexual assault be criminalized?

- What mechanisms could be introduced to address the continued failure of the legal system to effectively respond to sexual assault?

- What do you think victims of sexual assault really want from the justice system?

- Do reporting, attrition, conviction rates, and sentencing outcomes tell the whole story?

- How could understanding the collective victim's lived experience of the justice system help change that system?

- Do victims want harsher penalties?

- What is the impact of being registered as a sex offender?

- Are sex offenders the lepers of the twenty-first century?

- How do you think the whole-of-government SARS strategy could have been improved to obtain better results on its key performance indicators?

- How could introducing alternative resolution pathways for some sexual assaults, within an overall criminal justice response, have resulted in different outcomes?

*The Sexual Assault Reform Strategy Final Evaluation Report*, prepared by the Department of Justice of Victoria, dated January 2011, can be found online here: http://www.justice.vic.gov.au/home/justice+system/laws+and+regulation/criminal+law/sexual+assault+reform+strategy+-+final+evaluation+report

As I stated above, SARS was not perceived as a failure. It was an ambitious attempt to alter the criminal justice response. I have related here what is recorded in the final evaluation report. I have argued that an existential social work approach would have adopted different approaches for minor offenders, and this is now being piloted. This would have framed the strategy as working beyond the confines of a criminal justice response in providing better outcomes for all those affected by sexual offences, including the perpetrators. Powerful forces within the adversarial criminal justice system were effective in using the system itself to oppose the perceived punitive aims of the overall strategy against defendants charged with sexual offences. In hindsight, my personal view is that an overall strategy seeking to embrace better outcomes for all participants, using alternatives to criminal justice responses for lesser offences, may have received more support from those most opposed to the SARS reforms.

Finally, I want to examine a successful evaluation process and some of the impacts of a program's success.

# Lessons in evidence-based practice from a successful pilot program

Below in Table 7.1 is a summary of six consecutive, independent program evaluation reports conducted on the Victorian Youth Justice Group Conferencing Program over fifteen years, from its inception as a pilot program to a state-wide legislated program. In Chapter 5, I examined the history of this program to see what some of the reasons for its success were. Here I am examining the independent evaluation of the program. The body of the reports is 458 pages long, excluding the executive summaries, attachments, and appendices. The evaluations were conducted by reputable external consultants, including the University of Melbourne's Social Work Department, KPMG, and others.

## The context of the pilot program

Table 7.1, below, names the six reports, the key foci of the reports, and the program outcomes they related. They tell a story of gradual improvement in the pilot programs function over the fifteen years. In Chapter 5, I provided an insider's view of the many challenges faced by the program, including staff resignations, as well as the difficulty of maintaining referral numbers and of building the program's credibility. I also explained some of the factors that I think led to the expansion of the program. Over the ten-year life of the pilot program, the Department of Human Services evolved from a reluctant stakeholder in the management of the pilot to funding the program's expansion throughout the state.

In this chapter, the focus is on the evaluation of the pilot program. The reports documented below are not governmental reports used to justify a program: the first four reports were funded independently of government by a philanthropic donor and were evaluated by academic social work staff employed at the University of Melbourne. They employ detailed qualitative and quantitative research methods. The final two reports were funded by the government but were contracted out to external research consultancies.

**Table 7.1**  Evaluation of Youth Justice Group Conferencing (GC)
in Victoria 1997–2010

| Program evaluation report | What the report studied | Key outcomes |
|---|---|---|
| 1. Juvenile Justice Group Conferencing Report –An Evaluation of a Pilot Program; May 1997 | • The first 2 years of the pilot program, from April 1997–September 1997. 42 young people were tracked through program and follow-up.<br><br>• Direct observation of 15 conferences.<br><br>• Only 17 young people had completed the 12-month post-conference. | • Numbers too small for generalization of findings.<br><br>• Report's findings provide justification for expansion of program into broader geographical areas and inclusion of young people charged with serious offences in first court appearance.<br><br>• Family decision making highlighted. |
| 2. Juvenile Justice Group Conferencing in Victoria Phase Two; December 1997 | • 61 young people in 59 conferences tracked throughout program with 12-month follow-up.<br><br>• Comparison group of young people on probation.<br><br>• Focus group with young people who had completed the program. | • Significant increase in throughput of young people since first study.<br><br>• Convenors spending less preparation time for group conferences.<br><br>• Young people re-offend less after GC, but not significantly so.<br><br>• Cost per conference significantly reduced and compares well with probation costs. |
| 3. Juvenile Justice Group Conferencing Project Evaluation; June 1999 | • 71 young people over 4 years, with 12-month follow-up post-GC. | • Factors associated with success in GC identified.<br><br>• Recidivism similar to probation, but less likely to result in further supervisory orders (real diversion from intrusion into juvenile justice system occurring). |

*Continued*

**Table 7.1** (Continued)

| | | |
|---|---|---|
| 4. Report on the Juvenile Justice Group Conferencing Program Stage 1; April 2005 | • 50 young people undergoing a GC between April 2003 and June 2004 are compared to 36 young people deemed suitable for GC but did not proceed to GC (deemed, control group of 11 young people) and 25 probationers.<br><br>• 6-month follow-up for re-offending rates comparison. | • 82% of young people undergoing GC are diverted from supervisory orders.<br><br>• Only 12% re-offended post conference.<br><br>• Higher rates of re-offending apparent in probation population.<br><br>• GC 'strongly supported' by key stakeholders in system.<br><br>• Jesuits Metropolitan program fails to meet performance targets for referrals. |
| 5. Report on the Juvenile Justice Group Conferencing Program; January 2006 | • 86 young people undergoing GC between April 2003 and June 2004, with 54 of these followed up 12 months post-GC for recidivism, compared to 53 in control group deemed suitable but did not proceed, or were given probation for first court appearance. | • 86% directly diverted from supervisory orders as a result of GC.<br><br>• Significant reduction in seriousness of re-offending as a result of GC in comparison to control and probation populations. |
| 6. Review of the Youth Justice Group Conferencing Program Final Report; September 2010 | • 372 young people from April 2007 to June 2009 undergoing GC process, compared to 129 young people receiving probation or youth supervision order in the same period.<br><br>• Re-offending rates compared with both groups at 6 months and 12 months post-intervention. | • State-wide program now exceeding its performance targets.<br><br>• Demand for program has significantly increased.<br><br>• 75% diverted appropriately for youth justice supervision– detention programs.<br><br>• GC clients 'much less likely to re-offend' than young people placed on supervisory orders. |

What are some of the policy lessons from this successful piloting of a new initiative? First, numbers matter. No amount of lived experience or storytelling of astounding outcomes in group conferences would impress government enough to make it willing to enact the state-wide expansion, legislative provision, and ongoing funding of the program without a quantitative evaluation to prove that this program achieved the government's objectives in diversion from the juvenile justice system at a reasonable cost to the taxpayer.

The pilot experience demonstrates the considerable time it takes to get a new program going and to build the kind of street-level credibility that is rewarded with increased referrals from lawyers and magistrates. The program had to find its niche within the system. Further, the program interfaced with every aspect of the youth justice system: police, courts, detention centres, lawyers, and magistrates, but also young offenders and their supporters, including families and schools, as well as with victims and their supporters, and victim support agencies. All these stakeholders must have felt that the program has benefits for them to have continued their participation and support.

The convenors of the process consisted, mainly, of social workers with extensive youth work experience. The convenors needed to learn new skills and new ways of dealing with the group conference members and to understand how the program helped people change.

The success of the pilot program does highlight for me the costs involved in compromising goals to achieve success. Throughout the pilot phase, support for and familiarity with the program grew within the Department of Health and Human Services (DHHS) and among all the key stakeholders. Paradoxically, as it lurched from funding crisis to threat of extinction, this support and familiarity challenged the DHHS authorities to decide their position on the program. Short-term funding periods took place during which the program was resuscitated by the DHHS. As the funding body, they were able to reshape the primary goals of the program back towards youth justice objectives, like diversion and lower sentences. Family decision making and victim involvement became secondary. The reformulation of the goals of the program enabled the DHHS to embrace it and perceive it as part of the 'approved' repertoire of responses to youthful offending. By the end of the fifteen-year process, the DHHS was fully funding, leading and managing the contracting for the program.

Despite the hard-nosed real-life political experience concerning the importance of numbers, and about re-offending and diversion being the only things that mattered in the final EBP evaluation, I also wish to share with you the crucial importance of another vital ingredient of success; that key politicians observed conferences to see the lived experience. They became supporters, retelling the stories of what they had seen for many years in crucial settings. In practice, the family decision making aim has not been lost in the redesign of the key goals of the program. What keeps workers doing restorative justice is the power of group synergy created by the participants, who were well briefed in the guided process.

Sensible EBP researchers also recognize the role played by economic, resource, and political factors in shaping program implementation and evaluation (Munro, 2002). But what was missing from the evidence-based 'scientism' of the DHHS's focus on recidivism and diversion as the sole criteria of evaluation? The whole lived experience of the restorative justice process as a new paradigm of criminal justice was ignored. The DHHS justified the narrowing of the focus of the research on the basis that previous reports had already found high levels of satisfaction among all participants.

It *may* be the case that the evaluations proves that the juvenile justice group conferencing program got better results than the existing supervisory orders, but it could also be the case that there were hidden biases in the manner in which the research compared dissimilar populations. The young people who eventually completed the program, first, consented to the process of potentially meeting their victims, and, second, were assessed as suitable by the Convenor. Further, they actually had to complete the process to be counted as participants on the evaluation.

Here are some of the aspects of the program that were largely ignored in this narrow evidence-based assessment:

- The convenors assessed participants (victims, victims' supporters, the young person, their family, and supporters of the young person) for risk and contribution. Crucial decisions were made that affected the outcomes of the process, potentially leading to key participants being missed or excluded.

- The purpose of the group conference was to present an agreed upon outcome plan for the Children's Court to endorse that addressed the harm of the offending on the victim(s) and helped to prevent further offending. Statistics can be produced regarding how many conferences resulted in agreement on an outcome plan (no small feat) and how many were fully or partially implemented or completed. Ignoring or missing this element of the process fails to appreciate one of the key advantages of the process – the direct and creative forms of reparation made by the offenders to the victims.

- As it happened, it would have been difficult for the juvenile justice authorities not to expand the program, given the strength of the support among the key stakeholders. However, it was by no means inevitable. You only have to look at the failure of restorative justice to make serious inroads into the adult correctional system to see that nothing is inevitable. In contrast, restorative practices have emerged as a significant social movement across a range of other human services areas, including community-based crime prevention and problem solving, mental health, aged care, family support, and many others, including global issues and crimes against humanity. The funding decisions to expand the program were aided by the evidence on recidivism and diversion. This 'solid evidence' helped the politicians decide that their spending of new money, enacting of new legislative provisions, and expansion and support of the program was backed up by the facts.

- In the final report, considerable stress was placed on the crucial element of convenor skill and knowledge as the key element in the success of group conferencing. While I agree with this conclusion, it also fails to take into account that the process is a new form of social group work and that the success of its outcomes depends on the contributions of all the participants in keeping the event alive and on its meaning in the implementation of the outcome plan.

- By the end of the fifteen years of research on the program, it was found that it was exceeding important performance requirements, such as the number of group conferences completed. I remember the pressure, in those early years, when getting referrals was a major challenge. Restorative justice demands more of us, and it may be centuries before we know the real effects of this new approach. In the meantime, small beachhead programs like this one are needed to keep the dream alive. Today, most young offenders, and nearly all adult offenders, are still dealt with in a corrective manner. Tragically, our state's poor handling of youth residential correctional services has deteriorated still further, to the point that adult corrections has assumed control of the system. The youth justice group conferencing program remains one of the few positive programs in youth justice in Victoria today.

In summary, the above case study of a successful and thoroughly evaluated pilot program continues to highlight, for me, some of the limitations of the EBP movement in social work.

You may well ask what a restorative justice pilot program has to do with an existential approach to social work practice. Houston (2014), for example, has made connections between strengthening phenomenology in social work and the part played by restorative practices and family group conferences in emphasizing the links between the life world of clients and the systems they interface with. I have already mentioned how restorative practices empower participants and encourage client self-determination and responsibility-taking. Certainly, existential theory did not influence the development of restorative practices. The program evaluation is mentioned here because of my personal and intimate knowledge of this evaluation process and of the strengths and limitations of the EBP approach taken.

Social work has always been interested in empirical evidence and in the outcomes of interventions. I argue that an existential approach is not anti-empirical or anti-scientific; the more reasonable EBP researchers accept all the key elements of the existential approach, and recognize that researchers influence the outcomes of research through their own preconceptions, interests, and questions – they are not neutral observers. They bring their own theoretical assumptions to the research, which helps shape all its aspects. They also aim to test the assumptions of the program and to establish its successes and failures (Munro, 2002).

Finally, I made the pragmatic point that we live in a political and economic era in which resources are limited and evidence of successful implementation of program ideas is required before the political system will confidently fund new initiatives. An existential view accepts the reality of our world but also seeks to change that world by taking a more comprehensive view of what constitutes evidence for the purposes of evidence-based practice.

# Conclusion

Existential social work practice builds from its foundation in the real world of the lived experience of practitioners and of their clients, worlds that are separated but also interconnected. The goal of existential social work practice is to broaden the understanding of evidence for EBP to include other voices, and neglected areas of human experience, such as the emotions and meanings of experience. Program failure is part of the reality of program delivery and needs to be discussed and understood. Success also comes at a cost, but the effort to achieve success in social programs is well worth it. Finally, it is important to realize that the more progressive EBP researchers accept all the key points of an existential approach to research and program evaluation.

## KEY POINTS FROM CHAPTER 7

1   Existential social work research is grounded in the lived experience of clients and social workers.
2   Narrow versions of evidence-based practice (EBP) can restrict their definition of evidence to scientific knowledge, leaving out other crucial dimensions of program success and failure. These narrow approaches to EBP can also ignore marginalized voices, mood, emotion, intention, and spiritual, moral, and ecological measures. An existential approach to EBP values these other forms of evidence.
3   Long-term prospective studies find that people actively shape part of their destinies through the choices they make, and that they can address trauma and other struggles by choosing how they respond to these circumstances. Adult development is a crucial determinant of peoples' ability to cope and thrive. Structural inequalities and oppressions created by unjust social conditions, such as low wages and poor working conditions, are major factors perpetuating disadvantage.
4   In program evaluation, knowing what services clients actually receive is important.
5   An exclusive focus on outcomes can be counter-productive to good social work practice.
6   In existential social work, the focus is on the elements we can control, such as our personal influence, and on helping to shape informal supports and to create improved formal supports for clients.
7   Program failures and successes both have potential value to research.

# 8
## CONCLUSION

During the First World War, Gabriel Marcel, existentialism's only philosopher with military social work experience, contemporaneously with Heidegger, developed the concept of being-in-the-world, a fundamental idea in existential phenomenology. Marcel experienced overwhelming human suffering and pain as he tried to help the family members of soldiers missing in action to find their loved ones. It was when he challenged himself to remain present and available to each request, and to avoid treating people as a category or number, that he radically altered his philosophical stance from idealism to existentialism as we know it today; and all this in spite of the sheer, overwhelming number of displaced people (Griffiths, 2016).

Social work, in public human services areas, is faced with a not dissimilar challenge today. There are vast numbers of troubled and oppressed people interfacing with these systems, which are forced to develop and apply risk hierarchies to prioritize service to those in greatest need. People's lives are fragmented, dislocated, tenuous, and uncertain. Social work itself feels more fragmented. Marcel (1950) described our world as broken, because it lacks transcendence and is focused solely on problems and technical solutions. He gives the example of how this broken world creates repetitive jobs that lead to dehumanization and demoralization. While some writers, influenced by postmodern, poststructural thinking, suggest that we should embrace this new, fragmented social identity, I have argued here that an existential approach to our world helps us find a meaningful sense of unity in existence itself. An existential approach to social work finds this unity in the recognition that there is always more to reality than any theoretical perspective can encompass, including existentialism.

Social work's history provides the foundations, a history reflected in the existing welfare state – which continues to expand despite all the pessimism. But the past is not enough. There are many present challenges, like growing income inequality, personalization, technical innovation, the impacts of global dislocation and mass migration, and the negative impacts of globalization and global warming, along with fundamentalist terrorism and the continued use of violence to resolve conflicts. There is no roadmap for the future of social work in this age of existential risk. An existential approach to social work can only be one choice among a range of diverse theoretical approaches. Evidence-based or informed practice cannot contain all of social work; other legitimate types of evidence and voices need to be known as well.

The truth is always more than humanity can discover. True science is aware of its limitations and is always very careful to qualify its findings and their relevance. Even our clients' lived experiences, no matter how valuable, provide a limited perspective bounded by their horizons and consciousness. For example, in family violence, male perpetrators, unaware of their controlling behaviours, of their assumed male privilege, and of the extent of their abusive behaviours, are assisted through a gradual process of uncovering, surfacing, and challenging these views in a manner in which they feel supported and assisted in the process of re-storying.

Existential thought is being challenged by the existential risks that we face. Existentialism is no longer necessarily atheistic as an *a priori* condition. Spiritual thought is embraced in the context of our massive but finite world encompassed by the infinite.

Ethics are not my choice. Ethical foundations are built into our existence as interdependent beings and are to be found in the infinitely vulnerable and fragile faces of ourselves and others.

A recent work on trauma-informed care described the five key elements at play in all cultures and circumstances in a situation of mass trauma: promotion of a sense of safety, calm, self- and collective efficacy, connectedness, and the instilling of hope. Surely these five elements are crucial now to any current or future social work intervention.

Existential thought in social work is part of the resurgence in the importance of relationship in effective social work practice. Compared to the pioneers of casework, modern social work relationships are far more numerous, much shorter in duration, deal with more complex social change and control elements, and occur in a much broader (and growing) range of fields of service. This context demands even more from today's social workers. How can they stay genuinely present and available to all their clients, listening to their stories and responding so that the person really feels understood and unique to the worker? How can we help them make sense of the interventions they are participating in so that they can best engage with them? Can today's social workers balance the demands of technology and accountability with their clients' needs, or do they allow the broken world of immediacy and demand to control them?

I began this work by praising the Functionalist School of social work for focusing on the inherent limitations of social work practice and for finding, within those limitations, a way to engage creatively by working with clients' own will-power. Social work is both broader in its focus and more limited in its depth than psychotherapy. Our focus in the existential approach is on the pre-reflective and conscious mind in the world, not on the unconscious (if it exists at all). Most people in their daily lives do not reflect before acting – they act or react instinctively to events, sometimes with little awareness of their motivations and emotions. In the words of my current team leader, the purpose of existential social work is to help people become 'card carrying adults', to help them take more responsibility for their emotions and actions, and to learn to reflect before acting so that they can make wiser choices for the benefit of others, as well as themselves.

Social workers need to take more responsibility for the impacts of their interventions on others, including for the unforeseen and unintended impacts, and for our failures to act. This approach should not deter our resilience in promoting social change as much as we work to maintain social control. In advocating social change, social workers embrace others in social movements and collectively work to bring about new services, more fairness, and different solutions to existing problems, as well as better service outcomes.

Our choice is to embrace non-violent democratic social movements, based on the existential ethics of reminding our partners in those movements of the fragile and vulnerable face of the other, even when it is the face of an enemy. This demands of social workers that we advocate for a society that refuses to be defined by affluence, competition, and 'winners'. In social work, nobody gets left behind. By tapping into the energy of collective, interconnected social action, social work can use the real global transformative power of the twenty-first century.

Gisela Konopka (2005) held social work to two essential principles: that every client counts, and that through our work we demonstrate the need for mutual responsibility in overcoming the challenges faced. Communities, groups, governments, businesses, and individuals all bear responsibility to bring out from each other our fullest potential. When this happens we touch the deepest yearnings within ourselves, for fullness, happiness, and joy, and we no longer feel that our lives are ruled by fear, contingency, or the precarious. The challenge for an existential approach to social work is to operate free of fear and anxiety by being fully present and available to our clients, knowing that we have some vital capacity to help them reach their fullest potential and to achieve a greater sense of belonging.

I began this work with a question: 'What does it mean to be a social worker in the twenty-first century?' I have used elements of my own lived experience in the field of family violence service and other fields of practice to answer that question. I have suggested that it is important to dwell within social work, finding inspiration, nurturance and even enjoyment in your work with other colleagues and in your identification with the inspiring aspects of social work's history.

While we are finite creatures, affected by our reality, we also have a wonderful capacity to gradually become more present and available to others in the present moment. We can transcend a focus on ourselves and become aware of how we can relate more constructively to others for their benefit. When we do this we transform our own world by finding our true purpose as social workers: to bring about a new world for our clients and ourselves, a world in which social justice and hope prevail.

# APPENDICES

## Appendix 1: The Leon Jedwab story

The story below describes the occasion of my meeting Leon Jedwab, a Holocaust survivor, at the Jewish Holocaust Centre in Melbourne. It is included here as an example of the existential value of hope in our lives. Existential thinkers want us to seize opportunities to make a difference in the world. The stark possibilities we face – under-employment, inequality, environmental catastrophe, and death – are the very circumstances, according to Gabriel Marcel (2010), in which hope can flourish: 'There can be no hope except where the temptation to despair exists. Hope is the act by which this despair is actively or victoriously overcome' (pp. 30–31). For Marcel, hope is a mysterious creative force in the world, existing only in communion with others. It was this creative force, born of undying hope, that helped Leon Jedwab, now over 90 years old, to survive the Holocaust, despite being imprisoned in Nazi labour and concentration camps throughout the Second World War.

Leon's source of hope was the belief that he would be reunited with his father and two of his five siblings after the war. They had managed to escape to Australia before the internments began. The idea was that Leon's father, Ide, would scope out a possible move for the whole family. Given Australia's reputation as 'a wild place with kangaroos' and 'no kosher food', the family had some misgivings, Leon recalled. But war broke out in September 1939 during Ide's visit, and Ide was deterred from returning to his family in Poland by a concerned shipping company representative, who had heard reports of atrocities. 'I'm not selling you a ticket,' the representative told Ide. 'It's too risky. You have no idea what is happening over there.'

Back in Poland, Leon and his mother, Szejna Rajsel, and his two younger siblings, Riva and Moisha, were rounded up by the Nazis. Only Leon, just 15 at the time, was selected to work in Hohensalza labour camp. His mother and two younger siblings were murdered. For the next five years, Leon was shifted between concentration camps and labour camps.

How could a 15 year old survive such an experience? Leon was clear on this point: he never lost hope. Believing that he might be reunited with his family in Australia if he survived the ordeal helped Leon maintain hope through all the abuse and deprivations. He told himself, 'If I survive it, at least I have a place to go to,' he says. As he spoke, Leon visibly relived his memories, especially the trauma of the infamous death march from Auschwitz to Buchenwald during which so many died just before the end of the war.

The story of Leon's survival is of a series of inspired, quick-witted actions. Here we see the meaning of Marcel's existential idea. In the face of almost daily threats to his life, Leon Jedwab went to extraordinary lengths to out-wit the Nazis. Here are four examples of Leon's ability to use the creative inspiration of his hope in his most dire moments of need.

Leon was determined to stay close to his friend Chaim, who was interned with him. Before the war, Chaim had been engaged to Leon's sister, and during their incarceration, Chaim became Leon's dearest friend. On one occasion, they came close to separation when Leon was sent 'to the left', while Chaim was sent 'to the right'. Incredibly, Leon snuck behind the SS guards to re-join Chaim in the line.

Then there was his escape from the bathhouse. It was here that the Germans held people before their murder in the gas chamber. Leon held a picture of it, his hand shaking as emotion welled up. He pointed to the small barred window he had climbed through to escape. Stick thin with malnutrition, Leon had slipped through the bars and back to Chaim, who had not been picked for death.

Leon's fate had looked set when he was placed in an open truck by the camp authorities. This group, too, was destined for death. But, Leon revealed as he pointed shakily to another photo, a picture of a downpipe, he had managed to dodge death again. (The building in the photograph still exists at the Auschwitz historic site.) When the truck stopped at an office for the drivers to fill out various records before leaving the camp, Leon noticed a broom that had been left beside that downpipe. He leapt from the truck, snatched up the broom, and instantly pretended to be sweeping the footpath, as the truck departed. Leon had escaped certain death again.

Near the very end of his internment, Leon had become gravely ill. He knew he could not cope with the work detail. When he told the guard,

'I am sick, I can hardly walk,' the guard called him a liar, and kicked him down a flight of stairs. Leon landed in a mass of corpses, destined for the crematorium. He didn't move. The guard presumed he had died from the fall. Despite the horror of the experience of lying among the dead, Leon 'got up eventually and went back to Chaim'.

On a day-to-day basis, Leon staved off despair, hunger, and thirst by keeping busy and working hard at whatever he was required to do. This kept him focused and helped him to ignore the gruesomeness and enormity of his situation. During his time in the Nazi work camps, Leon worked building railways and locomotives and in coal mining; 'I was busy with whatever I worked. I put my mind to it. It helped me forget my hunger and thirst. This is how I survived.' For Gabriel Marcel, 'hope means first accepting the trial as an integral part of the self, destined to be absorbed and transmuted by the inner workings of a certain creative process' (p. 33).

In the early days of his internment, relatives were still able to send Leon ration cards (although it was illegal for Jews to have them). He bribed guards with cigarettes to leave the camps in search of food and took the ration cards to a Latvian baker, Alexander Assmuss, in the local town, but the man recognized him as a Jew. Leon lowered his eyes and humbly accepted his fate. Rather than hand Leon over to the Gestapo, the baker asked if Leon could procure tobacco for him from the camps; Assmuss was a heavy smoker. Astonishingly, Leon was inspired to bargain with the baker! He asked for two loaves of bread, one that he shared with Chaim and the other that he used in bartering more tobacco to continue the deal the next day.

Leon came closest to despair during the death march from Auschwitz–Birkenau to the Buchenwald camp. He watched as his Hebrew teacher, also on the march, gave up, sat down, and was shot in the head by a soldier. (The Germans shot anyone who refused to keep walking and threw their bodies into the nearest ditch.) The Germans marched the concentration camp prisoners through icy fields in wooden shoes, retreating from the Soviet advance. On seeing his teacher murdered, Leon too sat down and said to Chaim, 'I can't stand this anymore.' Chaim got him up and said, 'You've got me still.' As Leon put it, 'as long as somebody had somebody' hope endured. Chaim had saved his life.

A few steps farther on, Leon noticed an object sparkling in the frozen fields. It was a cracked gold ring. The ring gave him hope, Leon recalled, because he could get cash for it if he survived. Both Leon and Chaim survived the march, but Chaim was to die in Leon's arms just nineteen days after they had been liberated from Buchenwald. Leon also lost the ring – it was stolen from him in the barracks – but, Leon says, 'The ring had done its job': it had given him a reason to believe he had a future.

Ten days before the liberation, there had been 71,000 people in the concentration camp at Buchenwald. Ten days after the liberation there were 21,000. Fifty thousand people had lost their lives to the frantic efforts of the Nazis to implement their 'Final Solution'. Leon has returned to Poland, and to Buchenwald, on two occasions since the liberation, with his wife, who survived the war by using false Aryan papers to escape. Leon showed us the US Army certificate that registered him as a concentration camp survivor, interned from 18 September 1940 to 11 April 1945. After the liberation, an aunt in Israel found his name in the list of survivors and informed Leon's father in Australia. Leon almost cried remembering these details and the reunion with his father and brothers in Sydney.

## Finding meaning in his experience as a survivor of the Holocaust

Existential thought addresses the issue of meaning but has been associated with the view that life is meaningless. In fact, existentialism is about the idea of finding one's own meaning.

What sense could possibly be made of such an experience as Leon's and those of other Holocaust survivors? For Leon, the answer is a very personal one.

One of the first war acts of the German army was to destroy Jewish religious objects and seize synagogues. In Poland, Leon showed us before-and-after pictures of the transformation of a synagogue into a private swimming pool for German soldiers. The Torah, the five books of the Hebrew Bible, was hand written from right to left and read and recited every Saturday in synagogues. The Germans burned, shot, and tore up these priceless artefacts. Only fragments of these parchments remained following the liberation; most ended up in museums in Poland and Germany. Leon attempted to obtain one of these fragments and was eventually successful. It now resides in the most holy place inside the Melbourne Jewish Holocaust Centre.

Leon had his own personal explanation for the symbolic significance of this fragment of the Torah. In the middle of the second column is the most holy Jewish prayer, the Shema Yisrael. Leon explained that this prayer 'was probably uttered in the moments when our brothers and sisters perished in the Holocaust'. Leon's interpretation of the Shema Yisrael shares a connection with the most profound experience of existential psychotherapist Viktor Frankl, author of *Man's Search for Meaning* (2004), an account of his own Holocaust experience. (Leon, incidentally, had never read Frankl nor heard of this book.) Frankl (2004) describes his deepest concentration camp experience as losing the written manuscript of his first book, which was hidden in his coat when he arrived at Auschwitz. He describes this as the 'loss of my mental child' (p. 118). This experience was part of the stripping of prior identity that all camp residents were to undergo. It created a loss of meaning in Frankl's life. But what followed created an answer to the question of life's meaning; 'I had to surrender my clothes and in turn inherit the worn out rags of an inmate who had already been sent to the gas chambers immediately after his arrival at the Auschwitz railway station. Instead of the many pages of my manuscript, I found in a pocket of the newly acquired coat one single page torn out of a Hebrew prayer book, containing the most important Jewish prayer, Shema Yisrael. How should I have interpreted such a "coincidence" other than as a challenge to *live* my thoughts instead of merely putting them on paper?' (Frankl, 2004, p. 119, emphasis in original).

For Leon this fragment of the Torah, saved from Nazi destruction, is symbolic of his personal search for the meaning behind the terrible suffering undergone by the Jewish people during the Holocaust. Leon also sought out the only remaining descendent of Alexander Assmuss, the Latvian baker who had chosen not to hand Leon over to the Nazis and who had dealt with him as a human being. Leon invited Alexander's grandson, Wolfgang Haupt, a chef, and his wife Regina to Australia for a ten-day visit. Leon also wanted Wolfgang to take back to Germany memories of a thriving Jewish community that had survived Hitler.

Leon lives with a reminder of the Holocaust every day: the number 144768 tattooed on his arm. Chaim's number was 144769. For Leon, the memories are as real today as if they were of yesterday. It is now more than seventy years since the liberation, and unlike many survivors Leon is still happy to share his story: 'I want to leave something after I've gone,' he says. His pledge is to keep telling this story so that the world never repeats the mistake of allowing ideology to take precedence over humanity.

What meaning can we draw from Leon's stories? They are the stories of a young man who found a way to creatively keep hope alive in circumstances specifically designed to extinguish it, by remaining in hopeful communion with Chaim and his remaining family. Keeping hope alive was a matter of hourly, even moment-to-moment survival. He was not just being optimistic; there were absolutely no guarantees. Leon's hope gave him the creative inspiration that eventually ensured his return to his father and brothers. As Gabriel Marcel (2010) wrote, 'to expect is in some way to give' (p. 43). In Marcel's view, hope requires humanity to be open to communion 'to accomplish … the transcendent act, the act establishing the vital regeneration of this experience affords the pledge and the first fruits' (p.61). These are the gifts of Leon Jedwab's story and of the act of hope. Even greater than the hope that kept Leon alive is the effort he has put into making sense of his experience in the real, symbolic coincidence he shares with existential therapist Viktor Frankl in finding meaning in suffering through the survival of the spirit of the Jewish people and its triumph over pure evil.

Edited by Kath Walters

# Appendix 2: Glossary of existential terms

| Term | Meaning |
|------|---------|
| Alienation | Alienation refers to a disconnection from ourselves, from others, from the world, and from God. Existentialism is regarded as a philosophical response to this alienation experience, which reached a peak in the twentieth century after two world wars, the depression, nuclear terror, and the failure of communism. In the twenty-first century, many people feel even more alienated, reflected in a sense of homelessness or lack of grounding in the world. Social workers can feel alienated from their work, from their field of service, or from their profession. |
| Anxiety | More than simple worry about things, anxiety is our apprehension towards our freedom that reflects the possibility of failure, loss, success, or other outcomes. Normal anxiety is seen as the fuel that drives us forward, if we overcome it by taking action and giving things a try. Anxiety is different from fear, which has an object of focus. In existential thought, anxiety is behind the experience of lack of meaning, boredom, being shaken to the core, and a general mood of uneasiness, which drives people to seek distractions. |
| Authenticity | An existential value that describes the quality of a person who accepts responsibility for being who they are and for making the most of their life, without concern for how others might judge them. Someone who is genuine and whose words and actions are congruent is described as authentic. A social program or organization could be described as authentic if it acted congruently with its stated aims and objectives. |
| Bad faith | A term developed by Sartre to describe human behaviour that pretends (or acts as if) it had no choice or responsibility for its actions. A social worker who pretends that their job defines them and prescribes all their actions would be acting in bad faith. |
| Being | For Hegel, being is the most abstract concept and is part of a process for all things, which involves them coming into existence (being), then developing further (becoming), and then coming to an end (nothing).<br><br>Hegel also identified the possibility of the infinite, which encompasses finite being. With the concept of true infinity comes the possibility of 'being as fullness', as found in the work of Stein.<br><br>Asking about the being of social work is asking an ontological question about its essence or meaning. |

| Being-in-the-world | A central concept that is fundamental to existential phenomenology and has some connections to similar concepts such as Person-in-the-world (Marcel) and Life World (Husserl). It means that humans exist in a world and cannot be separated from it. Scientism and some forms of positivist thought assume that consciousness can be separated from what it observes. Existentialism rejects this subject–object divide as an abstraction. Atheistic existentialists are not open to the inclusion of transcendence or encompassing meaning allowing for the possibility of hidden or spirit dimensions in the world, as well as the material or natural world. Their concept of transcendence is limited to the concept of self-determination and freedom, which is problematic as it posits egoistic freedom that may trample upon others' freedom. |
|---|---|
| Being-in-a-social work-world | A term created for this book to describe the lived experience of the direct service social worker working in a team in a field of service in a human services organization. |
| Being thrown | A term identified mostly with Heidegger that describes our experience of coming into a world with an existing facticity (a time period, location, gender, class, particular family, etc.) The opposite of being thrown is being held or dwelling (defined below), which has some connection to the holding environment concept used in social work to refer to the safety and security provided in programs that enable people to grow. |
| Consciousness | In existential thought, consciousness is intentional, is in the world, and is of other objects, such as other humans and happenings. |
| Contingency | Contingency is the idea that anything can happen. Nothing is certain. We can all experience an accident or illness at any time that could put our whole life on hold. |
| Dasein | Human existence. |
| Dwelling | Levinas uses this term to describe how a human's first experiences in the world as an infant (providing they are not abused or neglected) are of dwelling in the world, a sense of being comforted, secure, and looked after. It is used in this book when I speak of dwelling in social work through understanding of its history and feeling supported by the profession. |

| Essence | The essence of something is *what* makes that thing unique. For example, Edith Stein, for her dissertation, studied the problem of empathy. Using a phenomenological approach, Stein was able to show that empathy not only helps us understand others to some extent but is also essential to our growth as human beings. |
|---------|---|
| Existence | The quality of being. Existence refers to things or people that exist. For example, before social work existed, there were other forms of helping, such as friendly visitors and hospital almoners. Gradually social work as a profession came into existence through trial and error, reflection, research, and people giving up secure employment as nurses and teachers to become the first social workers. Social work struggled into existence. To exist is to struggle, to make an effort every day in our work, life, and play. We make something of ourselves within our world and facticity, the givens of our developing world. |
| Existence precedes essence | A famous description by Sartre of his existentialism, by which he means that we define who we are by our thoughts and actions, projects, and intentions. Humans are not predetermined by anyone or anything or any essence within themselves. There is always a possibility of free choice, even in the most extreme situations. |
| Existential | Relating to existence. The existential social work perspective builds on our existence as human beings-in-the-world, meaning that as subjects we are not separate from the world. We are open to the world, including our glimpses into the mystery (or non-problematic) of the world. |
| Existentialism | A specific philosophy based on our existence in the world. The founder of existentialism is considered to be the philosopher Soren Kierkegaard for his re-emphasis on subjective knowledge, but the term is mostly associated with Sartre and de Beauvoir and with their advocacy of freedom and self-determination as a fundamental quality of all human life. This term can also refer to a philosophical movement associated with a range of existential thinkers. Developing in the twentieth century, it continues to evolve and to inspire new thinking, such as eco-existentialism, which Deborah Bird Rose describes as bringing together two major shifts, an end to certainty and an end to atomism. See Kevin Aho's, *Existentialism: An Introduction* (2014), for how existentialism is developing globally this century. |

| Existential social work | Existential social work focuses on the lived relational existence of people, which is always more than any totality of thought can explain. It aims to support people to create their fullest potential in the concrete world. Existential social work is not simply the application of existential therapy to social work practice, nor is it simply the application of existential concepts to social work practice. Existential social work is an openness to the lived reality or mystery of social work. |
|---|---|
| Existentialist | A person who advocates existentialism as a philosophy. Existential social work writer Neil Thompson describes his approach as 'existentialist' social work practice because only existential concepts developed within modern existential thought as theory can be included in this approach. |
| Existential therapies | Sometimes called existential psychotherapy; a range of diverse therapies inspired by existential thought and its application to therapy. |
| Existential issues | Anything concerned with our existence can be an existential issue, but common ones include death, freedom, isolation, and meaninglessness. In social work practice, chronic ill health requiring pain management and dying can result in clients experiencing existential concerns or crises.<br><br>All clients try to make sense of their involvement in social work programs, and social workers play an important role in helping to shape this sense-making process. |
| Existential threats | Currently, global warming, species extinction, terrorism, and war, including the threat of nuclear war, are forms of existential threat. They have a small chance of occurring suddenly, but a huge potential impact on human life if they do.<br><br>Clients can experience social work intervention as an existential threat; for example, a child protection investigation could be experienced by a family as an existential threat to that family. Thus social work needs to face the impact of existential threats in the twenty-first century within our practice. |
| Facticity of the world | All the givens of our world that place restrictions on our freedom. For example, for me, facticities include the historical period I am living through in this finite life, my age, and work history that don't allow me to become an astronaut, no matter how hard I work at it. |

| Face of the other | A concept created by Levinas to describe our inherent interpersonal and social being as human beings that obliges us to focus our concerns on others given our direct visceral experience of our own and others' fragility, frailty, and potential for hurt and offence. |
| --- | --- |
| | Levinas states that when we look deeply into the face of the other we can see their finite weaknesses but also their infinite and unique value. That is why our first philosophy becomes ethical behaviour, which begins with not harming or killing one another. |
| Freedom | A primary existential value, which is inherent in the notion of being human. |
| Lived experience | A fundamental existential and phenomenological concept, which has now entered mainstream social work thought. In existential phenomenology, lived experience is the foundation of all other knowledge, including science, which builds upon lived experience by experimentation and other methods of analysis. |
| Ontological | Ontology is the search for the meaning of our existence and thus for the answer to the fundamental question of the meaning of being or why things exist, why people die, and how we grow and develop. In the medieval world, other beings held more importance than humanity, such as angels and the supreme being, or God. These beings helped define the ontological significance of humans. In the modern age, human beings became the primary beings of concern, and existential thought reflects this concern. Ontology is also described as the metaphysics of being, which refers to our beliefs about being and the meaning of life. |
| Phenomenology | Phenomenology refers to the study of phenomena. It focuses on the world as experienced. It seeks to describe our lived experiences in great detail to determine what is essential about them. |
| Self-determination | A mainstream social work objective, referring to helping clients to become more responsible and self-directed. |
| True infinity | An existential concept created by Hegel to describe his understanding of the infinite, which, by definition, must encompass the finite or it would be a spurious infinity. This idea contrasts with traditional theological thought, which understood God or eternal being as completely separate from all finite beings and thus as separate from the world. |
| Worked matter | A term created by Sartre to describe how our institutions, programs, machines, and other technologies are formed by human praxis and become restrictions on freedom and on new development. |

# Appendix 3: Biographies of key existential writers and social workers

| Existential writers | |
|---|---|
| de Beauvoir, Simone | de Beauvoir is best known for her application of existential thought to the cause of feminism in her classic work *The Second Sex* (2011), which documents the ontological oppression of women by patriarchy over the history of mankind. Along with Maurice Merleau-Ponty, de Beauvoir argued for the ambiguous nature of human life, not because it is purely subjective, but rather because it is intersubjective and inherently reciprocal. |
| Frankl, Viktor | Viktor Frankl was a leading existential psychiatrist, as well as a Holocaust survivor and founder of logotherapy, which is a type of existential therapy that focuses on making sense of our experiences and finding meaning in our existence. |
| Hegel, Georg | Hegel was a leading German idealist philosopher and was highly influential on existential thinking from its very beginnings with Kierkegaard. Hegel also influenced critical thinking through his dialectical approach, which helped shape Marxism. A dialectical approach seeks to expose the contradictions within things that provide the dynamics for change and transition over time. The materialist and naturalistic perspective underlying critical thought tends to denigrate Hegel's idealism. However, Hegel was also a deeply religious thinker and felt that he had discovered a new idea in the conceptualization of true infinity. Based upon the Christian revelation, Hegel felt that the finite world is not separate from the infinite but is fully encompassed by it. The fundamental concept of being-in-the-world in existential phenomenology allows for infinite and finite being to be present in the world. The existential writer Maurice Merleau-Ponty was the first existential thinker to name Hegel as a pioneer of this philosophy. |
| Heidegger, Martin | Heidegger is the highly controversial founder of existential phenomenology. He felt that the whole of Western philosophy had erred by ignoring the fundamental question of existence or being: why something exists rather than nothing. He examined this question through the being of humans, called *Dasein* in German. He carefully described how the human being actually experiences the world in everyday life. Heidegger argued that being is disclosed to humans differently throughout historical time and that we now live in a technological age that treats all being as 'standing reserve'. He is famous for creating a new terminology that grew alongside his insights into human beings; one of the basic terms he used is the concept of 'Being-in-the-world' (see Glossary). |

| Levinas, Emmanuel | Levinas was a highly influential phenomenological thinker who built his existential philosophy in response to his profound disappointment in Heidegger's identification with Nazism. He challenged Heidegger's obsession with being by pointing to the presence of the 'face of the other', which places infinite obligations upon us to avoid doing harm and to assist others in meeting their needs. He is known for the statement that 'ethics is first philosophy', which is based on the recognition of the world's interdependent nature. |
|---|---|
| Marcel, Gabriel | Marcel is the only existential writer to have experienced military social work in the First World War. Marcel was the first writer to use the word 'existentialism' to describe the movement that grew in the twentieth century from the dismissal of the subject–object divide created by idealist and positivist empirical thinkers. See my article on his influence in social work practice in the bibliography (Griffiths, 2016). |
| Rank, Otto | Otto Rank was one of the first psychoanalysts and was influential in the development of the Functional School of social work through his connection with Jessie Taft (see Chapters 1 and 2). |
| Sartre, Jean Paul | Along with his life-long companion, Simone de Beauvoir, Sartre is the most famous existential thinker in the world, mostly for his advocacy of freedom and self-determination as an inherent existential condition of being human. This is the view that no matter what the circumstances or beliefs we hold, we must take responsibility for how we respond to any situation, even when we make no choice or allow others to choose for us. His first novel, *Nausea*, elaborates on the contingency of our human existence, the idea that reality can suddenly change for no apparent reason or cause. At any point, anything can happen; for example, we might experience an accident. Sartre has influenced many social workers, notably Neil Thompson, and has been highly influential across the globe for his advocacy of social movements for liberation from oppression. |
| Stein, Edith | Stein was an assistant to the founder of phenomenology, Edmund Husserl. Despite being a brilliant student, she was kept from reaching her full potential by discrimination on the basis of her sex and her Jewish ethnicity, being denied many academic positions at universities. Stein continued to write, but little of her work was published until she was canonized as a Catholic Saint after her murder in the Holocaust. Her collected works have now been published. Her critique of Heidegger's classic *Being and Time* was not included in the collected works but can be found here: https://www.maynoothuniversity.ie/sites/default/files/assets/document/MPP%204%20(2007).pdf. What Stein does in this document is stress the personal being of the human. At the same time, Stein argues, we are communal beings, and we develop as human beings and spiritual beings over time, leading to fullness of being to the point of complete union with eternal being. This evolving development allows us to gain the perspective that life is not ultimately precarious, as we are held to being by a mysterious force (Sutton, 1992). |

| Existentially informed social workers | |
|---|---|
| Konopka, Gisela | One of the founders of group work in social work, Konopka did not believe in identification with any theory in social work because of the necessary limitations of all theories and their application. I have identified her as existential in her thinking because of her clear ethical approach to social work in her stressing of the importance of the uniqueness of the individual and of the need for all members of society to help to solve its problems. Konopka emphasized the art of social work and dismissed its scientific pretensions. She also stressed the importance of philosophical issues in social work. |
| Krill, Donald | Donald Krill was one of the first American existential social workers and has continued to write and explain the existential viewpoint in social work for the last 40 years (see Chapter 3). |
| Lantz, Jim | Jim Lantz was a leading existential family therapist and social worker who wrote extensively on existentially informed social work practice and the practice of logotherapy. He was influenced by the thought of Gabriel Marcel and Viktor Frankl. |
| Taft, Jessie | The founder of the first existential social work school, described as the Functional School of social work. The Functional School was in conflict with the Diagnostic School of social work, which was aligned with the psychoanalytic approach to social work practice. |
| Thompson, Neil | Neil Thompson is a leading existentialist social worker. He has written numerous books extending beyond social work, applying his existentialist ideas to issues such as leadership and human resource management. Thompson adopts a critical existentialist perspective on social work practice inspired by the critical Marxist existential period of Jean Paul Sartre. |
| Wilkes, Ruth | Ruth Wilkes was an English social worker with a philosophical bent who was strongly influenced by Immanuel Kant, Simone Weil, and Soren Kierkegaard. Her focus was on a critique of social work's current obsessions with improving clients and achieving better outcomes, the impact of managerialism, and the failure of modern social work to advocate for the inherent value of the marginalized and despised, client groups that social work was created to advocate for. |

# REFERENCES

Aho, K. 2014, *Existentialism: An Introduction*, Polity Press, Cambridge.

Alder, C. and Wundersitz, J. (eds), 1995, *Family Conferencing and Juvenile Justice*, Australian Institute of Criminology, Canberra.

Alinski, S. 1971, *Rules for Radicals: A Pragmatic Primer for Realistic Radicals*, Random House, New York.

Anderson, T. 1993, *Sartre's Two Ethics*, Open Court Publishing Company, Chicago.

Anglicare Victoria and Success Works Pty. Ltd. 1999, *Juvenile Justice Group Conferencing Project Evaluation*, Anglicare, Melbourne.

Applegate, J. and Bonovitz, J. 1995, *The Facilitating Partnership*, Jason Aronson, London.

Australian Public Service Commission, 2017, Tackling Wicked Problems: A Public Policy Perspective (URL: http://www.enablingchange.com.au/wickedproblems. pdf) [Accessed 08/05/2017].

Backhaus, G. and Psathas, G. 2007, *The Sociology of Radical Commitment: Kurt H Woff's Existential Turn*, Lexington Books, Lanham.

Barber J. 1991, *Beyond Casework*, Macmillan Education, London.

Barnes, H. 1997, *The Story I Tell Myself: A Venture in Existentialist Autobiography*, University of Chicago Press, Chicago.

Bartlett, H. 1971, 'Social Work Fields of Service', in *Encyclopedia of Social Work*, Vol. 2 (16th edn) (ed Morris, R.), National Association of Social Workers, New York, pp. 1477–1481.

Biestek, F. 1957, *The Casework Relationship*, Loyola University Press, Chicago.

Biestek, F. and Gehrig, C. 1978, *Client Self-Determination in Social Work*, Loyola University Press, Chicago.

Bisno, H. 1956, 'How Social Will Social Work Be?' *Social Work*, vol. 1, no. 2, pp. 12–18.

Bisno, H. & Cox, F. 1997, 'Social Work Education: Catching Up with the Present and the Future', *Journal of Social Work Education*, vol. 33, no. 2, pp. 373–387.

Bloom, M. 1993, 'A Research Odyssey: The Multi-Faceted Work of Ludwig L. Geismar', in *Single-System Designs in the Social Services: Issues and Options for the 1990s* (ed Bloom, M.) Haworth, New York, pp. 5–17.

Bloom, M. and Fischer, J. 1982, *Evaluating Practice: Guidelines for the Accountable Professional*, Prentice Hall, Englewood Cliffs.

Bradford, K. A. 1969, *Existentialism and Casework,* Exposition Press, New York.

Brandon, D. 1990, *Zen in the Art of Helping,* Penguin, London.

Brandon, D. and Jordan, B. (eds), 1979, *Creative Social Work,* Blackwell, Oxford.

Brendtro, L. 2006, 'The Vision of Urie Bronfenbrenner', *Reclaiming Children and Youth,* vol. 15, no. 3, pp. 162–166.

Brown, J. 1971, *Freud and the Post-Freudians,* Penguin, Harmondsworth.

Buber, M. 1970, *I and Thou,* Charles Scribner's Sons, New York.

Buber, M. 2000, *I and Thou,* Scribner, New York.

Burns, K. 2013, *The Dust Bowl,* DVD, Florentine Films, Special Broadcasting Services, Washington.

Camus, A. 1958, *Exile and the Kingdom,* H. Hamilton, London.

Camus, A. 1972, 'The Myth of Sisyphus', in *Existentialism from Dostoevsky to Sartre* (13th edn) (ed Kaufmann, W.), World Publishing Company, New York, pp. 375–378.

Camus, A. 2000, *The Rebel,* Penguin, London.

Carkhuff, R. and Berenson, B. 1967, *Beyond Counselling and Therapy,* Holt, Rinehart and Winston, New York.

Carroll, M. 1994, 'Implementational Issues: Considering the options for Victoria', in *Family Conferencing and Juvenile Justice* (eds Alder, C. and Wundersitz J.), Australian Institute of Criminology, Canberra, pp. 167–180.

Cohn, H. 2002, *Heidegger and the Roots of Existential Therapy,* Continuum, London.

Coll, B. 1980, 'Hoey, Jane Margueretta' in *Notable American Women: The Modern Period,* Vol. 4 (eds Sicherman, B., Hurd Green, C., Kantron, I. and Walker, H.), Belknap Press of Harvard University Press, Cambridge, pp. 341–343.

Coll, B. 1995, *Safety Net,* Rutgers University Press, New Brunswick.

Cooper, M. 2003, *Existential Therapies,* Sage, London.

Corey, G. 2009, *Theory and Practice of Counselling and Psychotherapy,* Thomson, Brooks/Cole, Belmont.

Coull, V., Giesmar, L. and Waff, A. 1982, 'The Role of the Family in the Resocialization of Juvenile Offenders', *Journal of Comparative Family Studies,* vol. 13, no. 1, pp. 63–75.

Davies, M. 1985, *The Essential Social Worker* (2nd edn), Wildwood House, Aldershot.

de Beauvoir, S. 2010, *The Second Sex,* Vintage, London.

Department of Human Services, 2011, *Child Protection Workforce, The Case for Change,* Victorian Government, Melbourne.

Department of Human Services, 2012, Family Violence Risk Assessment and Risk Management Framework and Practice Guides 1–3, Edition 2 (URL: http://www.dhs.vic.gov.au/about-the-department/documents-and-resources/policies,-guidelines-and-legislation/family-violence-risk-assessment-risk-management-framework-manual) [Accessed 08/05/17].

Department of Human Services and KPMG, 2010, Review of the Youth Justice Group Conferencing Program (URL: http://www.dhs.vic.gov.au/for-service-providers/children,-youth-and-families/youth-justice/group-conferencing-information/review-of-the-youth-justice-group-conferencing-program-report) [Accessed: 08/05/17]

Department of Justice, 2011, Sexual Assault Reform Strategy, Final Evaluation Report (URL: http://www.justice.vic.gov.au/home/justice+system/laws+and+regulation/criminal+law/sexual+assault+reform+strategy+-+final+evaluation+report) [Accessed: 08/05/17].

Dixon, J. 2010, 'Comparative Social Welfare: The Existential Humanist Perspective and Challenge', *Journal of Comparative Social Welfare*, vol. 26, no. 2–3, pp. 177–187.

Ehrenreich, J. 1985, *The Altruistic Imagination*, Cornell University Press, London.

England, H. 1986, *Social Work As Art*, Allen and Unwin, London.

Farrar, R. 1994, *Sartrean Dialectics*, Rodopi, Amsterdam.

Fischer, J. 2009, *Towards Evidence Based Practice*, Lyceum Books, Chicago.

Flynn, T. 1997, *Sartre, Foucault and Historical Reason*, University of Chicago Press, Chicago.

Frankl, V. 2004, *Man's Search for Meaning*, Rider, Random House, Croydon.

Freire, P. 1972, *Pedagogy of the Oppressed*, Penguin Education, Middlesex.

Freire, P. 1975, *Pedagogy of the Oppressed*, Penguin Education, London.

Freud, S. (ed Breuer, J.) 2001, *The Standard Edition of the Complete Psychological Works of Sigmund Freud, Volume 2: Studies on Hysteria*, Vintage, London.

Frye, N. 1964, *The Educated Imagination*, Indiana University Press, Indianapolis.

Gadamar, H. 1989, *Truth and Method*, Bloomsbury, London.

Gilbert, N. and Terrell, P. 2010, *Dimensions of Social Welfare Policy*, Allyn and Bacon, Boston.

Goldstein, H. 1974, *Social Work Practice: A Unitary Approach*, University of South Carolina Press, Columbia.

Goldstein, H. 1984, 'A Cognitive-Humanistic Approach to Practice: Philosophical and Theoretical Foundations' in *Creative Change* (ed Goldstein, H.), Tavistock, New York, pp. 3–32.

Gray, M. and Webb, S. 2008, 'Social Work as Art Revisited', *International Journal of Social Welfare*, vol. 17, pp. 182–193.

Griffin, M. 2011, 'Paperwork is Swamping Child Protection Workers', *The Saturday Age*, 4 June, p. 7 (URL: http://www.theage.com.au/victoria/paperwork-is-swamping-child-protection-workers-20110603-1fky6.html) [Accessed 08/05/17].

Griffiths, M. 2001, 'Restorative Justice Conferencing: Reconstructing Practice with Male Juvenile Offenders', in *Working with Men in the Human Services* (eds Pease, B. and Camilleri, P.), Allen and Unwin, Sydney, pp. 134–146.

Griffiths, M. 2016, 'Applying Gabriel Marcel's Thought in Social Work Practice', *Marcel Studies*, vol. 1, no. 1, pp. 1–16.

Grimwood, T. 2016, *Key Debates in Social Work and Philosophy*, Routledge, New York.

Guttman, D. 1996, *Logotherapy for the Helping Professional: Meaningful Social Work*, Springer Publishing Co., New York.

Hamilton, G. 1951, *Theory and Practice of Social Case Work*, Columbia University Press, New York.

Healy, K. 2005, *Social Work Theories in Context*, Palgrave MacMillan, New York.

Hegel, G. 2009, *Hegel's Logic*, Marxists Internet Archive, Pacifica.

Heidegger, M. 1962, *Being and Time*, Harper and Row, New York.

Heidegger, M. 1971, 'Building Dwelling Thinking', in *Poetry Language Thought* (ed Heidegger, M.), Harper Perennial, New York, pp. 145–161.

Heidegger, M. 1977, *The Question Concerning Technology and Other Essays*, Harper Perennial, New York.

Herz, M. and Johansson, T. 2012, 'Doing Social Work: Critical Considerations on Theory and Practice in Social Work', *Advances in Social Work*, vol. 13, no. 3, pp. 527–540.

Hoey, J. 1938, 'Our Common Stake in the Development of the Social Security Program', *The Family*, vol. 18, no. 9, pp. 295–298.

Hoey, J. 1939, 'Aid to Families with Dependent Children', *The Annals of Political and Social Science*, vol. 202, March, pp. 74–81.

Hoey, J. 1943, 'The Conservation of Family Values in Wartime', *The Family*, vol. 24, no. 2, pp. 43–49.

Hoey, J. 1947, 'The Content of Living as a Basis for a Standard of Assistance and Service', *Social Casework*, vol. 28, no. 1, pp. 3–9.

Hoey, J. 1948, 'Public Assistance in 1948', *Social Casework*, vol. 29, no. 4, pp. 123–130.

Hoey, J. 1950, 'Social Work: Its Base, Skills, and Relation to Other Fields', *Social Casework*, vol. 31, no. 10, pp. 399–410.

Hoey, J. 1953, 'Public Welfare: Burden or Opportunity?', *Social Services Review*, vol. 27, no. 4, pp. 377–384.

Hoey, J. 1957, 'The Lack of Money: Its Cost in Human Values', *Social Casework*, vol. 38, no. 8, pp. 406–412.

Hoey, J. 1958, 'Book Review of Decisions about People in Need: A Study in Administrative Responsiveness in Public Assistance', *Social Services Review*, vol. 32, no. 2, pp. 195–197.

Houston, S. 2014, 'Getting Back to the Things Themselves: Strengthening Phenomenology in Social Work', in *Social Change and Social Work* (eds Harrikari, T., Rauhala, P. and Virokannas, A.), Ashgate, Farnham, pp. 87–99.

Irving, A. 1999, 'Waiting for Foucault: Social Work and the Multitudinous Truth(s) of Life', in *Reading Foucault for Social Work* (eds Chambon, A., Irving, A. and Epstein L.), Columbia University Press, New York, pp. 27–50.

Jenkins, A. 1990, *Invitations to Responsibility*, Duluth Centre, Richmond.

Jenkins, A. 2001, *Invitations to Responsibility*, Dulwich Centre, Adelaide.

Jenkins, A. 2009, *Becoming Ethical*, Russell House, Dorset.

Joblin, D. 1992, 'At the Limits of Biographical Knowledge: Sartre and Levinas', in *Shaping Lives: Reflections on Biography* (eds Donaldson, I., Read, P. and Walter, J.), Humanities Research Centre, ANU, Canberra, pp. 79–101.

Karpe, F. 1953, *The Psychology and Psychotherapy of Otto Rank*, Philosophical Library, New York.

Karpman, S. 1968, 'Fairy Tales and Script Drama Analysis', *Transactional Analysis Bulletin*, vol. 7, no. 26, pp. 39–43.

Keating, C. and Barrow, D. 2005, *Report on the Juvenile Justice Group Conferencing Program*, Stage 1, Draft, Effective Change Ptd. Ltd., Melbourne.

Keating, C. and Barrow, D. 2006, *Report on the Juvenile Justice Group Conferencing Program*, Effective Change Ptd. Ltd., Melbourne.

Keith-Lucas, A. 1953, 'The Political Theory Implicit in Social Casework Theory', *The American Political Science Review*, vol. 47, no. 4, pp. 1076–1091.

Keith-Lucas, A. 1957, *Decisions about People in Need*, University of North Carolina Press, Chapel Hill.

Keith-Lucas, A. 1975, 'An Alliance for Power', *Social Work*, vol. 20, no. 2, pp. 93–97.

Kierkegaard, S. 1980, *The Concept of Anxiety*, Princeton University Press, Princeton.

Kirby, W. 1921, *The Social Mission of Charity*, Catholic University of America Press, Washington.

Konopka, G. 1958, *Edward C. Lindeman and Social Work Philosophy*, University of Minnesota Press, Minneapolis.

Konopka, G. 1963, *Social Group Work*, Prentice Hall, Englewood Cliffs.

Konopka, G. 2005, 'The Significance of Social Group Work Based on Ethical Values', in *A Quarter Century of Classics (1978–2004): Capturing the Theory, Practice and Spirit of Social Work with Groups* (eds Malekoff, A. and Kurland, R.), Haworth Press, New York, pp. 17–28.

Kramer, R. 1995, 'The Birth of Client-Centred Therapy: Carl Rogers, Otto Rank, and "The Beyond"', *Journal of Humanistic Psychology*, vol. 35, no. 54, pp. 54–110.

Kramer, R. (ed), 1996, *The Psychology of Difference: Otto Rank*, Princeton University Press, Princeton.

Krill, D. 1969, 'Existential Psychotherapy and the Problem of Anomie', *Social Work*, vol. 14, no. 2, pp. 33–49.

Krill, D. 1978, *Existential Social Work*, Free Press, New York.

Krill, D. 1987, 'Existential Approach', in *Encyclopedia of Social Work*, Vol. 1 (18th edn), National Association of Social Workers (NASW), Silver Spring, pp. 517–519.

Krill, D. 2011, 'Existential Social Work', in *Social Work Treatment* (5th edn) (ed Turner, J. F.), Oxford University Press, New York, pp. 179–203.

Krill, D. 2014, 'Existential Social Work', *Advances in Social Work*, vol. 15, no. 1, pp. 117–128.

Laing, R. D. 1971, *The Politics of the Family and Other Essays*, Tavistock Publications, London.

Lantz, J. 1988, 'The Use of Frankl's Concepts in Family Therapy', *Journal of Independent Social Work*, vol. 2, no. 2, pp. 65–80.

Lantz, J. 1994a, 'Marcel's 'Availability' in Existential Psychotherapy with Couples and Families', *Contemporary Family Therapy*, vol. 16, no. 6, pp. 489–501.

Lantz, J. 1994b, 'Mystery in Family Therapy', *Contemporary Family Therapy*, vol. 16, no. 1, pp. 53–66.

Lantz, J. 1994c, 'Primary and Secondary Reflection in Existential Family Therapy', *Contemporary Family Therapy*, vol. 16, no. 4, pp. 315–327.

Lantz, J. 1996, 'Cognitive Theory and Social Work Treatment', in *Social Work Treatment: Interlocking Theoretical Perspectives* (4th edn) (ed Turner, F. J.), Free Press, New York, pp. 94–115.

Lantz, J. 1999, 'Marcel's Testimony in Existential Psychotherapy with Couples and Families', *Contemporary Family Therapy*, vol. 21, no. 4, pp. 469–483.

Lantz, J. 2000, *Meaning Centred Marital and Family Therapy*, Charles C Thomas, Springfield.

Lantz, J. 2001, 'Existential Theory', in *Theoretical Perspectives for Direct Social Work Practice: A Generalist–Eclectic Approach* (ed. Lehmann, P.), Springer, New York, pp. 240–254.

Lantz, J. 2004, 'Research and Evaluation Issues in Existential Psychotherapy', *Journal of Contemporary Psychotherapy*, vol. 34, no. 4, pp. 331–340.

Laub, J. and Sampson, R. 1993, *Crime in the Making*, Harvard University Press, Cambridge.

Laub, J. and Sampson, R. 2003, *Shared Beginnings, Divergent Lives*, Harvard University Press, Cambridge.

Lear, J. 2006, *Radical Hope*, Harvard University Press, Cambridge.

Levinas, E. 1969, *Totality and Infinity*, Duquesne University Press, Pittsburgh.

Levinas, E. 1995, *The Theory of Intuition in Husserl's Phenomenology*, Northwestern University Press, Evanston.

Lieberman, E. 1985, *Acts of Will*, The Free Press, New York.

Lipsky, M. 2010, *Street Level Bureaucracy*, Russell Sage, New York.

Lubove, R. 1965, *The Professional Altruist*, Harvard University Press, New York.

Macdonald, H. 2011, 'Levinas in the Hood: Portable Social Justice', *The Humanistic Psychologist*, vol. 39, pp. 305–311.

Marcel, G. 1950, *The Mystery of Being 1: Reflection and Mystery*, St Augustine's Press, South Bend.

Marcel, G. 1966, *The Philosophy of Existentialism*, The Citadel Press, New York.

Marcel, G. 2010, *Homo Viator*, St Augustine's Press, South Bend.

Margolin, L. 1997, *Under the Cover of Kindness: The Invention of Social Work*, University Press of Virginia, Charlottesville.

Markiewicz, A. 1997, *Juvenile Justice Group Conferencing in Victoria. An Evaluation of a Pilot Program, Phase 2*, Anglicare, Melbourne.

Marston, G. and McDonald, C. 2012, 'Getting beyond 'Heroic Agency' in Conceptualising Social Workers as Policy Actors in the Twenty-First Century', *British Journal of Social Work*, vol. 42, no. 6, pp. 1022–1038.

Marx, K. 1852, *The Eighteenth Brumaire of Louis Bonaparte*, Marxists.org (URL: http://www.marxists.org/archive/marx/works/1852/18th-brumaire/) [Accessed 20/10/2013].

May, R. 1967, *The Art of Counseling*, Abingdon Press, New York.

May, R. 1977, *The Meaning of Anxiety*, Pocket Books, New York.

May, R. 1983, *The Discovery of Being*, W. W. Norton and Co., New York.

Meyer, C. 1976, *Social Work Practice*, The Free Press, Collier Macmillan, London.

Miller, J. 2003, 'We Work Together, We Think Together, We Act Together', *Journal of Progressive Human Services*, vol. 14, no. 1, pp. 15–39.

Mission of St James and St John, 1995, *Juvenile Justice Pilot Program on Group Conferencing*, Melbourne.

Moreau, J. 1979, 'A Structural Approach to Social Work Practice', *Canadian Journal of Social Work Education*, vol. 5, no. 1, pp. 78–94.

Moyer, B. 2001, *Doing Democracy*, New Society Publishers, Gabriola Island.

Munro, E. 2002, 'The Role of Theory in Social Work Research: A Further Contribution to the Debate', *Journal of Social Work Education*, vol. 38, no. 3, pp. 461–470.

Munro, E. 2010, 'Learning to Reduce Risk in Child Protection', *British Journal of Social Work*, vol. 40, pp. 1135–1151.

O'Hare, T. 2009, *Essential Skills of Social Work Practice*, Lyceum Books, Chicago.

Overton, A. 1953, 'Serving Families Who "Don't Want Help"', *Social Casework*, vol. 34, pp. 304–309.

Overton, A. and Tinker, K. 1959, *Casework Notebook*, Family Centered Project, St Paul.

Parton, N. 2006, 'Changes in the Form of Knowledge in Social Work: From the 'Social' to the 'Informational'?', *British Journal of Social Work*, vol. 38, no. 2, pp. 253–269.

Parton, N. 2012, 'The Munro Review of Child Protection: An Appraisal', *Children and Society*, Vol. 26, pp. 150–162.

Payne, M. 2005, *Modern Social Work Theory*, Palgrave Macmillan, London.

Piven, F. and Cloward, R. 1971, *Regulating the Poor*, Vintage Books, Random House, Toronto.

Piven, F. and Cloward, R. 1979, *Poor People's Movements*, Vintage Books, Random House, New York.

Pozzuto, R. and Arnd-Caddigan, M. 2008, 'Social Work in the U.S: Sociohistorical Context and Contemporary Issues', *Australian Social Work*, vol. 61, no.1, pp. 57–71.

Pringle, H. and Pringle, K. 1952, 'The Case for Federal Relief', *Saturday Evening Post*, 19 July, pp. 79–82.

Ragg, N. 1980, 'Respect for Persons and Social Work: Social Work as 'Doing Philosophy'', in *Social Welfare: Why and How* (ed Timms, N.), Routledge and Kegan, London, pp. 211–232.

Randall, E. 2007, 'Existential Theory', in *Theoretical Perspectives for Direct Social Work Practice* (2nd edn) (eds Coady, N. and Lehmann P.), Springer, New York.

Rank, O. 1927, 'Social Adaptation and Creativity', in *The Psychology of Difference* (ed Kramer, R.) (1996), Princeton University Press, Princeton.

Rank, O. 1932, *Art and Artist*, Norton and Company, New York.

Rank, O. 1935, 'Neurosis as a Failure in Creativity', in *The Psychology of Difference* (ed Kramer, R.) (1996), Princeton University Press, Princeton, pp. 251–299.

Rank, O. 1936, *Will Therapy*, Norton and Company, New York.

Reamer, F. 1993, *The Philosophical Foundations of Social Work*, Columbia University Press, New York.

Reynolds, B. 1951, *Social Work and Social Living*, National Association of Social Workers, Washington.

Reynolds, B. 1963, *An Uncharted Journey*, Citadel Press, New York.

Richmond, M. 1922, *What is Social Casework?*, Russell Sage Foundation, New York.

Robinson, V. 1930, *A Changing Psychology in Social Casework*, University of North Carolina Press, Chapel Hill.

Robinson, V. 1962, *Jessie Taft: Therapist and Social Work Educator*, University of Pennsylvania Press, Philadelphia.

Rogers, C. 1980, *A Way of Being*, Houghton Mifflin Company, Boston.

Rose, D. 2011, *Wild Dog Dreaming*, University of Virginia Press, Charlottesville.

Rossiter, A. 2011, 'Unsettled Social Work: The Challenge of Levinas's Ethics', *British Journal of Social Work*, vol. 41, pp. 980–995.

Rubin, A. and Babbie, E. 2014, *Research Methods for Social Work*, Brooks/Cale, Belmont.

Sakamoto, I. and Pitner, R. 2005, 'Use of Critical Consciousness in Anti-Oppressive Social Work Practice: Disentangling Power Dynamics at Personal and Structural Levels', *British Journal of Social Work*, vol. 35, pp. 435–452.

Saltiel, D. 2016, 'Observing Front Line Decision Making in Child Protection', *British Journal of Social Work*, vol. 46, pp. 2104–2119.

Sartre, J. 1963, *Search for a Method*, Alfred A Knopf, New York.

Sartre, J. 1968, *Search for a Method*, Vintage Books, New York.

Sartre, J. 1982, *Critique of Dialectical Reasoning*, Verso, London.

Sartre, J. 2010, 'A Fundamental Idea of Husserl's Phenomenology: Intentionality' in *Critical Essays (Situations 1)*, Seagull Books, Calcutta, pp. 40–46.

Satir, V. 1967, *Conjoint Family Therapy*, Science and Behavior Books, Palo Alto.

Satir, V. 1976, *Making Contact*, Celestial Arts, Berkeley.

Smalley, R. 1967, *Theory for Social Work Practice*, Columbia University Press, New York.

Stein, E. 1989, *On the Problem of Empathy*, ICS Publications, Washington.

Stein, E. 2007, 'Martin Heidegger's Existential Philosophy', *Maynooth Philosophical Papers*, no. 4, pp. 55–98.

Stein, E. 2010, 'Otto Rank: Pioneering Ideas for Social Work Theory and Practice', *Psychoanalytic Social Work*, vol. 17, pp. 116–131.

Steinberg, A. 2007, *Phenomenology and Mysticism*, Indiana University Press, Bloomington.

Steinberg, A. 2014, *Moral Emotions, Reclaiming the Evidence of the Heart*, North West University Press, Evanston.

Stretch, J. 1974, 'Existentialism: A Proposed Philosophical Orientation for Social Work', in *Towards Effective Social Work Practice* (ed. Glicken, M.), MSS Information, New York, pp. 112–119.

Sutton, R. 1992, *Human Existence and Theodicy*, P. Lang, New York.

Taft, J. 1928, 'The Spirit of Social Work', *The Family*, vol. 9, no. 4, pp. 103–107.

Taft, J. (ed), 1940, *Social Case Work with Children*, Pennsylvania School of Social Work, Camden, New Jersey.

Taft, J. 1942, 'The Relation of Function to Process in Social Case Work', in *Training for Skill in Social Case Work*, Oxford University Press, London, pp. 100–116.

Taft, J. 1958, *Otto Rank,* The Julian Press, New York.

The Children, Young People and Families Research Unit, 1997, *Juvenile Justice Group Conferencing in Victoria: An Evaluation of a Pilot Program*, School of Social Work, University of Melbourne, Melbourne.

Thompson, N. 1992, *Existentialism and Social Work*, Ashgate, Aldershot.

Thompson, N. 2000, 'Existentialist Practice', in *Social Work Models, Methods, and Theories* (2nd edn) (eds Stepney, P. and Ford, D.), Russell House Publishing, Dorset, pp. 201–213.

Thompson, N. 2002, 'Social Movements Social Justice and Social Work', *British Journal of Social Work*, vol. 32, pp. 711–722.

Thompson, N. 2006, *Anti-Discriminatory Practice,* Palgrave MacMillan, Hampshire.

Thompson, N. 2009, *Understanding Social Work*, Palgrave Macmillan, New York.

Thompson, N. 2010, *Theorizing Social Work Practice*, Palgrave Macmillan, New York.

Thompson, N. and Thompson, S. 2008, *The Social Work Companion*, Palgrave Macmillan, London.

Tierney, L. 1976, *Excluded Families* (PhD Thesis), School of Social Work, Columbia University, New York.

Tillich, P. 1974, *The Courage To Be*, Fontana, London.

Timms, N. 1964, *Social Casework*, Routledge and Kegan Paul, London.

Timms, N. 1997, 'Taking Social Work Seriously: The Contribution of the Functional School', *British Journal of Social Work*, vol. 27, pp. 723–737.

Timms, N. 2014, 'Interview with Noel Timms', *Qualitative Social Work*, vol. 13, pp. 749–756.

Timms, N. and Mayer, J. 1970, *The Client Speaks*, Routledge and Kegan Paul, London.

Timms, N. and Timms, R. 1977, *Perspectives in Social Work*, Routledge and Kegan Paul, London.

Towle, C. 1945, *Common Human Needs*, Federal Security Agency, Social Security Board, Bureau of Public Assistance, Washington.

Trattner, W. 1974, *From Poor Law to Welfare State*, Free Press, Collier Macmillan, London.

Trevithick, P. 2012, *Social Work Skills and Knowledge: A Practice Handbook*, Open University Press, Maidenhead.

Truax, C. and Carkhuff, R. 1967, *Toward Effective Counseling and Psychotherapy*, Aldine, Chicago.

Turner, R. 1973, 'Dialectical Reason', *Radical Philosophy*, no. 4, pp. 30–33.

Vaillant, G. 2012, *Triumphs of Experience: The Men of the Harvard Grant Study*, Harvard University Press, Cambridge.

Van Deurzen, E. and Kenward, R. 2005, *Dictionary of Existential Psychotherapy and Counselling*, Sage, London.

Victorian Government, 2016, *Royal Commission into Family Violence, Volumes 1–6*, Victorian Government Printer, Melbourne (URL: http://www.rcfv.com.au/Report-Recommendations) [Accessed 08/05/17].

Victorian Juvenile Justice Group Conferencing: Pilot Project, 1998, *Report of the Project Steering Committee 1994–1997*, Victorian Government, Melbourne.

Vinson, T. 2007, 'The Web of Social Disadvantage', *Developing Practice*, vol. 19, Winter, Spring, pp. 56–65 (URL: search.informit.com.au/documentSummary;res=IELHEA;dn=796335332380455) [Accessed 08/07/17].

Vlais, R. 2014, 'Domestic Violence Perpetrator Programs: Education, Therapy, Support, Accountability 'or' Struggle?', *No To Violence* (URL: http://ntv.org.au/resources/) [Accessed 08/07/17].

Wakefield, J. 1998, 'Foucauldian Fallacies: An Essay Review of Leslie Margolin's Under the Cover of Kindness', *Social Services Review*, December, pp. 545–587.

Wallace, R. 2005, *Hegel's Philosophy of Reality, Freedom and God*, Cambridge University Press, New York.

Waugh, W. 2004, 'The Existentialist Public Administrator', *International Journal of Organization Theory and Behavior*, vol. 7, no. 3, pp. 432–451.

Weiss, D. 1974, *Existential Human Relations*, Dawson College Press, Montreal.

Weil, S. 1987, *The Need for Roots*, Ark Paperbacks, London.

Weil, S. 2001, *Oppression and Liberty*, Routledge, New York.

Wilkes, R. 1981, *Social Work with Undervalued Groups*, Tavistock, New York.

Williams, L. and Joyner, M. 2008, *Encyclopedia of Social Work*, Oxford University Press, Oxford.

Wilson, K., Ruch, G., Lymbery, M. and Cooper, A. 2008, *Social Work: An Introduction to Contemporary Practice*, Pearson Longman, New York.

Winnicott, D. 1986, *Holding and Interpretation*, Hogarth Press, London.

Wisnewski, J. 2013, *Heidegger*, Rowman and Littlefield, Lanham.

Wolff, K. 1976, *Surrender and Catch: Experience and Inquiry Today*, Reidel, Boston.

Wootton, B. 1959, 'Contemporary Attitudes in Social Work', in *Social Science and Social Pathology* (ed Wootton, B.), Allen and Unwin, London, pp. 268–297.

Wrathall, M. 2005, *How to Read Heidegger*, Granta Books, London.

Yalom, I. 1980, *Existential Psychotherapy*, Basic Books, Harper Collins Publishers, New York.

Yalom, I. 1998, *The Yalom Reader*, Basic Books, New York.

Yalom, I. 2005, *The Theory and Practice of Group Psychotherapy*, Perseus Books, New York.

Yelloly, M. 1980, *Social Work Theory and Psychoanalysis*, Van Nostrand Reinhold, New York.

# INDEX

*Tables are denoted by page numbers in italics.*

Printed by Printforce, the Netherlands